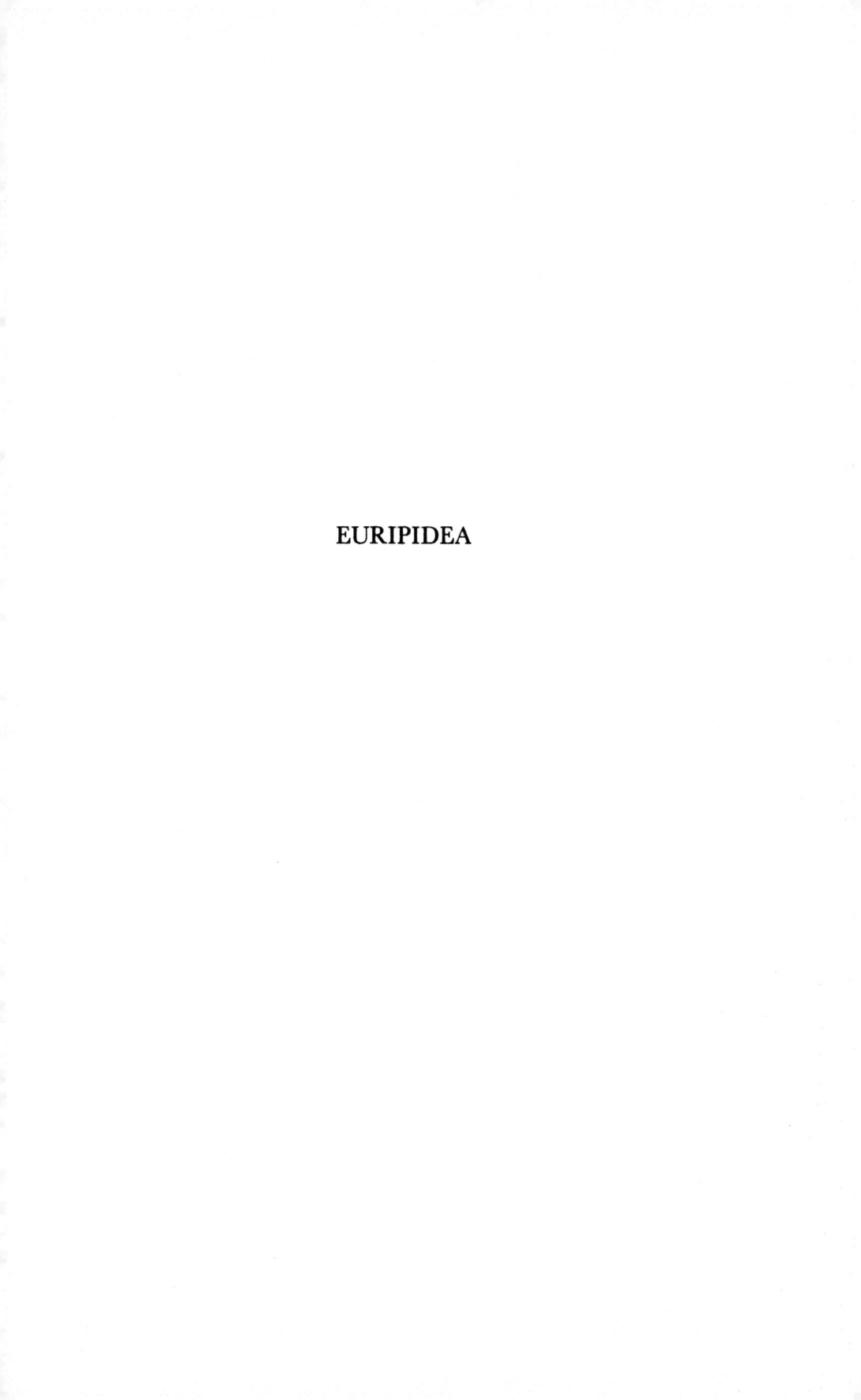

# EURIPIDEA

# MNEMOSYNE
## BIBLIOTHECA CLASSICA BATAVA

COLLEGERUNT

J.M. BREMER · L.F. JANSSEN · H. PINKSTER

H.W. PLEKET · C.J. RUIJGH · P.H. SCHRIJVERS

BIBLIOTHECAE FASCICULOS EDENDOS CURAVIT

C.J. RUIJGH, KLASSIEK SEMINARIUM, OUDE TURFMARKT 129, AMSTERDAM

SUPPLEMENTUM CENTESIMUM TRICESIMUM SECUNDUM

DAVID KOVACS

EURIPIDEA

# EURIPIDEA

BY

DAVID KOVACS

E.J. BRILL
LEIDEN · NEW YORK · KÖLN
1994

The paper in this book meets the guidelines for permanence and durability of the Committee on Production Guidelines for Book Longevity of the Council on Library Resources.

ISSN 0169-8958
ISBN 90 04 09926 3

© *Copyright 1994 by E.J. Brill, Leiden, The Netherlands*

*All rights reserved. No part of this publication may be reproduced, translated, stored in a retrieval system, or transmitted in any form or by any means, electronic, mechanical, photocopying, recording or otherwise, without prior written permission from the publisher.*

*Authorization to photocopy items for internal or personal use is granted by E.J. Brill provided that the appropriate fees are paid directly to Copyright Clearance Center, 27 Congress Street, Salem MA 01970, USA. Fees are subject to change.*

PRINTED IN THE NETHERLANDS

## CONTENTS

Preface . . . . . . . . . . . . . . . . . . . . . . . . . . . . . vii

Abbreviations . . . . . . . . . . . . . . . . . . . . . . . . . . ix

### PART I: TESTIMONIA VITAE ET ARTIS SELECTA
### (SOURCES FOR THE LIFE OF EURIPIDES)

| | | |
|---|---|---|
| A. | Lives and fragments of lives . . . . . . . . . . . . . . . | 3 |
| B. | Date and place of birth and parentage . . . . . . . . | 29 |
| C. | Boyhood . . . . . . . . . . . . . . . . . . . . . . . . . | 31 |
| D. | Early pursuits . . . . . . . . . . . . . . . . . . . . . . | 33 |
| E. | Student or companion of philosophers . . . . . . . . | 33 |
| F. | Tragic contests . . . . . . . . . . . . . . . . . . . . . | 39 |
| G. | Other poems . . . . . . . . . . . . . . . . . . . . . . | 55 |
| H. | Euripides and Sophocles . . . . . . . . . . . . . . . | 57 |
| I. | Euripides and Agathon . . . . . . . . . . . . . . . . | 59 |
| J. | Euripides and Timotheus . . . . . . . . . . . . . . . | 59 |
| K. | Euripides and Cephisophon . . . . . . . . . . . . . | 61 |
| L. | Legal troubles . . . . . . . . . . . . . . . . . . . . . | 61 |
| M. | Visit to Macedon and death . . . . . . . . . . . . . | 63 |
| N. | Euripides in the comic poets . . . . . . . . . . . . . | 67 |
| O. | Other judgements . . . . . . . . . . . . . . . . . . . | 115 |
| P. | Miscellanea . . . . . . . . . . . . . . . . . . . . . . | 123 |
| Q. | Epigrams . . . . . . . . . . . . . . . . . . . . . . . | 127 |
| R. | Fictitious letters . . . . . . . . . . . . . . . . . . . . | 129 |

## PART II: TEXTUAL DISCUSSIONS

    *Cyclops* .................................. 145
    *Alcestis* ................................. 159
    *Medea* ................................... 167

Bibliography

    List of Editions Used ....................... 173
    Other Works ............................... 175

Indices

    Indices to the Testimonia
        Index of Names ........................ 177
        Index of Sources ....................... 178

    Indices to the Textual Discussions
        Index of Subjects ...................... 180
        Index of Greek Words .................. 181
        Index of Passages Cited ................ 181

# PREFACE

This book is intended as a companion volume to my Loeb Euripides, Volume One. It contains two sections. The first is a collection of testimonia to the life and literary career of Euripides, together with an English translation. I gathered this material in connection with the section of my Introduction on the life of Euripides and translated it with a view to making it a part of the volume. In the event, it proved impossible to include it. I publish it here for several reasons, apart from a pardonable desire not to see my labor wasted. Although Nauck gathered most of the references in the Preface to his Teubner edition, no one has printed the texts themselves in one place. Classical scholars will not need a translation of this material, but others may find profit or amusement in seeing the ancient biographical tradition at work. In addition, some of the material, such as the spurious *Letters of Euripides*, has never been translated into English. I have not included all the testimonia I could find—a complete collection will be available in the *TrGF* series when Richard Kannicht's Euripides volume appears—but all the principal lineaments in antiquity's view of Euripides' life may be seen here, together with enough context to be able to divine how much—or how little—authority each item possesses. As I try to show in the above-mentioned Loeb Introduction, the history of Euripidean interpretation would have been much different if interpreters had been warier of accepting what this tradition says at face value.

I print the text of the testimonia from the standard editions listed in the Bibliography. I have noted deviations from these editions or worthwhile conjectures in footnotes.

The second part discusses passages in *Cyclops*, *Alcestis*, and *Medea* where the text I adopt calls for explanation. James Diggle's OCT, now complete, marks a great advance over previous editions, not least because Diggle is not diffident about questioning the soundness of the text in places where his predecessors have dogmatically slumbered. But some of the questions he raises admit of other solutions, and there are further places where doubts about the text should be aired, established conjectures challenged, or new defenses of the tradition advanced. I have also listed in their proper place the location of earlier discussions of mine.

The preparation of this work was made possible in part by a grant from the National Endowment for the Humanities, an independent federal agency. Without their support for this project and for the Loeb Euripides, progress would have been much slower.

I would like to express my gratitude to Sir Hugh Lloyd-Jones for helpful comment and encouragement, to James Diggle for his hospitality and illuminating discussion in Cambridge, and Sir Charles Willink for both hospitality and many acute suggestions. None of these, obviously, is to be blamed for errors that remain.

University of Virginia                                      David Kovacs

## ABBREVIATIONS

Ancient authors and works are abbreviated as in LSJ, periodicals as in *L'année philologique*, and metrical symbols as in M. L. West, *Greek Metre* (Oxford, 1982). See also under List of Editions Used.

| | |
|---|---|
| Austin | C. Austin, ed., *Comicorum Graecorum Fragmenta in Papyris Reperta* (Berlin, 1973). |
| D.-K. | H. Diels and W. Kranz, *Die Fragmente der Vorsokratiker*, 6th ed., 3 vols. (Berlin, 1951-2, rpt. Dublin, 1966). |
| *GP* | J. D. Denniston, *The Greek Particles*$^2$ (Oxford, 1959) |
| K.-G. | R. Kühner and B. Gerth, *Ausführliche Grammatik der griechischen Sprache* (Hannover and Leipzig, 1898) |
| Mullach | F. W. A. Mullach, ed., *Fragmenta philosophorum Graecorum* (Paris, 1881). |
| N$^2$ | A. Nauck, ed., *Tragicorum Graecorum Fragmenta: Supplementum adiecit Bruno Snell* (Hildesheim, 1964). |
| Radt 3 | S. Radt, ed., *Tragicorum Graecorum Fragmenta*, vol. 3: Aeschylus (Göttingen, 1985). |
| Radt 4 | S. Radt, ed., *Tragicorum Graecorum Fragmenta*, vol. 4: Sophocles (Göttingen, 1977). |
| *RE* | A. Pauly, G. Wissowa, and W. Kroll, edd., *Real-Encyklopädie der classischen Altertumswissenschaft* |
| Smyth | H. W. Smyth, *Greek Grammar*, rev. by G. Messing (Cambridge, Mass., 1956) |
| Winiarczyk | M. Winiarczyk, ed., *Diagorae Melii et Theodori Cyrenaei reliquiae* (Leipzig, 1981). |

PART ONE

TESTIMONIA VITAE ET ARTIS SELECTA:
SOURCES FOR THE LIFE OF EURIPIDES

# TESTIMONIA VITAE ET ARTIS SELECTA

**1** Γένος Εὐριπίδου καὶ βίος, *Euripide I*, ed. Méridier, pp. 1-5 [=i 1-6 Schwartz]

(1) Εὐριπίδης ὁ ποιητὴς υἱὸς ἐγένετο Μνησαρχίδου καπήλου καὶ Κλειτοῦς λαχανοπώλιδος, Ἀθηναῖος. (2) ἐγεννήθη δὲ ἐν Σαλαμῖνι ἐπὶ Καλλιάδου ἄρχοντος κατὰ τὴν οε΄ ὀλυμπιάδα, ὅτε ἐναυμάχησαν τοῖς Πέρσαις οἱ Ἕλληνες. (3) ἤσκησε δὲ κατ' ἀρχὰς μὲν παγκράτιον ἢ πυγμήν, τοῦ πατρὸς αὐτοῦ χρησμὸν λαβόντος ὅτι στεφανηφόρους ἀγῶνας νικήσει, καί φασιν αὐτὸν Ἀθήνησι νικῆσαι. (4)†ἀναγνοὺς†[1] δὲ ἐπὶ τραγῳδίαν ἐτράπη, καὶ πολλὰ προσεξεῦρε, προλόγους φυσιολογίας ῥητορείας ἀναγνωρισμούς, ὡς δὴ ἀκουστὴς γενόμενος Ἀναξαγόρου καὶ Προδίκου καὶ Πρωταγόρου, καὶ Σωκράτους ἑταῖρος. (5) δοκεῖ δὲ αὐτῷ καὶ Σωκράτης [ὁ φιλόσοφος] καὶ Μνησίλοχος συμπεποιηκέναι τινά, ὥς φησι Τηλεκλείδης [fr. 41 K.-A.]·

Μνησίλοχός ἐστ' ἐκεῖνος ὃς φρύγει τι δρᾶμα καινὸν
Εὐριπίδῃ[2], καὶ Σωκράτης τὰ φρύγαν' ὑποτίθησιν.

οἱ δὲ τὰ μέλη αὐτῷ φασι Κηφισοφῶντα[3] ποιεῖν ἢ Τιμοκράτην Ἀργεῖον. (6) φασὶ δὲ αὐτὸν καὶ ζωγράφον γενέσθαι καὶ δείκνυσθαι αὐτοῦ πινάκια ἐν Μεγάροις· (7) γενέσθαι δὲ αὐτὸν καὶ πυρφόρον τοῦ Ζωστηρίου Ἀπόλλωνος. (8) γεννηθῆναι δὲ τῇ αὐτῇ ἡμέρᾳ [καὶ Ἑλλάνικον][4] ἐν ᾗ ἐνίκων τὴν περὶ Σαλαμῖνα ναυμαχίαν οἱ Ἕλληνες· (9) ἄρξασθαι δὲ ἀγωνίζεσθαι γενόμενον ἐτῶν κε΄.[5] (10) μετέστη δὲ ἐν Μαγνησίᾳ καὶ προξενίᾳ ἐτιμήθη καὶ ἀτελείᾳ. (11) ἐκεῖθεν δὲ εἰς Μακεδονίαν περὶ Ἀρχέλαον γενόμενος διέτριψε καὶ χαριζόμενος αὐτῷ δρᾶμα ὁμωνύμως ἔγραψε καὶ μάλα ⟨εὖ⟩[6]

---

[1] μεταγνοὺς vel ἀνὰ χρόνους Nauck: ἀπογνοὺς Goosens
[2] aliquot testes, probantibus K.-A.: -δου ceteri
[3] Welcker: ἰοφῶντα vel σιοφῶντα codd.; cf. 26 infra.
[4] del. Wilamowitz
[5] Nauck: κϛ΄ codd.
[6] Nauck

# SOURCES FOR THE LIFE OF EURIPIDES

A. *Lives and Fragments of Lives*

**1** 'Euripides' Origins and Life', transmitted in some mss. of Euripides

(1) Euripides the poet was the son of Mnesarchides, a shopkeeper, and of Cleito, a seller of vegetables; he was Athenian. (2) He was born on Salamis in the year Calliades was archon [480/79] in the 75th Olympiad, when the Greeks fought the sea-battle against the Persians. (3) He trained at first in the pankration[1] or in boxing since his father had received an oracle that he would win contests that bestow crowns, and it is said that he was victor at Athens. (4) Having studied (?) he turned to tragedy and made a number of innovations, such as prologues, discussions of natural science, displays of rhetorical skill, and recognition-scenes, as you might expect from one who had been a pupil of Anaxagoras, Prodicus, and Protagoras and a companion of Socrates. (5) It is thought that Socrates and Mnesilochus were collaborators with him in some of his works, as Teleclides says:

> That man there is Mnesilochus, who is roasting up a new play for Euripides, and Socrates is laying the firewood.[2]

Others say that Cephisophon or Timocrates of Argos wrote the lyric parts of his plays. (6) They say that he was also a painter and that paintings of his were on display in Megara; (7) further that he was torch-bearer of Apollo Zosterios; (8) that he was born on the same day as the Greeks won the sea-battle at Salamis; (9) that he began to enter the competitions at the age of twenty-five. (10) He took up a new home in Magnesia, where he received the honor of being *proxenos*[3] and of exemption from taxation. (11) From there he went to Macedonia and spent time in the circle of Archelaus, and as a favor to him he wrote the drama that has the same name as his;[4] he en-

---

[1] A sport that combined boxing and wrestling.
[2] The text of this fragment has been altered either here or in Diogenes Laertius, T 17 below.
[3] A *proxenos* was 'official friend' to citizens of another state when they were visiting the *proxenos'* home city.
[4] Cf. also Diomedes, p. 488 Keil.

ἔπραττε παρ' αὐτῷ, ὥστε[1] καὶ ἐπὶ τῶν διοικήσεων ἐγένετο. (12) ἐλέγετο δὲ καὶ βαθὺν ⟨τὸν⟩[2] πώγωνα θρέψαι καὶ ἐπὶ τῆς ὄψεως φακοὺς ἐσχηκέναι. (13) γυναῖκα δὲ γῆμαι πρώτην Μελιτώ, δευτέραν δὲ Χοιρίλην. (14) καὶ υἱοὺς κατέλιπε τρεῖς, Μνησαρχίδην μὲν πρεσβύτατον ἔμπορον, δεύτερον δὲ Μνησίλοχον ὑποκριτήν, νεώτατον δὲ Εὐριπίδην, ὃς ἐδίδαξε τοῦ πατρὸς ἔνια δράματα. (15) ἤρξατο δὲ διδάσκειν ἐπὶ Καλλίου ἄρχοντος, ὀλυμπιάδος πα' ἔτει α'· πρῶτον δὲ ἐδίδαξε τὰς Πελιάδας, ὅτε καὶ τρίτος ἐγένετο [=*TrGF* DID C9]. (16) τὰ πάντα δ' ἦν αὐτῷ δράματα Ϙβ', σῴζεται δὲ οη'. τούτων νοθεύεται τρία, Τέννης Ῥαδάμανθυς Πειρίθους. (17) ἐτελεύτησε δέ, ὥς φησι Φιλόχορος [*FGrH* 328 F 220], ὑπὲρ τὰ ο' ἔτη γεγονώς, ὡς δὲ Ἐρατοσθένης [*FGrH* 241 F 12], οε', καὶ ἐτάφη ἐν Μακεδονίᾳ. (18) κενοτάφιον δὲ αὐτοῦ [ἐν][3] Ἀθήνησιν ἐγένετο, καὶ ἐπίγραμμα [*AP* 7.45] ἐπεγέγραπτο Θουκιδίδου τοῦ ἱστοριογράφου ποιήσαντος ἢ Τιμοθέου τοῦ μελοποιοῦ·

    Μνῆμα μὲν Ἑλλὰς ἅπασ' Εὐριπίδου· ὀστέα δ' ἴσχει
      γῆ Μακεδών, τῇ γὰρ[4] δέξατο τέρμα βίου.
    πατρὶς δ' Ἑλλάδος Ἑλλάς, Ἀθῆναι. πολλὰ δὲ μούσαις
      τέρψας ἐκ πολλῶν καὶ τὸν ἔπαινον ἔχει.

(19) φασὶ δὲ καὶ κεραυνωθῆναι ἀμφότερα μνημεῖα. (20) λέγουσι δὲ καὶ Σοφοκλέα ἀκούσαντα ὅτι ἐτελεύτησεν αὐτὸν μὲν ἱματίῳ φαιῷ προελθεῖν, τὸν δὲ χορὸν καὶ τοὺς ὑποκριτὰς ἀστεφανώτους εἰσαγαγεῖν ἐν τῷ προαγῶνι καὶ δακρῦσαι τὸν δῆμον.

(21) ἐτελεύτησε δὲ τὸν τρόπον τοῦτον. ἐν τῇ Μακεδονίᾳ κώμη ἔστι καλουμένη Θρᾳκῶν διὰ τό ποτε κατῳκηκέναι ἐνταῦθα Θρᾷκας. ἐν ταύτῃ ποτὲ τοῦ Ἀρχελάου Μολοττικὴ κύων ἦλθεν ἀποπλανηθεῖσα· ταύτην Θρᾷκες ὡς ἔθος θύσαντες ἔφαγον. καὶ δὴ ὁ Ἀρχέλαος ἐζημίωσεν αὐτοὺς ταλάντῳ. ἐπεὶ οὖν οὐκ εἶχον, Εὐριπίδου ἐδεήθησαν ἀπολύσεως τυχεῖν, δεηθέντος τοῦ βασιλέως. χρόνῳ δὲ ὕστερον Εὐριπίδης ἐν ἄλσει τινὶ πρὸ τῆς πόλεως ἠρέμει. Ἀρχελάου δὲ ἐπὶ κυνηγέσιον ἐξελθόντος, τῶν σκυλάκων

---

[1] Nauck: ὅτε codd.
[2] supplevi
[3] del. Nauck
[4] Jacobs: ᾗπερ vel ἡ γὰρ codd.

joyed great success in his court, so that he was put in charge of financial administration. (12) It is said that he wore his beard full and had moles over his eyes,[1] (13) and that his first wife was Melito and his second Choirile. (14) He left behind three sons: the eldest, Mnesarchides, a trader, the second, Mnesilochus, an actor, and the youngest, Euripides, who produced some of his father's plays.

(15) He began to put on plays in the year Callias was archon [456/5], in the first year of the 81st Olympiad. His first production was *The Daughters of Pelias*, and on that occasion he came in third. (16) The total number of his plays was ninety-two, of which seventy-eight survive. (17) Three of these are regarded as spurious: *Tennes, Rhadamanthys,* and *Pirithous.* (18) He died, as Philochorus[2] affirms, at more than seventy years of age, at seventy-five according to Eratosthenes,[3] and was buried in Macedonia. There was a cenotaph in Athens[4] with an inscription on it by Thucydides the historian or Timotheus the lyric poet:

> All Hellas is the tomb of Euripides, but his bones rest in the land of Macedon, for it was there that he died. His home was Athens, the Hellas of Hellas. Since he gave delight on many occasions with his poetry, from many lips too does he win praise.

(19) They say that both monuments were also struck by lightning.[5] (20) They also say that Sophocles, on hearing of his death, himself went forth dressed in a dark-grey cloak and brought on his chorus and his actors in the *proagon*[6] without garlands, and that the people wept.

(21) He died in the following manner. There is in Macedonia a place called Thracian Village, so called because Thracians once settled there. One day a Molossian hound of Archelaus wandered off into the village. This dog the Thracians, as was their custom, sacrificed and ate. Archelaus then fined them a talent. Since they did not have the money, they begged Euripides to win forgiveness for them by pleading with the king. Some time later he was taking his rest in a grove that stands before the city. When Archelaus went out for a

---

[1] Cf. Aristophanes, *Frogs* 1246.
[2] Athenian historian of the fourth to third century.
[3] The famous Hellenistic astronomer, chronologist, and polymath of the third to second century.
[4] Cf. Pausanias 1.2.2.
[5] On the significance of this, see T 95.
[6] The ceremony preliminary to the tragic contest.

ἀπολυθέντων ὑπὸ τῶν κυνηγῶν καὶ περιτυχόντων Εὐριπίδῃ, διεσπαράχθη καταβρωθεὶς ὁ ποιητής. ἦσαν δὲ ἔκγονοι οἱ σκύλακες τῆς ὑπὸ Θρᾳκῶν ἀναιρεθείσης κυνός, ὅθεν καὶ ἡ παροιμία ἐστὶ παρὰ τοῖς Μακεδόσι "κυνὸς δίκη".

(22) φασὶ δὲ αὐτὸν ἐν Σαλαμῖνι σπήλαιον κατασκευάσαντα ἀναπνοὴν ἔχον εἰς τὴν θάλασσαν ἐκεῖσε διημερεύειν φεύγοντα τὸν ὄχλον· ὅθεν καὶ ἐκ θαλάττης λαμβάνει[1] τὰς πλείους τῶν ὁμοιώσεων. (23) σκυθρωπὸς δὲ καὶ σύννους καὶ αὐστηρὸς ἐφαίνετο καὶ μισόγελως καὶ μισογύνης, καθὰ καὶ Ἀριστοφάνης αὐτὸν αἰτιᾶται· "στρυφνὸς ἔμοιγε προσειπεῖν [Εὐριπίδης]". (24) λέγουσι δὲ αὐτὸν γήμαντα τὴν Μνησιλόχου θυγατέρα Χοιρίλην καὶ νοήσαντα τὴν ἀκολασίαν αὐτῆς γράψαι δρᾶμα τὸν πρότερον Ἱππόλυτον, ἐν ᾧ τὴν ἀναισχυντίαν θριαμβεύει τῶν γυναικῶν, ἔπειτα δὲ αὐτὴν ἀποπέμψασθαι. λέγοντος δὲ τοῦ γήμαντος αὐτήν "σωφρονεῖ παρ' ἐμοί", "δύστηνος εἶ", ἔφη, "εἰ [γυναῖκα][2] δοκεῖς παρ' ᾧ μὲν αὐτὴν σωφρονεῖν, παρ' ᾧ δὲ μή".

ἐπιγῆμαι δὲ αὐτὸν δευτέραν, ἣν εὑρὼν ἀκολαστοτέραν προχειροτέρως εἰς τὴν κατὰ τῶν γυναικῶν βλασφημίαν ἐθρασύνετο. (25) αἱ δὲ γυναῖκες ἐβουλήθησαν αὐτὸν κτεῖναι εἰσελθοῦσαι εἰς τὸ σπήλαιον ἐν ᾧ γράφων διετέλει. (26) διαβάλλεται δὲ ὑπὸ φθόνου ὡς τὸν Κηφισοφῶντα εἶχε συμποιοῦντα αὐτῷ τὰς τραγῳδίας. (27) λέγει δὲ καὶ Ἕρμιππος [fr. 94 Wehrli] Διονύσιον τὸν Σικελίας τύραννον μετὰ τὴν τελευτὴν τοῦ Εὐριπίδου τάλαντον τοῖς κληρονόμοις αὐτοῦ πέμψαντα λαβεῖν τὸ ψαλτήριον καὶ τὴν δέλτον καὶ τὸ γραφεῖον, ἅπερ ἰδόντα κελεῦσαι τοὺς φέροντας ἐν τῷ ⟨τῶν⟩[3] Μουσῶν ἱερῷ ἀναθεῖναι ἐπιγράψαντα τοῖς αὐτοῦ καὶ Εὐριπίδου ὀνόμασι· διὸ καὶ ξενοφιλώτατον κεκλῆσθαί φασι διὰ τὸ μάλιστα ὑπὸ ξένων φιλεῖσθαι· ὑπὸ γὰρ Ἀθηναίων ἐφθονεῖτο. (28) μειρακίου δέ τινος ἀπαιδευτοτέρου στόμα δυσῶδες ἔχειν ὑπὸ φθόνου αὐτὸν εἰπόντος, "εὐφήμει", ἔφη, "μέλιτος καὶ Σειρήνων γλυκύτερον στόμα".

---

[1] fort. λαμβάνει⟨ν⟩
[2] del. Schwartz
[3] Westermann

hunt and the young hounds, let loose by the huntsmen, came upon Euripides, the poet was torn in pieces and devoured. Now these hounds were the offspring of the hound the Thracians had killed. This is the origin of the Macedonian proverb 'a dog's revenge'.

(22) They say that he fitted out a cave on Salamis opening on the sea and that he passed his days there avoiding the crowd; and that is the reason he takes most of his similes from the sea. (23) He was regarded as sullen and pensive and stern, a hater of laughter and of women. Thus Aristophanes[1] finds fault with him as '[Euripides] for my taste sour to talk to'. (24) They say that when he had married Mnesilochus' daughter Choerile and had observed her licentiousness, he wrote his first *Hippolytus*, in which he loudly proclaims the shamelessness of women and thereafter divorced her. When the man who married her said, 'She is chaste in my house', he replied, 'You are a poor fool if you think that she

> is chaste with one man and with one a whore.[2]

They say he married a second wife, and finding her even more licentious, he became all the readier to speak ill of women. (25) But the women wanted to kill him, going into the cave in which he spent his time writing. (26) The charge was made against him out of envy that he had Cephisophon collaborating with him on his tragedies. (27) Hermippus[3] says further that Dionysius the tyrant of Sicily gave the heirs of Euripides after his death a talent for the poet's harp, writing tablet, and stylus, and that when he had seen them he ordered those who brought them to dedicate them in the sanctuary of the Muses, and that he made an inscription in his own and Euripides' name. It is for this reason that they call him 'most beloved of strangers' since he was especially loved by foreigners. For he was treated with ill-will by the Athenians. (28) When a rather boorish lad said out of ill-will that he had foul-smelling breath, he replied, 'Speak respectfully of a mouth sweeter than honey and the Sirens'.[4]

---

[1] The phrase comes in fact from a poem of the Hellenistic poet Alexander of Aetolia: see below T 5.8.
[2] This is a quotation, adapted, from Euripides' *Electra* 923-4.
[3] Biographer of the 3rd c. B.C.
[4] A quotation from Alexander of Aetolia: see below T 5.8.

(29) ἔσκωπτε δὲ τὰς γυναῖκας διὰ τῶν ποιημάτων δι' αἰτίαν τοιάνδε. εἶχεν οἰκογενὲς μειράκιον ὀνόματι Κηφισοφῶντα· πρὸς τοῦτον ἐφώρασε τὴν οἰκείαν γυναῖκα ἀτακτοῦσαν. τὸ μὲν οὖν πρῶτον ἀπέτρεπεν ἁμαρτάνειν. ἐπεὶ δ' οὐκ ἔπειθε, κατέλιπεν αὐτῷ τὴν γυναῖκα, βουλομένου αὐτὴν ἔχειν τοῦ Κηφισοφῶντος. λέγει οὖν καὶ ὁ Ἀριστοφάνης [fr. 596 K.-A.]·

 Κηφισοφῶν ἄριστε καὶ μελάντατε,
 σὺ γὰρ συνέζης ὡς τὰ πόλλ' Εὐριπίδῃ
 καὶ συνεποίεις, ὥς φασι, τὴν μελῳδίαν.

(30) λέγουσι δὲ καὶ ὅτι γυναῖκες διὰ τοὺς ψόγους οὓς ἐποίει εἰς αὐτὰς διὰ τῶν ποιημάτων τοῖς Θεσμοφορίοις ἐπέστησαν αὐτῷ βουλόμεναι ἀνελεῖν· ἐφείσαντο δὲ αὐτοῦ πρῶτον μὲν διὰ τὰς Μούσας, ἔπειτα δὲ βεβαιωσαμένου μηκέτι αὐτὰς κακῶς ἐρεῖν. ἐν γοῦν τῇ Μελανίππῃ [fr. 499 N²] περὶ αὐτῶν τάδε φησί·

 μάτην ἄρ' ἐς γυναῖκας ἐξ ἀνδρῶν ψόγος
 ψάλλει, κενὸν τόξευμα, καὶ κακῶς λέγει·
 αἱ δ' εἴσ' ἀμείνους ἀρσένων, (ἣ)[1] 'γὼ λέγω

καὶ τὰ ἑξῆς. (31) οὕτω δὲ αὐτὸν Φιλήμων ἠγάπησεν ὡς τολμῆσαι περὶ αὐτοῦ τοιοῦτον εἰπεῖν [fr. 118 K.-A.]·

 εἰ ταῖς ἀληθείαισιν οἱ τεθνηκότες
 αἴσθησιν εἶχον, ἄνδρες, ὥς φασίν τινες,
 ἀπηγξάμην ἂν ὥστ' ἰδεῖν Εὐριπίδην.

(32) Εὐριπίδης Μνησαρχίδου Ἀθηναῖος. τοῦτον οἱ τῆς ἀρχαίας κωμῳδίας ποιηταὶ ὡς λαχανοπώλιδος υἱὸν κωμῳδοῦσι. (33) γενέσθαι δὲ κατ' ἀρχὰς μὲν αὐτόν φασι ζωγράφον, σχολάσαντα δὲ Ἀρχελάῳ τῷ φυσικῷ καὶ Ἀναξαγόρᾳ ἐπὶ τραγῳδίας ὁρμῆσαι. (34) ὅθεν καὶ πλέον τι φρονήσας εἰκότως περιίστατο τῶν πολλῶν, οὐδεμίαν φιλοτιμίαν περὶ τὰ θέατρα ποιούμενος. διὸ τοσοῦτον αὐτὸν ἔβλαπτε τοῦτο ὅσον ὠφέλει τὸν Σοφοκλέα. (35) ἐπέκειντο δὲ καὶ οἱ κωμικοὶ φθόνῳ αὐτὸν διασύροντες. ὑπεριδὼν δὲ πάντα εἰς Μακεδόνας ἀπῆρε πρὸς Ἀρχέλαον τὸν βασιλέα, κἀνταῦθα ὀψιαίτερον ἀναλύων ὑπὸ βασιλικῶν ἐφθάρη κυνῶν. (36) ἤρξατο δὲ διδάσκειν κατὰ τὴν πα' ὀλυμπιάδα ἐπὶ ἄρχοντος Καλλίου. (37) πλάσματι δὲ μέσῳ χρησάμενος περιγέγονε τῇ ἑρμηνείᾳ ἄκρως εἰς

---

[1] Nauck

(29) He jeered at women in his poems for the following reason. He had a home-born slave named Cephisophon with whom he discovered his own wife misbehaving. At first he tried to dissuade her from wrong-doing. But when he failed, he left the woman to him since Cephisophon wanted to have her. And so Aristophanes says,

> Cephisophon most excellent and black, since you used to live most of the time with Euripides and used to help him write, as rumor has it, the lyric parts.

(30) They also say that the women, because of the criticisms he made against them in his poetry, attacked him during the Thesmophoria, wishing to kill him.[1] But they spared his life, first, because of the Muses, and second, because he gave them his assurance that he would no longer speak ill of them. At any rate in the *Melanippe* he says the following about them:

> To no purpose does the dispraise of women (vain arrowshot) resound from the mouths of men and revile them. For they are better than men, as I maintain,

and so forth. (31) Philemon[2] loved him so much that he had the hardihood to say this about him:

> If in very truth the dead possessed any perception, gentlemen, as some claim they do, I would have hanged myself in order to see Euripides.

(32) Euripides, son of Mnesarchides, of Athens. The poets of Old Comedy derided him for being the son of a vegetable-seller. (33) They say that he was to begin with a painter, but that having studied with Archelaus the physical philosopher and Anaxagoras he turned to tragedy. (34) It was for this reason that he was rather proud and pardonably stood aloof from the majority, showing no ambition as regards his audience. Accordingly this fact hurt him as much as it helped Sophocles. (35) The comic poets also attacked him, mocking him in ill-will. But he ignored it all and departed for Macedonia and the court of King Archelaus, and there returning rather late he was killed by the king's hounds. (36) He began to produce plays in the 81st Olympiad during the archonship of Callias [456/5]. (37) He adopted a middle style and showed himself superior

---

[1] This is the plot of Aristophanes' *Women at the Thesmophoria*, treated as biography. Cf. 25 above.
[2] A poet of New Comedy.

ἀμφότερον χρώμενος ταῖς ἐπιχειρήσεσι. καὶ τοῖς μέλεσίν ἐστιν ἀμίμητος παραγκωνιζόμενος τοὺς μελοποιοὺς σχεδὸν πάντας, ἐν δὲ τοῖς ἀμοιβαίοις περισσὸς καὶ φορτικός, καὶ ἐν τοῖς προλόγοις δὲ ὀχληρός, ῥητορικώτατος δὲ τῇ κατασκευῇ καὶ ποικίλος τῇ φράσει καὶ ἱκανὸς ἀνασκευάσαι τὰ εἰρημένα. (38) τὰ πάντα δὲ ἦν αὐτοῦ δράματα ϙβ΄, σῴζεται δὲ αὐτοῦ δράματα ξζ΄ καὶ γ΄ πρὸς τούτοις τὰ ἀντιλεγόμενα· σατυρικὰ δὲ η΄, ἀντιλέγεται δὲ καὶ τούτων τὸ α΄. νίκας δὲ ἔσχε ε΄.

**2** *Suda* s.v. Εὐριπίδης, E 3695 (ii 468 Adler)

(1) Εὐριπίδης Μνησάρχου ἢ Μνησαρχίδου καὶ Κλειτοῦς, οἳ φεύγοντες εἰς Βοιωτίαν μετῴκησαν, εἶτα ἐν τῇ Ἀττικῇ. (2) οὐκ ἀληθὲς δέ, ὡς λαχανόπωλις ἦν ἡ μήτηρ αὐτοῦ· καὶ γὰρ τῶν σφόδρα εὐγενῶν ἐτύγχανεν, ὡς ἀποδείκνυσι Φιλόχορος [*FGrH* 328 F 218]. (3) ἐν δὲ τῇ διαβάσει Ξέρξου ἐκυοφορεῖτο ὑπὸ τῆς μητρός, καὶ ἐτέχθη καθ' ἣν ἡμέραν Ἕλληνες ἐτρέψαντο τοὺς Πέρσας. (4) γέγονε δὲ τὰ πρῶτα ζωγράφος, εἶτα μαθητὴς Προδίκου μὲν ἐν τοῖς ῥητορικοῖς, Σωκράτους δὲ ἐν τοῖς ἠθικοῖς καὶ φιλοσόφοις. διήκουσε δὲ καὶ Ἀναξαγόρου τοῦ Κλαζομενίου. (5) ἐπὶ τραγῳδίαν δὲ ἐτράπη τὸν Ἀναξαγόραν ἰδὼν ὑποστάντα κινδύνους δι' ἅπερ εἰσῆξε δόγματα. (6) σκυθρωπὸς δὲ ἦν τὸ ἦθος καὶ ἀμειδὴς καὶ φεύγων τὰς συνουσίας· ὅθεν καὶ μισογύνης ἐδοξάσθη· (7) ἔγημε δὲ ὅμως πρώτην μὲν Χοιρίνην, θυγατέρα Μνησιλόχου· ἐξ ἧς ἔσχε Μνησίλοχον καὶ Μνησαρχίδην καὶ Εὐριπίδην. (8) ἀπωσάμενος δὲ ταύτην ἔσχε καὶ δευτέραν, καὶ ταύτης ὁμοίως ἀκολάστου πειραθείς. ἀπάρας δὲ ἀπ' Ἀθηνῶν ἦλθε πρὸς Ἀρχέλαον τὸν βασιλέα τῶν Μακεδόνων, παρ' ᾧ διῆγεν τῆς ἄκρας ἀπολαύων τιμῆς. (9) ἐτελεύτησε δὲ ὑπὸ ἐπιβουλῆς Ἀρριβαίου τοῦ Μακεδόνος καὶ Κρατεύα τοῦ Θετταλοῦ, ποιητῶν ὄντων καὶ φθονησάντων αὐτῷ πεισάντων τε τὸν βασιλέως οἰκέτην τοὔνομα Λυσίμαχον, δέκα μνῶν ἀγορασθέντα, τοὺς βασιλέως, οὓς αὐτὸς ἔτρεφε, κύνας ἐπαφεῖναι αὐτῷ. οἱ δὲ ἱστόρησαν οὐχ ὑπὸ κυνῶν, ἀλλ' ὑπὸ γυναικῶν νύκτωρ διασπασθῆναι πορευόμενον ἀωρὶ πρὸς Κρατερὸν τὸν ἐρώμενον Ἀρχελάου (καὶ γὰρ σχεῖν αὐτὸν καὶ ⟨        ⟩[1]

---

[1] lac. indicavi, e.g. ⟨περιπαθῶς⟩

in expression by using to a high degree the rhetorical proofs on both sides of a case. In his lyric songs he is inimitable and surpasses nearly all the lyric poets, whereas in his dialogue he is wordy and vulgar and in his prologues he is annoying, but he is highly rhetorical in his arrangement and variegated in his diction and a capable arranger of what is said. (38) The total of his plays is ninety-two, of which sixty-seven dramas[1] survive, and additionally three of disputed authorship. There are eight satyr-plays, and one of these, too, is disputed. He won five victories.

## 2 *Suda*, 'Euripides'

(1) Euripides, son of Mnesarchus or Mnesarchides and Cleito. His parents were exiled and became resident aliens in Boeotia and then in Attica. (2) It is not true that his mother was a vegetable-seller. In fact, she happened to belong to a very noble family, as Philochorus demonstrates. (3) During Xerxes' crossing over to Europe he was carried by his mother, and he was born on the day the Greeks routed the Persians. (4) He first became a painter, then a disciple of Prodicus in rhetoric and of Socrates in ethics and philosophy. He also heard lectures by Anaxagoras of Clazomenae. (5) He turned to tragedy after seeing Anaxagoras running into danger because of the opinions he had introduced. (6) He was sullen in nature and did not smile and avoided company, and for this reason he was regarded as a hater of women. (7) He nevertheless married a first wife, Choerine, daughter of Mnesilochus, and by her he had Mnesilochus and Mnesarchides and Euripides. (8) Divorcing her he married a second, and found her just as unchaste. He moved from Athens to the court of King Archelaus of Macedon. There he passed his life enjoying the highest honor. (9) He died owing to a conspiracy by Arrhibaeus of Macedon and Crateuas of Thessaly, who were poets and hostile to him. They persuaded a servant of the king by the name of Lysimachus, bought for ten minas, to let loose the royal hounds, which were in his care, against Euripides. Others say that it was not by hounds but by women that he was torn apart at night as he was going at a late hour to see Craterus, Archelaus' boy-love (for he was, they say, <passionately> disposed toward this kind of love),

---

[1] This may mean 'tragedies', a late-Greek usage.

περὶ τοὺς τοιούτους ἔρωτας), οἱ δὲ πρὸς τὴν γαμετὴν Νικοδίκου τοῦ Ἀρεθουσίου. (10) ἔτη δὲ βιῶναι φασὶν αὐτὸν οε΄, καὶ τὰ ὀστᾶ αὐτοῦ ἐν Πέλλῃ μετακομίσαι τὸν βασιλέα. (11) δράματα δὲ αὐτοῦ κατὰ μέν τινας οε΄, κατὰ δὲ ἄλλους Ϟβ΄. σῴζονται δὲ οζ΄. (12) νίκας δὲ ἀνείλετο ε΄, τὰς μὲν δ΄ περιών, τὴν δὲ μίαν μετὰ τὴν τελευτήν, ἐπιδειξαμένου τὸ δρᾶμα τοῦ ἀδελφιδοῦ αὐτοῦ Εὐριπίδου. ἐπεδείξατο δ' ὅλους ἐνιαυτοὺς κβ΄, καὶ τελευτᾷ ἐπὶ τῆς Ϟγ΄ ὀλυμπιάδος.

**3** Θωμᾶ τοῦ Μαγίστρου σύνοψις τοῦ βίου τοῦ Εὐριπίδου [i 11-13 Dindorf]

(1) Εὐριπίδῃ τῷ ποιητῇ πατρὶς μὲν Ἀθῆναι, πατέρες δὲ Μνήσαρχος κάπηλος καὶ Κλειτὼ λαχανόπωλις. (2) γεννηθεὶς δὲ ἐν Σαλαμῖνι τῇ πρὸ τῆς Ἀττικῆς νήσῳ ἐπὶ Καλλιάδου ἄρχοντος κατὰ τὴν οε΄ ὀλυμπιάδα, ὅτε καὶ τὸ τοῦ Ξέρξου ναυτικὸν κατεναυμάχησαν Ἀθηναῖοι, (3) πρῶτον μὲν ἤσκησε παγκράτιον καὶ πυγμήν, τοῦ πατρὸς αὐτοῦ χρησμὸν λαβόντος ὅτι στεφανηφόρους ἀγῶνας ὁ παῖς αὐτῷ νικήσει. ὃ δὴ καὶ εἰς ἔργον προύβη· ἐνίκησε γὰρ ταῦτα Ἀθήνησιν. (4) ἔπειτα εἰς λόγους ὡρμηκὼς ἐφοίτησε παρὰ Ἀναξαγόρᾳ καὶ Προδίκῳ καί τισιν ἄλλοις. (5) ἀγχίνους δὲ ὤν, εἴπερ τις, καὶ τῷ πονεῖν ἑαυτὸν ἐκδεδωκὼς εἰς τραγῳδίαν ἐτράπη καὶ ἔλαμψεν ἐπὶ ταύτῃ σεμνῶς· πολλὰ γὰρ εἰς τὴν τέχνην ἐξεῦρεν, ἃ οὐδεῖστισοῦν γε τῶν πρὸ αὐτοῦ· τό τε γὰρ ἐν ἀρχῇ τοῦ δράματος τὴν ὑπόθεσιν διατυποῦν καὶ τὸν ἀκροατὴν ὥσπερ χειραγωγεῖν εἰς τὸ ἔμπροσθεν Εὐριπίδου τέχνημα, τό τε σαφήνειαν καὶ πλάτος ἔχειν τὰ λεγόμενα καὶ τὴν ἑρμηνείαν ποικίλλειν ἐπιχειρήσεσί τε καὶ ῥυθμῷ χαρίεντι καὶ γνώμας εἰσάγειν συνεχεῖς καὶ μάλα τῷ ὑποκειμένῳ προσφόρους. 〈             〉[1] θαυμαστός. (6) ἔγραψε μὲν οὖν δράματα Ϟβ΄ τὰ πάντα, ἐν οἷς ἦν η΄ μόνα σατυρικά. (7) νενίκηκε δὲ ἐν πᾶσι τούτοις τοῖς δράμασι νίκας ε΄. (8) ἤρξατο δὲ τοῦ περὶ ταῦτα ἀγῶνος ἐτῶν κε΄ γεγονώς. (9) φασὶ δὲ αὐτὸν καὶ ζωγράφον γεγονέναι καὶ δείκνυσθαι αὐτοῦ πινάκια ἐν Μεγάροις. (10) γυναῖκα δὲ γήμας πρώτην μὲν Μελιτώ,

---

[1] lac. indicavi, e.g. ⟨ἦν δὲ ἐν τῷ ποιεῖν ἐλεινοὺς⟩

while others say that he was going to see the wife of Nicodicus of Arethusa. (10) They say that he lived seventy-five years and that the king removed his remains to Pella.[1] (11) He wrote, by some accounts, seventy-five plays, by others ninety-two. Seventy-seven survive.[2] (12) He won five victories, four during his lifetime and one after his death, his nephew Euripides putting on the play. He put on plays for twenty-two years in all. He died in the 93rd Olympiad.

## 3 Thomas Magister,[3] Summary of Euripides' Life

(1) Euripides the poet had Athens as his homeland and as parents Mnesarchus the tradesman and Cleito the vegetable-seller. (2) He was born in Salamis, the island in front of Athens, in the archonship of Calliades [480/79] in the 75th Olympiad when the Athenians defeated the fleet of Xerxes. (3) At first he trained in the pancration and in boxing since his father had received an oracle that his son would win victories in contests that bestow crowns. This actually proved true, for he was victorious at Athens. (4) Then turning to intellectual pursuits he studied with Anaxagoras and Prodicus and certain others. (5) Since he was exceedingly clever and put himself to hard work, he turned to tragedy and distinguished himself marvelously in that field. For he made many advances over his predecessors in the art. Sketching the plot at the beginning of the drama and taking the audience forward by the hand was an advance of Euripides, as was the clarity and breadth he gave to the speeches, his varying the style by means of rhetorical arguments and pleasing rhythm, and his introduction of frequent aphorisms highly germane to the subject. <           >[4] he was remarkable. (6) He wrote ninety-two plays in all, and in their number only eight were satyr-plays. (7) With all these plays he won five victories. (8) He began competing in this field at the age of twenty-five. (9) They say that he was also a painter and that paintings of his are on display in Megara. (10) He first married Melito, then, after their divorce,

---

[1] On the grave see also Vitruvius, *De arch.* 8.3.16, Pliny, *NH* 31.28, Ammianus Marcellinus 27.4.8; M. Lefkowitz, *GRBS* 20 (1979), 203.
[2] Some of these numbers are obviously corrupt. Dieterich emends to read, 'He wrote 92 plays, of which survive, by some accounts, 75, by others, 77'.
[3] 13th to 14th c.
[4] There is a lacuna, e.g. <In his portrayal of the pitiful, too,>.

ἔπειτα αὐτῆς ἀπελθούσης Χοιρίλην, υἱοὺς ἔσχε τρεῖς, Μνησαρχίδην ἔμπορον, Μνησίλοχον ὑποκριτήν, καὶ ὁμώνυμον ἑαυτῷ Εὐριπίδην περὶ λόγους διατρίβοντα. (11) ἦν δὲ σύννους καὶ στρυφνὸς τὸ ἦθος καὶ μισόγελως καὶ σκυθρωπός, καθὰ καὶ Ἀριστοφάνης σκώπτων φησί "στρυφνὸς ἔμοιγε προσειπεῖν [Εὐριπίδης]". (12) φωράσας δὲ τὸν αὐτοῦ ὑποκριτὴν Κηφισοφῶντα ἐπὶ τῇ γυναικὶ καὶ τὴν ἐντεῦθεν οὐ φέρων αἰσχύνην, σκωπτόμενος ὑπὸ τῶν κωμῳδοποιῶν, ἀφεὶς τὴν Ἀθήνησι διατριβὴν εἰς Μακεδονίαν ἀπῆρε παρὰ τὸν βασιλέα Ἀρχέλαον, καὶ δεχθεὶς ὑπ' αὐτοῦ κάλλιστα καὶ φιλοτιμηθεὶς μεγίστης ἠξιοῦτο τιμῆς. (13) διατρίβων οὖν ἐκεῖ, ἐπειδὴ ἔν τινι ἄλσει φροντίζων ἔτυχε, κατεβρώθη, ὥς φασιν, ὑπὸ τῶν τοῦ Ἀρχελάου κυνῶν, ἐξιόντος εἰς θήραν, ὑπὲρ τὰ ο' ἔτη γεγονώς. (14) ἐτάφη μὲν οὖν ἐν Μακεδονίᾳ, κενοτάφιον δὲ αὐτοῦ Ἀθήνησι γέγονεν, ἐφ' οὗ ἐπέγραψε Θουκυδίδης ὁ συγγραφεὺς ἢ Τιμόθεος ὁ μελοποιὸς τάδε [AP 7.45]·

    Μνῆμα μὲν Ἑλλὰς ἅπασ' Εὐριπίδου· ὀστέα δ' ἴσχει
      γῆ Μακεδών, τῇ γὰρ[1] δέξατο τέρμα βίου.
    πατρὶς δ' Ἑλλάδος Ἑλλάς, Ἀθῆναι. πολλὰ δὲ μούσαις
      τέρψας ἐκ πολλῶν καὶ τὸν ἔπαινον ἔχει.

(15) φασὶ δὲ ἐπὶ τῷ ἀκούσματι τῆς Εὐριπίδου τελευτῆς τοὺς μὲν Ἀθηναίους πάντας πενθῆσαι, Σοφοκλέα δὲ αὐτὸν μὲν καὶ φαιὸν ἐνδεδύσθαι χιτῶνα, τοὺς δὲ ὑποκριτὰς αὐτοῦ ἀστεφανώτους τῷ τότε εἰσαγαγεῖν προαγῶνι.[2] (16) οὕτω δ' αὐτὸν Φιλήμων ἠγάπησεν ὡς καὶ τάδε περὶ αὐτοῦ τολμῆσαι εἰπεῖν [fr. 118 K.-A.]·

    εἰ ταῖς ἀληθείαισιν οἱ τεθνηκότες
    αἴσθησιν εἶχον, ἄνδρες, ὥς φασίν τινες,
    ἀπηγξάμην ἄν, ὥστ' ἰδεῖν Εὐριπίδην.

οὕτως ἡγοῦντο πολλοῦ τινος ἄξιον.

**4 P. Oxy. 1176, Satyrus, *Vita Euripidis* (maiora tantum frustula)**

(1) fr. 1: ἀλλαχῇ πό[λλ' ἐρ]ητόριζε[ν ἐν] τοῖς λόγοι[ς ὢν] λογικὸ[ς καὶ] παραμιμή[σασθ]αι

---

[1] Jacobs: ᾗπερ vel ἡ γὰρ codd.
[2] ex T 1.20 correxi: πρὸς τὸν ἀγῶνα codd.

Choirile. He had three sons, Mnesarchides, a trader, Mnesilochus, an actor, and his namesake Euripides, who spent his time in intellectual pursuits. (11) He was pensive and morose in nature, sullen and a hater of laughter, as Aristophanes' mockery has it '[Euripides] for my taste sour to talk to'[1]. (12) Having caught his actor Cephisophon lying with his wife and being unable to bear the shame thus caused since he was mocked by the comic poets, he left his life in Athens and went off to the court of King Archelaus. There he was splendidly received and highly favored and thought deserving of the greatest honor. (13) While he was living there, when he happened to be meditating in some grove or other, he was reportedly devoured at more than seventy years of age by the hounds of Archelaus, who had gone out on a hunt. (14) He was buried in Macedonia, but there is a cenotaph to him in Athens on which stands the following epigram by Thucydides the historian or Timotheus the lyric poet:

> All Hellas is the tomb of Euripides, but his bones rest in the land of Macedon for it was there that he died. His home was Athens, the Hellas of Hellas. Since he gave delight on many occasions with his poetry, from many lips too does he win praise.

(15) They say that when the news of Euripides' death was heard, all the Athenians mourned, and that Sophocles even wore a dark-grey cloak himself and brought on his actors without their garlands in the *proagon* that was then taking place. Philemon loved him so much that he had the hardihood to say this about him:

> If in very truth the dead possessed any perception, gentlemen, as some claim they do, I would have hanged myself in order to see Euripides.

So highly did men regard him.

**4** Satyrus, principal fragments of a *Life of Euripides* in dialogue form[2]

(1) fr. 1: ...in other ways he was very much the speech-writer in the dialogue portions of his plays, being prosaic in style and (capable of) imitating...

---

[1] See above, p. 7, n. 1.
[2] Most recent edition, with commentary, is by G. Arrighetti, *Studi Classici e Orientali* 13 (1964). See the review by S. R. West, *Gnomon* 38 (1966), 546-50 and also M. R. Lefkowitz, 'Satyrus the Historian', *Atti del XVII Congresso Internazionale di Papirologia* (Naples, 1984), pp. 339-43.

(2) fr. 8 II: ἀλ]λὰ καὶ [ηὔξ]εν καὶ ἐ[τε]λείωσεν ὥστε τοῖς μετ' αὐτὸν ὑπερβολὴν μὴ λιπεῖν. [κ]ατὰ μὲν οὖν [τ]ὴν τέχνην [ἀ]νὴρ τοιοῦτος. διὸ καὶ Ἀριστοφάνης [fr. 656 K.-A.] ἐπιθυμεῖ τὴν γλῶσσαν αὐτοῦ μετρῆσαι "δι' ἧς τὰ [λεπ]τὰ ῥήματ' [ἐξεσμ]ήχετο". [ἔτι δ]ὲ καὶ τὴν [ψυ]χὴν μέγας [ἦν] σχεδὸν [ὡς] ἐν τοῖς [ποι-ή]μασιν[1]. [προσ]εμάχε[το γὰ]ρ ὥσπερ [προ]είρη[κ]α

(3) fr. 37 I: [οὐκ ἐπὶ] τοῖς [ἰ]δίοις ἀγαθοῖς [ὑ]ψηλὸς ὢν [ο]ὐκ ἐπὶ τοῖς [ἀλ]λοτρίοις [ψό]γοις ταπει[νού]μενος· ἐ[τίμ]α[2] δὲ τὸν [Ἀνα]ξαγόραν [δαιμ]ονίως

(4) fr. 37 III: "...σο[ὶ τ]ῶι π[άν]των μεδ[έον]τι χλόην π[ε]λανόν τε φέρ[ω] Ζεὺς εἴ[θ'] "Αιδης ὀνομ[άζηι]" [fr. 912 N[2]]. ἀκριβῶς ὅλως περιείληφε[ν] τὸν Ἀναξ[α]γόρειον [διά]κοσμον [ἐν][3] τρισὶν περι[όδοις·][4] καὶ ἄλληι γ[έ] πηι διαπορ[εῖ] τί πότ' ἐστι τὸ προεστηκὸς τῶν οὐρανίων· "Ζεὺς [εἴ]τ' ἀνάγκ[η φύσεω]ς εἴτ[ε νοῦς βροτῶν ..." [Troades 886]

(5) fr. 38 I: -σασθαι [τὸν] Ἡρακλέα· [καὶ] δὴ καὶ τὴν [αὐ]τὴν[5] ἐπιφ[υομέν]ην τοῖς προειρημένοις [ἐπε]ὶ λέγει [fr. 913 N[2]]. "τίς [ἀτι]μόθεος [κ]αὶ [πα]ραδαίμ[ων ὃς] τάδε λεύσ[σω]ν οὐ προδι[δά]σκει ψυχὴν [αὐ]τοῦ θεὸν ἡ[γεῖ]σθαι, μετε[ωρ]ολόγων δ' ἐ-[κὰ]ς ἔρριψεν [σκολιὰ]ς ἀπά[τας ὧν] τολ[μηρὰ γλ]ῶσσ' εἰ[κοβολ]εῖ [περὶ τῶν ἀ]φα[νῶν..."

(6) fr. 38 IV + 39 I: μετῆλθεν [δ]ὲ πρὸς τ[ὸ αἰ]σχ[ρ]ὸν π[αρὰ τῶι] ὄ[χ]λωι τ[ῶι] θαυμά[ζει]ν τὸν Σω[κρά]τη πολὺ [μάλιστ]α ὥστ' ἀπ[οφα]ινόμενο[ς ἐν] τῆι Δανάη[ι π]ερὶ πλεονε[ξί]ας μόνον [αὐ]-τὸν πάν[τ]ων ἐποιή[σα]τ' ἐξαίρετον

(7) fr. 39 II: [τ]όνδ[ε τ]ὸν [τ]ρόπο[ν· "—λ]άθρα[ι] δὲ τού[τ]ων δρωμένων τίνας φοβῆι; —τοὺς μείζονα βλ[έ]ποντας ἀ[ν]θρώπων θεούς" [fr. 1007c N[2]]. (B) Εἴη ἂν ἡ τοιαύτη ὑπόνοια περ[ὶ] θεῶν [Σω]κρατική· τῶι γὰρ ὄντι τὰ [θ]νητοῖς ἀόρατα τοῖς ἀθανάτοις

---

[1] Hunt
[2] S. R. West
[3] Hunt-Wilamowitz
[4] Hunt-Wilamowitz
[5] Hunt

(2) fr. 8 II: ...but he also augmented it and brought it to perfection in such a way as to leave no room for his successors to improve on them. This was his nature as an artist. That is why Aristophanes longs to measure his tongue 'with which he licked his fine-spun words into shape'. Furthermore, he was also great in his soul, comparably with his poetry. For, as I have already said, he was engaged in a fight against...

(3) fr. 37 I: ...<not> being made proud over his own good qualities nor cast down by the censures of others. And he honored Anaxagoras to a remarkable extent...

(4) fr. 37 III: '...to thee who rulest all I bring herbs and an offering of batter, whether thou art called Zeus or Hades'. Here he gives a wholly accurate summary in three verse-periods of the cosmic doctrine of Anaxagoras. And in another place he is in doubt what is the power that presides over the gods: 'Zeus, whether thou art the necessity of nature or the mind of mortals...'

(5) fr. 38 I: ...Heracles...and further the same...as what was said before when he says, 'What a godless and ill-fated wretch is he that as he looks on these things does not teach his soul beforehand to believe in God and has not cast from himself the twisted deceits of those who ponder things above, men whose bold tongues talk idly and at random about things unseen...'

(6) fr. 38 IV + 39 I: ...and he came into disgrace in the eyes of the multitude for admiring Socrates to the very highest degree, with the result that when, in the *Danae*, he gave his opinion about avarice, he made Socrates alone exempt from it...

(7) fr. 39 II: ...in this fashion: '(1st speaker) Since these things are being done in secret, whom do you fear? (2nd speaker) The gods whose sight is greater than that of mortals'. (B) This kind of opinion about the gods will be Socratic; for in reality things invisible to

εὐκάτοπτα. (Α) Καὶ μὴν καὶ τὸ [μισο]τυραννεῖν [καὶ τὰ πλή]θη καὶ [τὰς δυναστ]είας [τῶν ὀλίγ]ων

(8) fr. 39 III: [εἰ]π[ό]ντι, κα[ὶ δὴ] κα[ὶ] τὸ μη[δένα] τῶν ἀστῶ[ν με]τεωρίζει[ν ὑπὲ]ρ τ[ὸ] μέτρ[ιον μ]ηδὲ τύραν[νον] ποιεῖν καὶ [ἀστ]οῖς φαύλοις μὴ διδόναι πάροδον πρὸς τὰ ἔντιμα. μέγιστον γὰρ ἕλκος πόλεως κακὸς ῥήτωρ, δημαγωγὸς πέρα τῆς ἀξίας π⟨ρο⟩αγόμενος[1]. ἀλλὰ μήν, ὦ Διοδώ[ρα,] καὶ περ[ὶ τ]ῆς κοινῆς [τ]ῶν ['Α]θη[ναίω]ν [ἀ]βουλ[ίας

(9) fr. 39 IV: "...[οὐ]χὶ τ[ο]ῦτον τ[ὸν τρ]όπον, ἄλλο[υ[2] δὲ τ]ῆι πονηρ[ίαι] π[ρ]οσχρώμεθα [καὶ] τῶι[3] μάλισ[θ' ὅσ'] ἂν λέγ[ηι] πισ[τεύ]ομεν, λέγ[οντ]ες ο[ὐ] πονη[ρ]ά, μ[άλα][4] δὲ χρώ[μενοι,] κἄπειτ[α τῆς] ἐκκλησία[ς κα]τηγορεῖ ἕκασ[τος] ἡμῶν ἧς ἕκασ[τος] αὐτὸς ἦν" [fr. adesp. 294(b) Austin]. (Β) Πολλὰ καὶ παρὰ τῶν κωμικῶν ποιητῶν, ὡς ἔοικεν, ἅμα αὐστηρῶς λέγεται καὶ πολιτικῶς. (Α) Πῶς γὰρ οὔ; πάλιν γοῦν ὁ μὲν Εὐριπίδης εὖ μάλα πρὸς ἀλκὴν καὶ εὐψυχίαν παρακαλεῖ τοὺς νέους ὑποβάλ[λ]ων αὐτοῖς ὁρμὰς Λακωνικὰς καὶ θυμοποι[ῶν] τὸ πλῆθ[ο]ς οὕτως [fr. 1007d N[2]]· "κτήσασθ' ἐν ὑστέροισιν εὔ[κ]λειαν χρόνοι[ς, ἅ]πασαν ἀντλήσαντες ἡμέρα[ν πόν]ον, ψυχαῖς..."

(10) fr. 39 VI: "...[καὶ τῶι] τεκόν[τι] π[α]τρὶ δυσμενέστατοι· δ⟨ό⟩μων γὰρ ἄρχε[ι]ν εἰς ἔρωτ' ἀφιγμένοι τοῖς φιλτάτοις κυρ[ο]ῦσι πολεμιώτατοι· σμικρ[οὶ] γέροντι πα[ῖ]δες ἡδίους πατρί" [fr. 1007e-f N[2]]. (Β) Φαίη τις ἂν ἀμέλει κα[τ]ά γε τῶν πλείστων [νῦ]ν κακῶς ἠγμένων μ[α]ντευόμενος. σπουδάζουσι γὰρ ὅτι τάχος οἱ τοιοῦτοι τοῦ τε πατρὸς καὶ τῶν ὑπαρχόντων ποιήσασ[θαι τ]ὴν ἐκφο[ρὰν

(11) fr. 39 VII: πρὸς γ[υ]ναῖκα καὶ πατρὶ πρὸς υ[ἱὸ]ν καὶ θερά-[πον]τι πρὸς δ[εσ]πότην, ἢ τ[ὰ κ]ατὰ τὰς π[ερι]πετείας, β[ια]σμοὺς παρθ[έ]νων, ὑποβολὰς παιδίων, ἀναγνωρισμοὺς διά τε δακτυλίων καὶ διὰ δεραίων· ταῦτα γάρ ἐστι δήπου τὰ συνέχοντα τὴν

---

[1] Hunt-Wilamowitz
[2] ἀλλ' οὐδὲ Austin
[3] ὅτ]ε τωι legit Austin
[4] Richards

mortals are easily seen by the gods. (A) Yes, and what is more to hate tyrants and <to regard with suspicion?> multitudes and the power of oligarchs...

(8) fr. 39 III: ...and furthermore to exalt none of the citizens above what is moderate and to make no one a tyrant and not to give worthless citizens access to high office. For the greatest wound a city can suffer is an evil politician, a demagogue advanced beyond his worth. But, Diodora, about the common folly of the Athenians...

(9) fr. 39 IV: '...not thus, but we make use of the wickedness of another and we trust completely whatever he says, not speaking evil ourselves but very much doing it. And then each man of us accuses the assembly of which he himself was a member'. (B) It seems that also in the comic poets one can find many things written in an astringent public spirit. (A) But of course. And then again Euripides admirably exhorts the young to valor and courage, urging Spartan charges on them and making the multitude bold, in this fashion: 'Acquire in after days fair renown by enduring labor the livelong day, and in your hearts...'

(10) fr. 39 VI: '...and most hostile to the father that begat them. For conceiving a desire to rule the house, they are in fact most inimical to their near and dear. But small children are to their aged father a greater pleasure'. (B) So one would say, no doubt, prophesying about the majority of those now brought up badly. For such persons are eager to carry out their father for burial with all speed and to remove his property...

(11) fr. 39 VII: ...<the husband> towards the wife, and the father towards the son and the slave towards the master; or in the swift reversals of fortune, violations of maidens, palmings off of children, recognitions by means of rings and necklaces. For these are the things in which New Comedy consists, and Euripides developed them to perfection, Homer being the first to use a conversational ar-

νεωτέραν κωμωιδίαν, ἃ πρὸς ἄκρον ἦγα[γ]εν Εὐριπίδης. Ὁμήρου [ὄ]ντος ἀρχῆς καὶ στίχων γε συντάξεως λεκτικῆς· μαρτυρ[ε]ῖ δ' αὐτῶι καὶ τοῦτ' [ε]ἰκότως ὁ Φι[λ]ήμων ἐν[τα]υθί [fr. 153 K.-A.]· "Εὐρι[πί]δης πού φησιν, οὗτος [ὃς] μόνος δύ[να]ται λ[έ]γε[ιν"

(12) fr. 39 IX: [κεκτη]μέν[ος] δ' [αὐ]τόθι σπήλαιον τὴν ἀναπνοιὴν ἔχον εἰς τὴν θάλατταν, ἐν τούτωι διημέρευεν καθ' αὑ[τ]ὸν μεριμνῶν ἀεί τ[ι] καὶ γράφων ἁπλῶς ἅπαν εἴ τι μὴ μεγαλεῖον ἢ σεμνὸν ἡ[τι]μακώς. ὁ γ[ο]ῦν Ἀριστοφ[άν]ης φησὶν ὥ[σ]περ ἐπ' αὐτῶι τούτω[ι] κεκ[λη]μένος "{τ}ο[ῖ]α μὲν π[οι]εῖ λέγε[ι]ν τοιός ἐστιν" [fr. 694 K.-A.]. [ἀλ]λὰ θεώ[με]νος κω[μωι]δίαν λ[έγεταί] ποτε

(13) fr. 39 X: ἀπήχθοντ' αὐτῶι πάντες, οἱ μὲν ἄνδρε[ς] διὰ τὴν δυ[σ]ομιλίαν, α[ἱ δὲ] γυναῖκε[ς δ]ιὰ τοὺς ψ[ό]γους τοὺς ἐν τοῖς ποιήμασιν. ἦλθεν δ' εἰς κίνδυνον ἀφ' ἑκατέρου τῶν γενῶν μέγαν. ὑπὸ μὲν γὰρ Κλέωνος τοῦ δημαγωγοῦ τὴν τῆς ἀσεβείας δίκην ἔφυγεν ἣν προειρήκαμεν, αἱ δὲ γυναῖκες ἐπισυνέστησαν αὐτῶι τοῖς Θεσμοφορίοις καὶ ἀθρόαι παρῆ[σ]αν ἐπὶ τὸν [τό]πον ἐν ὧι [σ]χολάζων [ἐ]τύγχανεν· [δι]ωρισμέναι [δὲ] ἐφε[ίσαν]το τἀν[δρὸ]ς ἅμα μὲν [ἀγ]ασθεῖσαι [τὰς] μούσας

(14) fr. 39 XII: "...[τῆι τῶ]ν γυ[ναι]κῶν· Ἀρ[χίκλ]εια ἐπε[στ]άτει, Λύσιλ[λ' ἐ]γραμμάτευεν, εἶπε Σωστράτη" [Ar. Thesmo. 374-5]. "εἴ τις ἐπιβουλεύει τι τῶι δήμωι κακὸν τῶι τῶν γυναικῶν ἢ ἐπικηρυκεύετ[αι] Εὐριπίδ⟨η Μήδοις⟩[1] τ' ἐπὶ βλάβη[ι] τινί" [ibid. 335-7]. (Α) Σαφῶς ὑπονενόηκας ὃ λέ[γ]ω καὶ παραλέλυκάς με [τ]ῆς ἐξηγήσε[ω]ς· προσώχ[θι]σεν δὲ τῶι [γ]ένει το[ύ]των χάριν· ἦν, ὡς ἔοικεν, π[α]ρ' αὐτῶι μειρακίσκος οἰκογενὴς ὄνομα Κηφισοφῶν. [πρ]ὸς τοῦτον οὖν [ἐ]φώρασε τ[ὴ]ν γυναῖκ[α τὴ]ν ἰδίαν [αὐτο]ῦ [ἀ]τακ[το]ῦ[σαν

(15) fr. 39 XIII: τἀδίκημ' ἐν[ε]γκών, ὡς μ[νη]μονεύου[σι,] τ[ὴ]ν μὲν ἄ[ν]θ[ρ]ωπον ἐκ[έ]λ[ευ]σεν τῶ[ι] νεανίσκ[ωι] συνοικεῖ[ν, ἐ]πειδήπερ [αὐ]τὴ[2] προ[είλε]το, "ἵνα μ[ὴ τὴν] ἐμὴν ο[ὗτ]ο[ς]

---
[1] Hunt
[2] Schmidt

rangement of his verses.[1] And Philemon properly attests to this character in him in saying, 'I think Euripides says, Euripides, who alone is able to speak...'

(12) fr. 39 IX: ...since he possessed a cave there with the mouth opening toward the sea, it was there that he passed his days thinking by himself and writing, simply disdaining everything that was not high and lofty.[2] At any rate, Aristophanes, as though summoned on purpose as a witness, says 'As are the speeches he gives his characters, so is the man'. But the story is told that once while he was watching a comedy...

(13) fr. 39 X: Everyone became his enemy, the men because he was so unpleasant to talk to, the women because of his abuse of them in his poetry. He ran into great danger from both sexes. For as we have mentioned he was prosecuted for impiety by Cleon the demagogue. And the women conspired against him during the Thesmophoria and came in a body to the place where he happened to be studying.[3] But with this stipulation they spared the man, first out of respect for the Muses...

(14) fr. 39 XII: '...<resolved by the assembly> of women, <Archi>cleia presiding, Lysilla being secretary, on the motion of Sostrate.' 'If anyone plots any harm against the women-folk or parlays with Euripides or the Mede for any harmful purpose.' (A) You have clearly understood my meaning and have saved me from having to explain it. He was put out with the sex for this reason. It seems there was, living in his house, a young home-born slave by the name of Cephisophon.[4] With him he discovered his own wife misbehaving...

(15) fr. 39 XIII: ...<When> he had borne the outrage <as best he could>, he told the woman, as the story goes, to live with the young man, since that was the way she chose, 'so that', he said, 'he may not

---

[1] Cf. T 84.
[2] Cf. T 1.22, 5.5.
[3] Cf. T 1.25, 1.30.
[4] Cf. T 1.29, 3.12.

ἔχηι", φησίν, "ἀλλ' ἐγὼ τὴν τούτου· δίκαιον γάρ, ἄνπερ βούλωμα[ι]". πρὸς ὅλον δὲ τὸ φῦλον δ[ι]ετέλει μαχόμενος ἐν τοῖς ποιήμασιν. (Β) Νὴ γελοίως γε. τί γὰρ ἄν τις εὐλογώτερο[ν] διὰ τὴν φθ[α]ρεῖσαν ψέγοι τὰς γυν[αῖ]κας ἢ διὰ τὸν φθείραντα τοὺς ἄνδρας; ἐπεὶ τ[άς] γε κακίας καὶ τὰς ἀρετὰς καθάπερ ἔλεγεν ὁ Σω⟨κρ⟩άτη⟨ς⟩[1] τὰς αὐτὰς [ἐν] ἀμφοῖν ἔ[στιν] εὑρεῖν· σ[κο]πεῖν δ' ἄξ[ιον

(16) fr. 39 XIV: [π]ρὸς αὐτὴν ὡς φαρμάτ[τ]οι φίλτρ[ο]ις [τ]ὸν Ὑστάσπην. μεταπεμψαμένη δὴ τὴν ἄνθρωπον ὅτ' εἶ[δεν] εἰσιούσης τὸ μέγεθος καὶ τὸ κάλλος, "χαῖρε", φησίν, "γύναι· ψευδεῖς ἄρ' ἦ[σ]αν αἱ [δια]βολαί· σὺ γὰρ [ἐν] τῶι π[ρ]οσώπωι τῶι σ[ῶι κ]αὶ τ[οῖ]ς ὀ[φ]θαλμοῖς ἔχεις τὰ φάρμακα". (Α) Εὖ γ', ὦ κρατίστη πασῶν καὶ τῶι ὄντι Εὔκλεια, δι[ό]τ[ι] τὰ τοιαῦτα τῶν ἠθῶν καὶ διὰ μνήμης ἔχεις κα[ὶ

(17) fr. 39 XV: -μαχε[ῖ]ν τέως ἐκράτησαν τῶν ἐναντίων· κατ' ἐμὲ μὲν [γ]ὰρ τοῦτο θε[τ]έον τὸ νίκημα τῶν γυναικῶν. οἱ μὲν γὰρ ἄνδρες ὅσον ἐφ' ἑαυτοῖς ἡττῶντο. (Α) Ἴ[σ]ως, ὦ Διοδώρ[α]· πλὴν ταῦτα μὲν συνηγορήσθω ταῖς γ[υ]ναιξίν· ἐπανάγωμεν δ[ὲ] πάλιν ἐπὶ τὸν Εὐριπίδην· ἐκεῖνος γὰρ ἅμα μὲν προσοχθίσας τῶι ἐπιχωρίωι φθόνωι τῶν πολιτῶν, ἅμα δὲ ἀχθόμενος ἐπὶ τῶι συννέμεσθαι πολλ[ά]κις Ἀκέστο[ρι κ]αὶ Δοριλάωι [καὶ] Μορσίμωι [καὶ] Μελανθίωι-- (Β) [Πρὸς] τοῦ Διὸς [τίν]ων ὀνόμα[τα λ]έγεις; ἢ ποι[ητά]ς; (Α) Ποιη[

(18) fr. 39 XVI: "...χ[. . .] δὲ Σοφοκλ[. .] λαβὼν πα[ρ' Αἰ]σχύλου ν[. . .]ρ ὅσον [. . . .]εσθ' ὅλον Εὐριπίδην, πρὸς τοισίδ' ἐμβα[λ]εῖν ἅλας, μ[εμ]νημένος δ' ὅπως ἅλας καὶ μὴ λάλας" [Aristoph. fr. 595 K.-A.]. (Β) Ἐοίκασιν ἀνδρὸς εἶναι τῶν ἀ[ντι]διδασκόντων αὐτῶ[ι,] καθάπερ εἶπας, ἀτ[ὰ]ρ σιναμώρως γε κἀνταῦθα πάλιν ὁ κωμω[ι]δοδιδάσκαλος ἐπέδακ[νε]ν τὸν Εὑρ[ιπ]ίδην. (Α) τοῦ ⟨δ'⟩[2] [ἐπ]ομένου χειμ[ῶ]νος ἄλλαι[. . .]. ἄλλοι

---

[1] Hunt-Wilamowitz
[2] Hunt

enjoy my wife but rather I his: for this is fair if I wish it thus'.[1] And he continued to fight against the whole sex in his poems. (Diodora) Laughably so. For why is it more reasonable for someone to find fault with women because of a woman seduced than with men because of the man who seduced her? For, as Socrates used to say, it is possible to find the same vices and the same virtues in both. But it is worthwhile to consider...

(16) fr. 39 XIV: ...<accused the woman to her> of drugging Hystaspes[2] with love-philtres. And when she had summoned the creature and seen her height and beauty as she entered the room, she said 'Welcome, woman. The slanders against you are false, as it now seems. For it is in your face and your eyes that you have those philtres'. (A) Well done, best of women and rightly named Eucleia, that you remember such traits of character and...

(17) fr. 39 XV: ...so long did they have the strength to fight their adversaries. For in my view this must be regarded as the victory of the women. The men, so far as in them lay, were defeated. (A) Perhaps, Diodora; but let this be the end of your brief on behalf of women and let us return to Euripides. He, partly in annoyance at the ill-will of his fellow-citizens and partly being vexed at his frequent association with Acestor and Dorilaus and Morsimus and Melanthius— (Di.) By Zeus, whose names are you speaking? Poets? (A) Yes, poets...

(18) fr. 39 XVI: '...take...Sophocles...from Aeschylus...a whole Euripides, and add in addition some salt, but take care to make that "salt," not "talkative women."'[3] (B) These charges seem, as you say, to be from one of his competitors. But even here the comic poet stung Euripides with harmful intent. (A) In the following winter...

---

[1] For interpretation, see S. R. West, *Gnomon* 38 (1966), 549-50 and D. Kovacs, *ZPE* 89 (1990), 15-18. Euripides proposes to cuckold Cephisophon where before he had been cuckolded by him.

[2] Probably the father of the Persian king Darius. This story has a parallel in Plutarch's *Advice to Bride and Groom* 141B. Its relevance to the life of Euripides may be to contrast Euripides' exaggerated reaction to his wife's infidelity with the calm response of Hystaspes' wife to that of her husband.

[3] The pun ἄλας /λάλας cannot be translated.

(19) fr. 39 XVII: "...ὅπου ποτ' οἰκεῖ σώματος λαχὼν μέρος, ἐν χερσὶ[ν], ἐ]ν σπλάγχν[οι]σιν ἢ παρ' [ὄ]μματα" [Eur. fr. 403 N²], προσυπέθηκεν τούτοις χλευαστικῶς "ὅπαι καθεύδουσ' ἁ κύων τὰν ῥῖν' ἔχει". οὗτο[ι] μὲν οὖν, ὅπερ εἶπα, πρὸς τὴν τῶν πολλῶν ἐπολιτεύοντο χάριν. ἐκεῖνός γε μὴν καθάπερ διαμαρτυρίαν θέμενος ἀπείπατο τὰς Ἀθήνας. (Β) Ποίαν ταύτην; (Α) Ἐν τῶιδε κατακεχωρισμένην τῶι στασίμωι [fr. 911 N²]· "χρύσεαι δή μοι πτέρυγες περὶ νώτω[ι κ]αὶ τὰ Σειρή[νω]ν πτε[ρόεν]τα πέδ[ι]λ' [ἁρμό]ζετα[ι, βάσομ]αι δ' ἀ[ν' αἰθέρα π]ουλὺ[ν ἀερθείς, Ζηνὶ..."

(20) fr. 39 XVIII: ἐξῆρχεν τὰς μελω[ιδία]ς, ἢ οὐκ [οἶσθα] ὅτι κα[ὶ τοῦ]τ' ἔσ[θ' ὅ] φη[σὶν] αὐτ[ός;] (Β) Πῶς οὖν; (Α) "Ζηνὶ συμμεί[ξω]ν ὁρμάν" λέγω[ν] μεταφορικῶς ἐμφαίνει τὸν μόναρχον, ἅ⟨μ⟩α[1] καὶ [συ]ναύξων τἀνδρὸς τὴν ὑπεροχήν. (Β) Κομψώ[τ]ε[ρ]α φαίνε[ι μοι] λέγειν ἤπε[ρ] ἀληθινώτερα· (Α) ⟨Πά⟩ρεστιν[2] ὡς θέλε[ι]ς ἐκδέχεσθαι. μετελθὼν δ' οὖν κατεγήρασε ἐν Μακεδονίαι μάλ' ἐντίμως ἀγόμενος παρὰ τῶι δυνάστηι τά τε λοιπ[ὰ] καὶ δὴ καὶ μν[η]μονεύε[ται ὅ]τι οὕτ[ως

(21) fr. 39 XIX: (Α) οὐ κακῶς εἴρηκας· τὰ μὲν γὰρ τῶν [Ἀ]θή[ν]{ι}ησιν [οὐ]δὲ λέγειν ἄξι[ο]ν, οἵ γε ποιητὴν τηλικοῦτον Μακεδόνων καὶ Σικελιωτῶν ὕστερον ἤισθοντο. λέγεται γοῦν, ὅτε Νικίας ἐστράτευσεν ἐπὶ Σικελίαν καὶ πολ[λ]οὶ τῶν Ἀθηναίων ἐγένοντ' αἰχμάλωτοι, συχνοὺς αὐτῶν ἀνασωθῆναι διὰ τῶν Εὐριπίδου ποιημάτων, ὅσοι κατέχοντες τῶν στίχων τινὰς διδάξε[ι]αν τοὺς υἱεῖς τῶν εἰληφότων ὑποχειρίους αὐτούς· οὕτως ἡ Σικελ[ί]α ἅπ[ασ]α τὸν Εὐ[ριπίδη]ν ἀπεθαύμασ]εν. καὶ [μὴν ὑ]π' Ἀρχε[λάου

(22) fr. 39 XX: "...ἔχε[ι] τὸ στόμα καὶ [καθ' ὑπ]ερβολ[ὴν δυσῶδες]". ὁ δ' ὑ[πολαβὼν,] "οὐκ εὐ[φη]μήσεις", εἶπεν, "ὦ παῖ; ποῖον δὲ στόμα τ{οι}ούτ[ο]⟨υ⟩[3] γέγονεν ἢ γένοιτ' ἂν ἥδιον, δι' οὗ γε δὴ τοιαῦτα μέλη τε καὶ ἔπη διαπορεύεται;" (Β) Ὅμοιος οὗτος, καθάπερ εἴρ⟨η⟩κας, δαιμ[ον]ίως ἐντ[. . . .]ακότι πρὸ[ς] τὸν ποιητήν. (Α) Ζῶντι μὲν δὴ ταῦθ' ὑπῆρξεν Εὐριπίδηι. τελευτῆς δὲ

---
[1] Hunt-Wilamowitz
[2] Hunt-Wilamowitz
[3] post Richards ego

(19) fr. 39 XVII: '...in whatever part of the body it dwells, in the hands or the inward parts, or next the eyes', he added mockingly to this 'wherever the bitch puts her nose when she sleeps'. So these, as I said, conducted themselves with a view to pleasing the many. He, however, after entering, as it were, a solemn protest, renounced Athens. (Di.) What protest was that? (A) It is set off by itself in the following choral ode, 'There are golden wings about my back and the winged sandals of the Sirens are fitted on my feet, and I shall go aloft far into the heavens, there with Zeus...'

(20) fr. 39 XVIII: ...began the songs. Or do you not know that it is this that he says? (Di.) What do you mean? (A) In saying 'mingle my flight with Zeus' he hints metaphorically at the monarch[1] and at the same time increases the man's preeminence. (Di.) It seems to me that you speak with more subtlety than truth. (A) You may understand it as you like. At any rate, he went over and spent his old age in Macedonia, enjoying very high honor with the king; and in particular the story is told that...

(21) fr. 39 XIX: (A) That is not a bad point: for it is not worth mentioning the judgement of those in Athens seeing that they learned he was such a great poet only later from the Macedonians and Sicilians. At any rate the story is that, when Nicias made the expedition against Sicily and many of the Athenians were taken captive, large numbers owed their lives to the poems of Euripides, those men, that is, who knew some of the lines by heart and taught them to the sons of their captors: so greatly did all of Sicily admire Euripides.[2] And what is more, by Archelaus he was...

(22) fr. 39 XX: '...his mouth is...and exceedingly malodorous'. But he said in reply, 'Hush, boy. What mouth has ever been or could be sweeter than this mouth through which pass songs and words such as these?'[3] (B) He resembles, as you say, someone < > towards the poet. (A) That is what befell Euripides during his lifetime. But the death he met with was most unpleasant and strange, as

---

[1] Archelaus: cf. T 1.11, 1.35, etc.
[2] Cf. T 92.
[3] Cf. T 1.28, 5.8.

μάλα δυσχεροῦς καὶ ἰδίας ἔτυχεν, ὡς οἱ λόγιοί τε καὶ γεραίτατοι μυθολο[γ]οῦσι Μακεδ[ό]νων. (Β) Πῶς λέ[γουσιν;] (Α) Ἔστ[ιν] ἐ[ν Μακεδονίαι

(23) fr. 39 XXI: ὃ δὴ[1] παρηιτήσατο. χρό[νωι δ' ὕ]στερ[ον] ὁ μ[ὲν] Εὐρι[πί]δη[ς ἔτυ]χεν ἀ[πω]τέ[ρω] τῆς πόλεως ἐν ἄλσει τινι καθ' αὑτὸν ἐρημαζόμενος, ὁ δ' Ἀρχέλαος ἐπὶ κυνηγίαν ἐξήιει. γενόμενοι δ' ἔξω τῶν πυλῶν οἱ θηρευταὶ λύσαντες τοὺς σκύλακας προαφῆκαν, αὐτο[ὶ δ' ἀ]πελείποντ[ο] κάτοπιν· ἐπιτυχόντες οὖν ο[ἱ] κύνες τῶι Εὐριπίδηι μονουμένωι διέφθειραν αὐτόν, ο[ἳ] δ' ἐπιπαρεγενήθησαν ὕστερον· ὅθεν ἔτι καὶ νῦν λέγεσθαί φασιν [τ]ὴν παροιμί[α]ν ἐν τοῖς Μα[κ]εδόσιν ὡς "ἔ[στι] καὶ κυνὸς [δί]κη". καὶ γὰ[ρ ἐκ] τῶν σκυ[λάκων

(24) fr. 39 XXII: τοῦ Τιμοθέου παρὰ τ[οῖ]ς Ἕλλη[σι]ν διὰ [τ]ὴν ἐ[ν τ]ῆι μου[σι]κῆ[ι] καινοτ[ο]μίαν καὶ κ[α]θ' ὑπερβολὴν ἀθυμήσαντος ὥστε κα[ὶ] τὰς χεῖρας ἑαυτῶι διεγνωκέναι προσφέρειν, μόνος Εὐριπίδης ἀνάπαλιν τῶν μὲν θεατῶν καταγελάσαι, τὸν δὲ Τιμόθεον α[ἰσ]θόμενος ἡλίκος ἐστὶν ἐν τῶι γένει παραμυθήσασθαί τε λόγους διεξιὼν ὡς οἷόν τε παρακ[λ]ητικωτάτους, καὶ δὴ καὶ τὸ τῶν Περσῶν προοίμιον συγγράψαι, τ⟨ῷ⟩ τε νικῆ[σ]αι παύσασθ[αι] καταφ[ρ]ο[νουμ]ενον [αὐτίκα τὸν] Τι[μόθεον

**5 Aul. Gell. 15.20**

(1) Euripidi poetae matrem Theopompus [*FGrH* 115 F 397] agrestia olera vendentem victum quaesisse dicit. (2) Patri autem eius nato illo responsum est a Chaldaeis eum puerum, cum adolevisset, victorem in certaminibus fore; id ei puero fatum esse. (3) Pater interpretatus athletam debere esse roborato exercitatoque filii sui corpore Olympiam certaturum eum inter athletas pueros deduxit. Ac primo quidem in certamen per ambiguam aetem receptus non est, post Eleusino et Theseo certamine pugnavit et coronatus est. (4) Mox a corporis cura ad excolendi animi studium transgressus auditor fuit physici Anaxagorae et Prodici rhetoris, in morali autem

---

[1] ὁ δὲ legit Hunt, ὁ δὴ Arrighetti: quae lectio si vera est, ὃ scribendum arbitror

the chroniclers and old men of Macedon tell the tale. (Di.) What do they say? (A) There is in Macedonia...

(23) fr. 39 XXI: ...and he won their release.[1] Some time later Euripides happened to be spending time alone in a grove some distance from the city, while Archelaus was going out to the hunt. And when the huntsmen were outside the gates of the city, they let loose their hounds and sent them ahead while they themselves were left behind. And when the hounds encountered Euripides, they killed him, and the huntsmen came along too late. And that, as the story goes, is why there is a proverb in Macedonia, 'There is a justice even for dogs'. For these <were descended> from the hounds...[2]

(24) fr. 39 XXII: ...when Timotheus <suffered criticism> among the Greeks for his innovation in music and was highly dispirited, so that he decided to do away with himself, only Euripides again ridiculed the spectators, and since he perceived how great the man was in his genre, he both consoled him, speaking the most encouraging words he could find, and wrote the proem to his *Persians*, and Timotheus, because of his victory, ceased to be despised...[3]

## 5 Aulus Gellius, *Attic Nights*

(1) Theopompus[4] says that the mother of Euripides the poet earned her livelihood by selling vegetables. (2) But when he was born his father received an oracular response from Babylonian soothsayers that when the boy grew up he would be a victor in contests, for that was his fate. (3) The father, concluding that he should be an athlete, trained and strengthened his son's body and took him to Olympia to compete among boy athletes. And at first he was not allowed to compete because of doubts about his age, but afterwards he competed in the Eleusinian and Thesean games and was crowned victor. (4) Thereafter passing from care for the body to a desire to cultivate his mind he became a student of Anaxagoras the physical philosopher and Prodicus the rhetorician, and of Socrates in moral

---

[1] Cf. T 1.21, 1.35, 2.9, 3.13, 5.9.
[2] The story doubtless continued as in T 1.21.
[3] Cf. T 57.
[4] Either the fourth-century historian or (less probably) the fifth-century comic poet.

philosophia Socratis. (5) Tragoediam scribere natus annos duodeviginti adortus est. Philochorus [*FGrH* 328 F 219] refert in insula Salamine speluncam esse taetram et horridam, quam nos vidimus, in qua Euripides tragoedias scriptitarit.

(6) Mulieres fere omnes in maiorem modum exosus fuisse dicitur, sive quod natura abhorruit a mulierum coetu sive quod duas simul uxores habuerat, cum id decreto ab Atheniensibus facto ius esset, quarum matrimonii pertaedebat. (7) Eius odii in mulieres Aristophanes quoque meminit ἐν ταῖς προτέραις Θεσμοφοριαζούσαις in his versibus [*Thesmo*. 453-6]:

νῦν οὖν ἀπάσαισιν παραινῶ καὶ λέγω
τοῦτον κολάσαι τὸν ἄνδρα πολλῶν οὕνεκα.
ἄγρια γὰρ ἡμᾶς, ὦ γυναῖκες, δρᾷ κακὰ
ἅτ' ἐν ἀγρίοισι τοῖς λαχάνοις αὐτὸς τραφείς.

(8) Alexander autem Aetolus [fr. 7 Powell] hos de Euripide versus composuit:

ὁ δ' Ἀναξαγόρου τρόφιμος χαιοῦ στρυφνὸς¹ μὲν ἔμοιγε προσειπεῖν
καὶ μισογέλως καὶ τωθάζειν οὐδὲ παρ' οἶνον μεμαθηκώς,
ἀλλ' ὅ τι γράψειεν ἅπαν² μέλιτος καὶ Σειρήνων ἐπεπνεύκει³.

(9) Is, cum in Macedonia apud Archelaum regem esset utereturque eo rex familiariter, rediens nocte ab eius cena canibus a quodam aemulo inmissis dilaceratus est, et ex his vulneribus mors secuta est. (10) Sepulchrum autem eius et memoriam Macedones eo dignati sunt honore, ut in gloriae quoque loco praedicarent: οὔποτε σὸν μνῆμα, Εὐρίπιδες, ὄλοιτό που,⁴ quod egregius poeta morte obita sepultus in eorum terra foret. Quamobrem cum legati ad eos ab Atheniensibus missi petissent, ut ossa Athenas in terram illius patriam permitterent transferri, maximo consensu Macedones in ea re deneganda perstiterunt.

**6 Marmor Parium, *FGrH* 239 A 50 [=*TrGF* DID D A50]**

ἀφ' οὗ Αἰσχύλος ὁ ποιητὴς τραγῳδίᾳ πρῶτον ἐνίκησε, καὶ Εὐριπίδης ὁ ποιητὴς ἐγένετο, καὶ Στησίχορος ὁ ποιητὴς εἰς τὴν Ἑλλάδα ἀ[φίκετ]ο, ἔτη ΗΗΔΔΙΙ ἄρχοντος Ἀθήνησι Φιλοκράτους.

---

¹ T 1.23: στριφνὸς codd.
² Nauck: γράψαι, τοῦτ ἂν codd.
³ Nauck: ἐτετεύχει codd.
⁴ fort. οὔποτε ⟨μὴ⟩ σὸν μνῆμ', Εὐριπίδη, ⟨ἐνθάδ'⟩ ὄληται.

philosophy. (5) He began to write tragedy at the age of eighteen. Philochorus reports that there is a foul and horrible cave on the island of Salamis, which I have seen, in which Euripides used to write his tragedies.

(6) It is said that he hated practically all women exceedingly, either because by nature he recoiled from intercourse with women or because he had had two wives at the same time—this being allowed by a decree of the Athenians—and was mightily tired of being married to them. (7) Aristophanes also mentions his hatred against women in the first *Thesmophoriazusae* in these verses:

> Now therefore my counsel and proposal to all you women is to punish this man and for more than one reason. Wild are the wrongs he commits against us since he himself was raised amidst wild vegetables.

(8) Alexander of Aetolia wrote these verses about Euripides:

> The protegé of doughty Anaxagoras is for my taste sour to speak to, and he hates laughter and has not learned to jest even over his cups, but whatever he wrote had the fragrance of honey and the Sirens.

(9) When he was in Macedonia at the court of King Archelaus, and the king treated him as his close friend, as he was returning one night from the king's dinner he was torn in pieces by dogs set upon him by a certain rival, and from these wounds death ensued. (10) His tomb and memory the Macedonians so honored that they said as a kind of boast, 'Your tomb, Euripides, will never perish', because an outstanding poet died and was buried in their land. Consequently when ambassadors sent by the Athenians asked that they allow his bones to be moved back to his native land, the Macedonians unanimously persisted in refusing their request.

### B. *Date and Place of Birth; Parentage*[1]

**6** *The Parian Marble*

Since Aeschylus' first victory in tragedy and the birth of Euripides the poet and the arrival of Stesichorus the poet in Greece, 222 years, when Philocrates was archon in Athens [485/4].[2]

---

[1] See also T 1.2, 2.3, and 3.2.
[2] See also T 25 and 67.

**7** Plut. *Quaest. Conv.* 8.1.1, 717C

Εὐριπίδου...γενομένου μὲν ἡμέρᾳ καθ' ἣν οἱ Ἕλληνες ἐναυμάχουν ἐν Σαλαμῖνι πρὸς τὸν Μῆδον,...

**8** Diog. Laert. 2.45

ἀμφότεροι δ' ἤκουσαν Ἀναξαγόρου, καὶ οὗτος [Σωκράτης sc.] καὶ Εὐριπίδης, ὃς καὶ τῷ πρώτῳ ἔτει τῆς ἑβδομηκοστῆς πέμπτης ὀλυμπιάδος ἐγεννήθη ἐπὶ Καλλιάδου.

**9** schol. Ar. *Ach.* 457

σκώπτει αὐτὴν [matrem Euripidis sc.] ὡς λαχανόπωλιν, τὴν Κλειτώ.

**10** Nic. Dam., *FGrH* 90 F 103(v), ap. Stob. vol. 4, p. 159 Wachsmuth-Hense

Βοιωτῶν ἔνιοι τοὺς χρέος οὐκ ἀποδιδόντας εἰς ἀγορὰν ἄγοντες καθίσαι κελεύουσιν, εἶτα κόφινον ἐπιβάλλουσιν αὐτῷ· ὃς δ' ἂν κοφινωθῇ, ἄτιμος γίνεται. δοκεῖ δὲ τοῦτο πεπονθέναι καὶ ὁ Εὐριπίδου πατὴρ Βοιωτὸς τὸ γένος.

**11** Harpocration, s.v. Φλυέα (i 302 Dindorf)

Φλυεῖς δῆμος τῆς Κεκροπίδος. ἐκ τούτου δὲ τοῦ δήμου ἦν Εὐριπίδης ὁ τῆς τραγῳδίας ποιητής.

**12** Theophr. fr. 119 Wimmer apud Athen. 10.24, 424EF

καὶ Εὐριπίδης ὁ ποιητὴς ἐν παισὶν ᾠνοχόησε. Θεόφραστος γοῦν ἐν τῷ περὶ μέθης φησί· "πυνθάνομαι δ' ἔγωγε καὶ Εὐριπίδην τὸν ποιητὴν οἰνοχοεῖν Ἀθήνησι τοῖς ὀρχησταῖς καλουμένοις. ὠρχοῦντο δ' οὗτοι περὶ τὸν τοῦ Ἀπόλλωνος νεὼν τοῦ Δηλίου τῶν πρώτων ὄντες Ἀθηναίων καὶ ἐνεδύοντο ἱμάτια τῶν Θηραϊκῶν. ὁ

**7 Plutarch, *Table-Talk***

Euripides...who was born on the day when the Greeks fought the sea-battle in Salamis against the Mede...[1]

**8 Diogenes Laertius, *Lives of the Philosophers***

Both were pupils of Anaxagoras, both he [Socrates] and Euripides, who was born in the first year of the 75th Olympiad, in the archonship of Calliades [480/79].

**9 Scholia to Aristophanes, *Acharnians* 457**

He makes fun of her [Euripides' mother] for being a vegetable-seller, Cleito.

**10 Nicolaus of Damascus quoted by Stobaeus, *Anthology***

Some of the Boeotians take those who are insolvent into the market-place, sit them down, and then put a basket over them. Whoever is 'basketed' in this way loses his citizen rights. It seems that this happened to Euripides' father, who was by birth a Boeotian.

**11 Harpocration, *Dictionary to the Orators***

Phlyeians, a deme of the tribe of Cecrops. Euripides the tragic poet came from this deme.

### C. *Boyhood*

**12 Theophrastus quoted by Athenaeus, *Scholars at Dinner***

Euripides the poet also served as wine-pourer among the lads. At any rate Theophrastus in his book about drunkenness says, 'I learn that Euripides the poet served as wine-pourer for the so-called *orchestai* [dancers]. These used to dance about the temple of Apollo Delios and were the sons of the leading men of Athens, and they

---

[1] Continued as T 69.

δὲ Ἀπόλλων οὗτός ἐστιν ᾧ τὰ Θαργήλια ἄγουσι. καὶ διασώζεται Φλυῆσιν ἐν τῷ δαφνηφορείῳ γραφὴ περὶ τούτων".

**13** Oenomaus fr. 1 Hammerstaedt ap. Euseb. *Praep. Evang.* 5.33, 227C

> ἔσται σοι κοῦρος, Μνησαρχίδη, ὅντινα πάντες
> ἄνθρωποι τίσουσι, καὶ ἐς κλέος ἐσθλὸν ὀρούσει
> καὶ στεφέων ἱερῶν γλυκερὴν χάριν ἀμφιβαλεῖται.

ὁ δὲ κοῦρος ἦν Εὐριπίδης.

**14** Vitruv. 8 pr.1

Euripides, auditor Anaxagorae, quem philosophum Athenienses scaenicum appellaverunt,...

**15** Diog. Laert. 9.54

πρῶτον δὲ τῶν λόγων ἑαυτοῦ ἀνέγνω [Πρωταγόρας sc.] τὸν περὶ θεῶν...ἀνέγνω δ' Ἀθήνησιν ἐν τῇ Εὐριπίδου οἰκίᾳ ἤ, ὡς τινές, ἐν τῇ Μεγακλείδου· ἄλλοι ἐν Λυκείῳ, μαθητοῦ τὴν φωνὴν αὐτῷ χρήσαντος Ἀρχαγόρου τοῦ Θεοδότου.

used to wear cloaks of the Theran sort.¹ This is the Apollo in whose honor they celebrate the Thargelia. There is an inscription about this preserved at Phlya in the *daphnephoreion*.'²

### D. *Early Pursuits*³

**13** Oenomaus quoted in Eusebius, *Preparation for the Gospel*

> You, Mnesarchides, shall have a son whom all men shall honor, and he shall rise up to good fame and clothe himself with the sweet grace of holy garlands.⁴

The son was Euripides.

### E. *Student or Companion of Philosophers*⁵

#### a) Anaxagoras⁶

**14** Vitruvius, *On Architecture*

Euripides, pupil of Anaxagoras, whom the Athenians called the philosopher of the stage,...

#### b) Protagoras

**15** Diogenes Laertius, *Lives of the Philosophers*

The first of his treatises that he [Protagoras] read aloud was that on the gods...He read it at Athens in the house of Euripides, or, as some report, in the house of Megaclides.⁷ Others say it was in the Lyceum, with his pupil Archagoras, son of Theodotus, lending his voice for this purpose.

---

¹ According to Pollux 7.48, 'Theran cloaks' were used in satyr-plays.
² See also T 1.8.
³ For Euripides as athlete see T 1.3, 3.3, 5.2-3, for Euripides as painter see T 1.6, 1.33, 2.4.
⁴ This is supposed to be the text of the oracle Euripides' father misunderstood: see T 1.3, 3.3, and 5.2.
⁵ See also T 1.4-5, 1.33, 2.4-5, 3.4, 4.3-7, 5.4, and 5.8; Archelaus A 2 D.-K.
⁶ See also Anaxagoras A 1.10, 20a, 20b, 33 D.-K. and Diodorus 1.7.7.
⁷ Otherwise unknown but probably a member of the philo-sophistic family of Callias and Megacles.

**16** Philochorus, *FGrH* 328 F 217, ap. Diog. Laert. 9.55 [=N², p. 490]

φησὶ δὲ Φιλόχορος, πλέοντος αὐτοῦ [Πρωταγόρου sc.] εἰς Σικελίαν, τὴν ναῦν καταποντωθῆναι, καὶ τοῦτο αἰνίττεσθαι Εὐριπίδην ἐν τῷ Ἰξίονι.

**17** Diog. Laert. 2.18

ἐδόκει δὲ [Σωκράτης sc.] συμποιεῖν Εὐριπίδῃ· ὅθεν Μνησίλοχος οὕτω φησί [Teleclides, fr. 41 K.-A.]·

> Φρύγες ἐστὶ καινὸν δρᾶμα τοῦτ' Εὐριπίδου,
> ⟨         ⟩ ᾧ καὶ Σωκράτης τὰ φρύγαν' ὑποτίθησι.

καὶ πάλιν [fr. 42 K.-A.],

> Εὐριπίδας σωκρατογόμφους.

καὶ Καλλίας Πεδήταις [fr. 15 K.-A.]·

> Α. Τί δή;[1] σὺ σεμνὴ καὶ φρονεῖς οὕτω μέγα;
> Β. Ἔξεστι γάρ μοι· Σωκράτης γὰρ αἴτιος.

Ἀριστοφάνης Νεφέλαις [fr. 392 K.-A.]·

> Εὐριπίδῃ δ' ὁ τὰς τραγῳδίας ποιῶν
> τὰς περιλαλούσας οὗτός ἐστι, τὰς σοφάς.

**18** Ael. *V. H.* 2.13

ὁ δὲ Σωκράτης σπάνιον μὲν ἐπεφοίτα τοῖς θεάτροις, εἴ ποτε δὲ Εὐριπίδης ὁ τῆς τραγῳδίας ποιητὴς ἠγωνίζετο καινοῖς τραγῳδοῖς, τότε γε ἀφικνεῖτο. καὶ Πειραιοῖ δὲ ἀγωνιζομένου τοῦ Εὐριπίδου καὶ ἐκεῖ κατῄει· ἔχαιρε γὰρ τῷ ἀνδρὶ δηλονότι διά τε τὴν σοφίαν αὐτοῦ καὶ τὴν ἐν τοῖς μέτροις ἀρετήν.

---

[1] distinxi, versus insequentis ratione habita

**16** Philochorus quoted in Diogenes Laertius

Philochorus says that when he [Protagoras] was sailing to Sicily, the ship sank, and that Euripides alluded to this in his *Ixion*.

### c) Socrates[1]

**17** Diogenes Laertius

It was thought that Socrates collaborated with Euripides on his plays. Hence Mnesilochus[2] says the following,

> The *Phrygians* here is a new play of Euripides...and Socrates is laying the fire for it;

and in another place,

> Euripideses with Socratic rivets.

Callias in his *Men in Fetters* says,

> A. What then? Are you so haughty and so proud?
> B. Yes, for I am allowed to be. Socrates is responsible.[3]

And Aristophanes in the *Clouds*[4] says,

> This is the man who composes tragedies for Euripides, the ones so talkative and so clever.

**18** Aelian, *Historical Miscellany*

Socrates seldom went to the theater, but if Euripides the tragic poet was competing in the new tragedy section,[5] he went. And once when Euripides was competing in the Piraeus, he even went there, for he took pleasure in the man for his wisdom and for his prowess in verse.

---

[1] See also T 8 and 21.
[2] By mistake for Teleclides.
[3] If the text is correct, the second speaker, who is female, must be the Muse of Euripides.
[4] The earlier version, now lost.
[5] Until 386 B.C. there was no regular production of 'old tragedies', i.e. revivals, hence the anecdote's reference to 'the new tragedy section' dates it to the fourth century or later.

**19** Cic. *Tusc. Disp.* 4.63

itaque non sine causa, cum *Orestem* fabulam doceret Euripides, primos tris versus revocasse dicitur Socrates.

**20** Diog. Laert. 3.6

ἔνθεν τε εἰς Αἴγυπτον [ἀπῆλθε Πλάτων sc.] παρὰ τοὺς προφήτας· οὗ φασὶ καὶ Εὐριπίδην αὐτῷ συνακολουθῆσαι καὶ αὐτόθι νοσήσαντα πρὸς τῶν ἱερέων ἀπολυθῆναι τῇ διὰ θαλάττης θεραπείᾳ· ὅθεν που καὶ εἰπεῖν [*I.T.* 1193]

θάλασσα κλύζει πάντα τἀνθρώπων κακά.

**21** Diog. Laert. 2.22

φασὶ δ' Εὐριπίδην αὐτῷ [Σωκράτει sc.] δόντα τὸ Ἡρακλείτου σύγγραμμα ἐρέσθαι, "τί δοκεῖ;" τὸν δὲ φάναι, "ἃ μὲν συνῆκα, γενναῖα· οἶμαι δὲ καὶ ἃ μὴ συνῆκα· πλὴν Δηλίου γέ τινος δεῖται κολυμβητοῦ".

**22** Clem. Alex. *Stromat.* 5.70.1, p. 373 St.

πάνυ θαυμαστῶς ὁ ἐπὶ τῆς σκηνῆς φιλόσοφος Εὐριπίδης τοῖς προειρημένοις ἡμῖν συνῳδός...

**19** Cicero, *Tusculan Disputations*

And so it is not without reason that when Euripides put on his *Orestes* Socrates is said to have called for an encore of the first three lines.

### d) Plato

**20** Diogenes Laertius

From there he [Plato] went to Egypt to the prophets. And they say that Euripides accompanied him, and when he fell sick there, was cleansed by the priests through their sea-cure; and that that doubtless is the reason he says [*Iphigenia among the Taurians* 1193],

> The sea washes all human ills away.

### e) Reads Heraclitus' works

**21** Diogenes Laertius

They say that Euripides gave him [Socrates] the work of Heraclitus and asked him, 'What do you think?' and that he replied, 'What I understand is noble. I suppose what I don't understand is too. Except that it needs a Delian diver to plumb its depths'.

### f) Called Philosopher of the Stage[1]

**22** Clement of Alexandra, *Miscellanies*

The philosopher of the stage, Euripides, is found to agree most remarkably with the foregoing statements...

---

[1] See also T 14 and Athenaeus 13.11, 561A.

**23** [Plut.] *de plac. phil.* 1.7, 880DE [=Aëtius *Plac.* 1.7.1, Diels *Dox. Gr.* p. 297]

Ἔνιοι τῶν φιλοσόφων, καθάπερ Διαγόρας ὁ Μήλιος καὶ Θεόδωρος ὁ Κυρηναῖος καὶ Εὐήμερος ὁ Τεγεάτης, καθόλου φασὶ μὴ εἶναι θεούς [=Diagoras T 47 Winiarczyk]...καὶ Εὐριπίδης δ' ὁ τραγῳδοποιὸς ἀποκαλύψασθαι μὲν οὐκ ἠθέλησε, δεδοικὼς τὸν Ἄρειον πάγον, ἐνέφηνε δὲ τοῦτον τὸν τρόπον· τὸν γὰρ Σίσυφον εἰσήγαγε προστάτην ταύτης τῆς δόξης καὶ συνηγόρησεν αὐτοῦ ταύτῃ τῇ γνώμῃ [Critias, *TrGF* 43 F 19.1-2]·

ἦν (γὰρ) χρόνος (φησὶν) ὅτ' ἦν ἄτακτος ἀνθρώπων βίος
καὶ θηριώδης ἰσχύος θ' ὑπηρέτης.

ἔπειτά φησι τὴν ἀνομίαν λυθῆναι νόμων εἰσαγωγῇ. ἐπεὶ γὰρ ὁ νόμος τὰ φανερὰ τῶν ἀδικημάτων εἴργειν ἠδύνατο, κρύφα δὲ ἠδίκουν πολλοί, τότε τις σοφὸς ἀνὴρ ἐπέστησεν, ὡς δεῖ ψευδεῖ λόγῳ τυφλῶσαι τὴν ἀλήθειαν καὶ πεῖσαι τοὺς ἀνθρώπους,

ὡς ἔστι δαίμων ἀφθίτῳ θάλλων βίῳ
νόῳ τ' ἀκούων καὶ βλέπων, φρονεῖ τ' ἄγαν [ibid. 17-18].

**24** *Suda* s.v. Ἀχαιός, Α 4683 (i 438 Adler) [=*TrGF* 20 T 1]

Ἀχαιός, Πυθοδώρου ἢ Πυθοδωρίδου, Ἐρετριεύς, τραγικός....ἦν δὲ νεώτερος Σοφοκλέους ὀλίγῳ τινί. ἐπεδείκνυντο δὲ κοινῇ σὺν καὶ Εὐριπίδῃ ἀπὸ τῆς πγ' Ὀλυμπιάδος.

### g) An atheist[1]

**23** Aëtius, quoted in pseudo-Plutarch, *Opinions of the Philosophers*

Some of the philosophers, such as Diagoras of Melos and Theodorus of Cyrene and Euhemerus of Tegea, say that there are no gods at all...And likewise the tragic poet Euripides, though he was not willing to reveal it for fear of the Areopagus, hinted at it in this fashion. He brought Sisyphus on stage as the spokesman for this belief and pled its cause by this sentiment of his, for he says,

> There was a time when the life of man was unruly, beast-like, and subject to violence.

Thereafter he says that lawlessness was abated by the introduction of laws. Since the law was able to prevent those injustices which are visible, but many were committing injustice in secret, then some wise man said that it was necessary to obscure the truth by a falsehood and to persuade mankind

> that divinity exists, flourishing in eternal life. He hears and sees by his intelligence and is very wise.

### F. *Tragic Contests*

#### a. First entry

See T 1.15, 1.36, and 5.5.

#### b. Competes with Sophocles and Achaeus, 447-444 and later

**24** *Suda*, 'Achaeus'

Achaeus, son of Pythodorus or Pythodorides, from Eretria, tragic poet...He was a little younger than Sophocles. He produced plays in competition with him and Euripides starting with the 82nd Olympiad [448/7-445/4].

---

[1] See also Athenagoras, *Apology* 5.1.

**25** Marmor Parium, *FGrH* 239 A 60 [=*TrGF* DID D A60]

ἀφ' οὗ Εὐριπίδης ἐτῶν ὢν ΔΔΔΔΙΙΙΙ (?) τραγῳδίᾳ πρῶτον ἐνίκησεν, ἔτη ΗΡΔΔΓΙΙΙ ἄρχοντος 'Αθήνησι Διφίλου· ἦσαν δὲ κατ' Εὐριπίδην Σωκράτης τε καὶ 'Αναξαγόρας.

**26** Plut. *De amore prolis* 4, 496F

οὐδὲ Εὐριπίδου καὶ Σοφοκλέους νίκας οἱ πατέρες ἔγνωσαν.

**27** Hypothesis Alcestidis [=*TrGF* DID C11]

ἐδιδάχθη ἐπὶ Γλαυκίνου ἄρχοντος 'Ολ(υμπιάδος) ⟨πε΄ ἔτει β΄⟩. πρῶτος ἦν Σοφοκλῆς, δεύτερος Εὐριπίδης Κρήσσαις, 'Αλκμέωνι τῷ διὰ Ψωφῖδος, Τηλέφῳ, 'Αλκήστιδι.

**28** Hypothesis Medeae [=*TrGF* DID C12]

ἐδιδάχθη ἐπὶ Πυθοδώρου ἄρχοντος 'Ολυμπιάδος πζ΄ ἔτει α΄. πρῶτος Εὐφορίων, δεύτερος Σοφοκλῆς, τρίτος Εὐριπίδης Μηδείᾳ, Φιλοκτήτῃ, Δίκτυι, Θερισταῖς σατύροις. οὐ σῴζεται.

### c. First Victory, 441

**25** *Parian Marble*

Since Euripides at the age of 44[1] won the tragic competition for the first time, 179 years, in the archonship of Diphilos at Athens [442/1]. Contemporary with Euripides were Socrates and Anaxagoras.

**26** Plutarch, *On Affection for Offspring*

Euripides' and Sophocles' fathers likewise did not know of their sons' victories.

### d. Cretan Women, Alcmeon in Psophis, Telephus, Alcestis, 438

**27** Argument to the *Alcestis*

It was put on in the archonship of Glaucinus [439/8] in the second year of the 85th Olympiad. Sophocles won first prize, Euripides was second with *Cretan Women, Alcmeon in Psophis, Telephus*, and *Alcestis*.

### e. Medea, Philoctetes, Dictys, The Reapers, 431

**28** Argument to the *Medea*

It was put on in the archonship of Pythodorus [432/1], the first year of the 87th Olympiad. Euphorion won first prize, Sophocles second, and Euripides was third with *Medea, Philoctetes, Dictys,* and the satyr-play *The Reapers*, which does not survive.

---

[1] This implies that Euripides was born in 486/5 or 487/6, one or two years earlier than the date given in T 6. See also T 67.

## 29 Hypothesis Hippolyti [=*TrGF* DID C13]

ἐδιδάχθη ἐπὶ Ἐπαμείνονος ἄρχοντος ὀλυμπιάδι πζ' ἔτει δ'. πρῶτος Εὐριπίδης, δεύτερος Ἰοφῶν, τρίτος Ἴων. ἔστι δὲ οὗτος Ἱππόλυτος δεύτερος, ⟨ὁ⟩ καὶ στεφανίας προσαγορευόμενος. ἐμφαίνεται δὲ ὕστερος γεγραμμένος· τὸ γὰρ ἀπρεπὲς καὶ κατηγορίας ἄξιον ἐν τούτῳ διώρθωται τῷ δράματι. τὸ δὲ δρᾶμα τῶν πρώτων.

## 30 Plut. *Vita Nic.* 9.7, 528E-529A

ἦσαν οὖν πρότερον πεποιημένοι τινὰ πρὸς ἀλλήλους ἐκεχειρίαν ἐνιαύσιον, ἐν ᾗ συνιόντες εἰς ταὐτὸ καὶ γευόμενοι πάλιν ἀδείας καὶ σχολῆς καὶ πρὸς ξένους καὶ οἰκείους ἐπιμιξίας, ἐπόθουν τὸν ἀμίαντον καὶ ἀπόλεμον βίον, ἡδέως μὲν ᾀδόντων τὰ τοιαῦτα χορῶν ἀκούοντες [Eur. fr. 369 N²]·

κείσθω δόρυ μοι μίτον ἀμφιπλέκειν ἀράχναις,...

## 31 Ael. *V. H.* 2.8 [=*TrGF* DID C14]

κατὰ τὴν πρώτην καὶ ἐνενηκοστὴν ὀλυμπιάδα, καθ' ἣν ἐνίκα Ἐξαίνετος ὁ Ἀκραγαντῖνος στάδιον, ἀντηγωνίσαντο ἀλλήλοις Ξενοκλῆς καὶ Εὐριπίδης. καὶ πρῶτός γε ἦν Ξενοκλῆς, ὅστις ποτὲ οὗτός ἐστιν, Οἰδίποδι καὶ Λυκάονι καὶ Βάκχαις καὶ Ἀθάμαντι σατυρικῷ. τούτου δεύτερος Εὐριπίδης ἦν Ἀλεξάνδρῳ καὶ Παλαμήδει καὶ Τρῳάσι καὶ Σισύφῳ σατυρικῷ. γελοῖον δέ (οὐ γάρ;) Ξενοκλέα μὲν νικᾶν, Εὐριπίδην δὲ ἡττᾶσθαι, καὶ ταῦτα τοιούτοις δράμασι. τῶν δύο τοίνυν τὸ ἕτερον· ἢ ἀνόητοι ἦσαν οἱ τῆς ψήφου κύριοι καὶ ἀμαθεῖς καὶ πόρρω κρίσεως ὀρθῆς, ἢ ἐδεκάσθησαν. ἄτοπον δὲ ἑκάτερον καὶ Ἀθηναίων ἥκιστα ἄξιον.

### f. Hippolytus, 428

**29** Argument to the *Hippolytus*

It was put on in the archonship of Epameinon [429/8], the fourth year of the 87th Olympiad. Euripides was first, Iophon second, and Ion third. This is the second *Hippolytus*, the one called *Hippolytus with a Garland*. It was plainly written later, for what was unseemly and deserving of criticism has been corrected in this play. The play is one of his masterpieces.

### g. *Erechtheus*, 423 or a little earlier

**30** Plutarch, *Life of Nicias*

They had previously made a one-year truce with one another, and in this truce, since they met together in the same place and tasted again of freedom and leisure and mingled with both foreigners and their own citizens, they longed for the untainted and peaceful life and listened with pleasure to choruses singing such things as

> Let my spear lie unused for the spider to cover with webs,...

### h. Alexander, Palamedes, Trojan Women, Sisyphus, 415

**31** Aelian

In the ninety-first Olympiad [416/5-413/2], in which the stade-race was won by Exaenetus of Acragas, Xenocles and Euripides were in competition with each other. And the winner was Xenocles, whoever in the world that is, with *Oedipus, Lycaon, Bacchae*, and the satyr-play *Athamas*. Second to him was Euripides with *Alexandros, Palamedes, Trojan Women*, and the satyr-play *Sisyphus*. A ridiculous result, is it not, for Xenocles to win and Euripides to lose, especially competing with plays of this quality? We must accordingly accept one or the other conclusion, either that those in charge of the vote were silly and ignorant and lacking in correct judgement or that they were bribed. Either supposition is bizarre and unworthy of the Athenians.

**32** schol. Ar. (a) *Av.* 842 et (b) *Vesp.* 1326

(a) μήποτε δὲ παρακωμῳδεῖ τὸν Εὐριπίδου Παλαμήδην οὐ πρὸ πολλοῦ δεδιδαγμένον.

(b) ὑστερεῖ δὲ ἡ τῶν Τρῳάδων κάθεσις [τῆς τῶν Σφηκῶν sc.] ἔτεσιν ζ'.

**33** Philochorus, *FGrH* 328 F 221, ap. Diog. Laert. 2.44

Εὐριπίδης δὲ καὶ ὀνειδίζει αὐτοῖς [τοῖς Ἀθηναίοις sc.] ἐν τῷ Παλαμήδει λέγων "ἐκάνετ' ἐκάνετε τὰν πάνσοφον, τὰν οὐδὲν ἀλγύνουσαν ἀηδόνα Μουσᾶν" [fr. 588 N²]. καὶ τάδε μὲν ὧδε· Φιλόχορος δέ φησι προτελευτῆσαι τὸν Εὐριπίδην τοῦ Σωκράτους.

**34** schol. Ar. *Thesm.* (a) 1012 et (b) 1060 [=*TrGF* DID C15(a)(b)]

(a) Ἀνδρομέδαν] πιθανῶς· συνδεδίδακται γὰρ τῇ Ἑλένῃ.

(b) Ἠχώ,...ἥπερ πέρυσιν...Εὐριπίδῃ...ξυνηγωνιζόμην] ἐπεὶ πέρυσιν ἐδιδάχθη ἡ Ἀνδρομέδα.

**35** schol. Ar. *Ran.* 53 [=*TrGF* DID C15(c)]

τὴν Ἀνδρομέδαν] διὰ τί δὲ μὴ ἄλλο τι τῶν πρὸ ὀλίγου [ante 405 sc.] διδαχθέντων καὶ καλῶν, Ὑψιπύλης, Φοινισσῶν, Ἀντιόπης; ἡ δὲ Ἀνδρομέδα ὀγδόῳ ἔτει προεισῆλθεν.

**32** scholia to Aristophanes' (a) *Birds* and (b) *Wasps*

(a) Perhaps he is parodying the *Palamedes* of Euripides, put on a short time before.[1]

(b) Nevertheless the entry of the *Trojan Women* into the competition was seven years later [than the *Wasps*].

**33** Philochorus quoted by Diogenes Laertius

But Euripides also upbraided them [the Athenians for the death of Socrates] in the *Palamedes* saying, 'You have slain, have slain the nightingale of the Muses, all wise, who causes no pain'. That is the report. But Philochorus says that Euripides died before Socrates.

i. Helen, Andromeda, 412

**34** scholia to Aristophanes' *Thesmophoriazusae*

(a) *Andromeda*] reasonably mentioned, since it was put on at the same time as the *Helen*.

(b) Echo, I who last year joined Euripides in the competition] since the *Andromeda* was put on the previous year [412].

j. *Antiope* and *Hypsipyle*, ca 411-408

**35** scholia to Aristophanes' *Frogs*

the *Andromeda*] But why not another play, one of those successful plays put on a short time before [i.e. before 405], such as *Hypsipyle, Phoenician Women,* or *Antiope*? The *Andromeda* was put on eight years before.

---

[1] Since *Birds* was put on in 414, we may date the *Palamedes* and its companions to 415, the first year of the 91st Olympiad: see T 31.

**36** Hypothesis Phoenissarum [=*TrGF* DID C16]

⟨ἐδιδάχθησαν⟩ ἐπὶ †Ναυσικράτους ἄρχοντος ⟨   ⟩ δεύτερος Εὐριπίδης ⟨   ⟩ καθῆκε διδασκαλίαν† περὶ τούτου. καὶ γὰρ ταῦτα ⟨   ⟩ ὁ Οἰνόμαος καὶ Χρύσιππος καὶ ⟨   ⟩ σῴζεται[1].

**37** schol. *Or.* 371 [=*TrGF* DID C18]

ὁ ποιητὴς τὸ ἄστατον τῆς Λακεδαιμονίων γνώμης κωμῳδεῖ...πρὸ γὰρ Διοκλέους, ἐφ' οὗ τὸν Ὀρέστην ἐδίδαξε, κτλ.

**38** Ar. *Ran.* 302-4 cum scholio

ΞΑ(ΝΘΙΑΣ)
   θάρρει· πάντ' ἀγαθὰ πεπράγαμεν,
   ἔξεστί θ' ὥσπερ Ἡγέλοχος ἡμῖν λέγειν,
   "ἐκ κυμάτων γὰρ αὖθις αὖ γαλῆν ὁρῶ".

schol: Ἡγέλοχος τραγῳδίας ὑποκριτής, ὃν καὶ ἐν τῷ Ὀρέστῃ Εὐριπίδου ⟨φασὶ⟩ προ⟨εκ⟩στάντος[2] αὐτῷ τοῦ πνεύματος ἐν τῷδε τῷ στίχῳ

   ἐκ κυμάτων γὰρ αὖθις αὖ γαλήν' ὁρῶ

[*Or.* 279] αἰφνιδίως ὀφθῆναι συνελόντα τὴν συναλοιφήν.

---

[1] fort. ὀλίγῳ πρότερον⟩ καθῆκε διδασκαλίαν περὶ τούτου ⟨τοῦ γένους⟩. καὶ γὰρ ταῦτα ⟨μυθολογοῦσιν⟩ ὁ Οἰνόμαος καὶ Χρύσιππος καὶ ⟨   ὃς οὐ⟩ σῴζεται.
[2] Fritzsche

k. Phoenician Women (with Oenomaus and Chrysippus?) 410 or 409[1]

**36** Argument to the *Phoenician Women*

It was put on in the archonship of Nausicrates[2] <    > Euripides came in second <    > entered a set of plays about this (?). And in fact these things <    > the *Oenomaus* and the *Chrysippus* and <    which is not> preserved.

l. Competes with Acestor, Dorilaus, Morsimus, and Melanthius shortly before 408

See T 4.17.

m. *Orestes*, 408

**37** Scholia to *Orestes*

The poet satirizes the instability of the Spartan character...For before the archonship of Diocles [409/8], in which he put on the *Orestes*...

**38** Aristophanes' *Frogs* with scholia

XANTHIAS
> Be of good cheer, our fortune is all good, and we may say, as Hegelochus did, 'After the storm once more I see a weasel'.

scholia: Hegelochus, the tragic actor, who, they say, in Euripides' *Orestes* ran out of breath in the line 'After the storm once more I see a calm' and was all at once perceived to have neglected the elision.[3]

---

[1] It is possible that the companion plays to *Phoenician Women* were *Hypsipyle* and *Antiope*. See T 35.
[2] We know of no such eponymous archon in the fifth century.
[3] I.e. Hegelochus pronounced γαλήν' (calm) γαλῆν (weasel) by neglecting to mark the elided syllable.

**39** schol. *Or.* 279

κεκωμῴδηται ὁ στίχος διὰ Ἡγέλοχον τὸν ὑποκριτήν· οὐ γὰρ φθάσαντα διελεῖν τὴν συναλοιφὴν ἐπιλείψαντος τοῦ πνεύματος τοῖς ἀκροωμένοις τὴν γαλῆν δόξαι λέγειν τὸ ζῷον, ἀλλ' οὐχὶ τὰ γαληνά. πολλοὶ μὲν οὖν αὐτὸ διέπαιξαν τῶν κωμικῶν, Ἀριστοφάνης ⟨  ⟩ καὶ Στράττις ἐν Ἀνθρωπορέστῃ [fr. 1 K.-A.]·

> καὶ τῶν μὲν ἄλλων οὐκ ἐμέλησέ μοι μελῶν,
> Εὐριπίδου δὲ δρᾶμα δεξιώτατον
> διέκναισ' Ὀρέστην, Ἡγέλοχον τὸν Κυντάρου
> μισθωσάμενος τὰ πρῶτα τῶν ἐπῶν λέγειν.

καὶ ἐν ἄλλοις παίζων φησίν [fr. 63 K.-A.]·

> γαλῆν' ὁρῶ. —ποῖ πρὸς θεῶν, ποῖ ποῖ γαλῆν;
> —γαληνά. —ἐγὼ δ' ᾤμην σε γαλῆν λέγειν ὁρῶ.

καὶ Σαννυρίων ἐν Δανάῃ [fr. 8 K.-A.]·

> τί οὖν γενόμενος εἰς ὀπὴν ἐνδύσομαι;
> ζητητέον. φέρ' εἰ γενοίμην ⟨—⟩ γαλῆ·
> ἀλλ' Ἡγέλοχος ⟨εὐθύς⟩ με μηνύσειεν ⟨ἂν⟩
> ὁ τραγικὸς ἀνακράγοι τ' ἂν [εὐθὺς] εἰσιδὼν μέγα·
> "ἐκ κυμάτων γὰρ αὖθις αὖ γαλῆν ὁρῶ".

**40** Arist. fr. 627 Rose ap. schol. Ar. *Ran.* 67 [=*TrGF* DID C22]

οὕτω γὰρ καὶ αἱ διδασκαλίαι φέρουσι, τελευτήσαντος Εὐριπίδου τὸν υἱὸν αὐτοῦ δεδιδαχέναι ὁμώνυμον ἐν ἄστει Ἰφιγένειαν τὴν ἐν Αὐλίδι, Ἀλκμαίωνα, Βάκχας.

**41** Varro fr. 298 Funaioli ap. Aul. Gell. 17.4.3

Euripiden quoque M. Varro ait, cum quinque et septuaginta tragoedias scripserit, in quinque solis vicisse.

**39** Scholia to *Orestes*

This line has become a comic target because of Hegelochus the actor. He did not make the elision soon enough, since his breath ran out, and to the audience he seemed to say *galen*, weasel, rather than *galena*, calm. Many of the comic poets made mirth of this, Aristophanes <         > and Strattis in his *Orestes as Mortal*:

> And he paid no attention to the other songs, but Euripides' most clever play, *Orestes*, he crushed to pieces by paying Hegelochus, son of Cyntarus, to speak the protagonist's role.

And elsewhere he says in jest:

> I see a *galen'*. —Where do you see a weasel?
> —*Galena*. —But I thought you said, 'I see a *galen*'.

And Sannyrion in his *Danae* says:

> What then can I become and slip into the hole? I must think. Suppose I become a weasel. But Hegelochus the tragic actor would immediately reveal my hiding-place and when he had seen me would shout with a loud voice, 'After the calm once more I see a weasel'.

### n. Plays first produced after the poet's death

**40** Aristotle quoted in the scholia to Aristophanes' *Frogs*

For the *Didascaliai* say that after Euripides' death his son of the same name put on at the City Dionysia *Iphigenia at Aulis, Alcmeon,* and *Bacchae*.

### o. Number of Victories[1]

**41** Varro quoted by Aulus Gellius

Marcus Varro says that although Euripides wrote 75 tragedies, he won victories with only five.

---

[1] See also T 1.38, 2.12, and 3.7.

**42** anonym. Περὶ τραγῳδίας

5. Ἡ δὲ παλαιὰ τραγικὴ μελοποιία γένει μὲν τῷ ἐναρμονίῳ ἐχρήσατο ἀμιγεῖ καὶ μικτῷ γένει τῆς ἁρμονίας καὶ διατόνων, χρώματι δὲ οὐδεὶς φαίνεται κεχρημένος τῶν τραγικῶν ἄχρις Εὐριπίδου· μαλακὸν γὰρ τὸ ἦθος τοῦ γένους τούτου. τῶν δὲ τόνων πλεῖστον μὲν ἡ παλαιὰ κέχρηται τῷ τε Δωρίῳ καὶ τῷ Μιξολυδίῳ, τῷ μὲν ὡς σεμνότητος οἰκείῳ, τῷ δὲ Μιξολυδίῳ ὡς συνεργῷ πρὸς τοὺς οἴκτους. κέχρηται δὲ καὶ ταῖς ἀνειμέναις τότε καλουμέναις ἁρμονίαις, τῇ τε Ἰαστὶ καὶ ἀνειμένῃ Λυδιστί. τοῦ δὲ Φρυγίου καὶ Λυδίου Σοφοκλῆς ἥψατο πρῶτος. κέχρηται δὲ τῷ Φρυγίῳ διθυραμβικώτερον. ὁ δὲ Ὑποφρύγιος καὶ ὁ Ὑποδώριος σπάνιοι παρ' αὐτῇ εἰσιν, ὡς...διθυράμβῳ προσήκοντες. πρῶτος δὲ Ἀγάθων τὸν Ὑποδώριον τόνον εἰς τραγῳδίαν εἰσήνεγκεν καὶ τὸν Ὑποφρύγιον. ὅ γε μὴν Λύδιος τῷ κιθαρῳδικῷ τρόπῳ οἰκειότερός ἐστι. συστήμασι δὲ οἱ μὲν παλαιοὶ μικροῖς ἐχρῶντο, Εὐριπίδης πρῶτος πολυχορδίᾳ ἐχρήσατο. ἐκαλεῖτο ὑπὸ τῶν μουσικῶν ⟨τῶν⟩ παλαιῶν ἀνάτρητος ὁ τρόπος οὗτος τῆς μελοποιίας· καὶ καθόλου εἰπεῖν Εὐριπίδης πολυειδέστερός ἐστι τῶν πρὸ αὐτοῦ καὶ πολυχρούστερος, καὶ ἐχρήσατο καὶ τοῖς προσήκουσι ῥυθμοῖς, καὶ βακχείοις ἁπλοῖς τε καὶ διπλοῖς, καὶ τῷ ἀπ' ἐλάττονος ἰωνικῷ, καὶ ἐπ' ὀλίγον προκελευσματικῷ.

12. ...καὶ κιθάρᾳ δὲ ἐν ταῖς τραγῳδίαις ἐχρήσατο καὶ Εὐριπίδης καὶ Σοφοκλῆς, Σοφοκλῆς δὲ καὶ λύρᾳ ἐν τῷ Θαμυρᾷ.

p. Technical innovations[1]

**42** Anonymous treatise on tragedy

Musical composition in ancient tragedy made use of the pure enharmonic genus and also a mixture of the enharmonic and the diatonic, but clearly no one until Euripides uses the chromatic genus.[2] For the character of that harmony is soft. Of the modes ancient tragedy makes the greatest use of the Dorian and the Mixolydian, the former as proper to grandeur, and the Mixolydian as contributory to lamentation. It also makes use of the harmonies that were at that time called 'relaxed', the Ionic and the relaxed Lydian. Sophocles was the first to make use of the Phrygian and the Lydian. Tragedy also uses the Phrygian in a more dithyrambic manner. The Hypophrygian and the Hypodorian are rare in tragedy as being...suitable for dithyramb. Agathon was the first to introduce the Hypodorian and the Hypophrygian. The Lydian mode is more proper to the manner of the cithara-player. The ancients used to use short metrical systems, and Euripides was the first to make use of polychordy. This way of writing music was called 'pierced through and through'.[3] Speaking generally Euripides uses more scales and melodic colors than his predecessors. He also used the proper rhythms, both the single and the double bacchius and the ionic *a minore* and to a slight extent the proceleusmatic.

............

...Both Euripides and Sophocles made use of the cithara also in their tragedies, and Sophocles even used the lyre in his *Thamyras*.

---

[1] See also T 1.4 and 3.5.
[2] Introduction of the chromatic genus is ascribed in Plut., *Quaest. Conv.* 3.1, to Agathon.
[3] According to Borthwick, cited by Browning, this means 'like an anthill', a metaphor applied to the new music at Aristoph. *Thesmo.* 100.

**43** Suda s.v. Νικόμαχος, Ν 397 (iii 469 Adler) [=Nicomachus, TrGF 36 T 1]

Νικόμαχος, Ἀθηναῖος, τραγικός· ὃς Εὐριπίδην παραδόξως[1] καὶ Θέογνιν ἐνίκησε.

**44** Plut. *Quomodo adolescens poetas audire debeat* 12, 33C

ὅθεν οὐδ' αἱ παραδιορθώσεις φαύλως ἔχουσιν αἷς καὶ Κλεάνθης ἐχρήσατο καὶ Ἀντισθένης, ὁ μὲν [Ἀντισθένης sc.] τοὺς Ἀθηναίους ἰδὼν θορυβήσαντας ἐν τῷ θεάτρῳ "τί δ' αἰσχρὸν εἰ μὴ τοῖσι χρωμένοις δοκεῖ;" [Eur. fr. 19 N²] παραβάλλων εὐθὺς "αἰσχρὸν τό γ' αἰσχρόν, κἂν δοκῇ κἂν μὴ δοκῇ".

**45** Plut. ibid. 4, 19E [=N², p. 490]

ὁ Εὐριπίδης εἰπεῖν λέγεται πρὸς τοὺς τὸν Ἰξίονα λοιδοροῦντας ὡς ἀσεβῆ καὶ μιαρόν, "οὐ μέντοι πρότερον αὐτὸν ἐκ τῆς σκηνῆς ἐξήγαγον ἢ τῷ τροχῷ προσηλῶσαι".

**46** Seneca, *Ep.* 115.15

Cum hi novissimi versus [Eur. *Danae* fr. 324 N²] in tragoedia Euripidis pronuntiati essent, totus populus ad eiciendum et actorem et carmen consurrexit uno impetu, donec Euripides in medium ipse prosilivit petens ut expectarent viderentque quem admirator auri exitum faceret. Dabat in illa fabula poenas Bellerophontes quas in sua quisque dat.

**47** Plut. *Amatorius* 13, 756BC

ἀκούεις δὲ δήπου τὸν Εὐριπίδην ὡς ἐθορυβήθη ποιησάμενος ἀρχὴν τῆς Μελανίππης ἐκείνην [fr. 480 N²]

Ζεὺς ⟨ὅστις ὁ Ζεύς,⟩ οὐ γὰρ οἶδα πλὴν λόγῳ,

---

[1] unus ex codicibus: παραδόξως Εὐ. plerique codices

## q. Miscellaneous theatrical notices[1]

**43** *Suda*, 'Nicomachus'

Nicomachus, an Athenian tragic poet. He defeated Euripides surprisingly and also Theognis.

**44** Plutarch, *How the Young Man Should Study Poetry*

And so the corrections which Cleanthes and Antisthenes made use of are not bad. Antisthenes, seeing that the Athenians had cried out in the theater at the line,
> What's shameful if the doers think it not?

added at once,
> The shameful is shameful, whether 'tis thought or no.

**45** Plutarch, ibid.

It is said that Euripides replied to those who reviled his *Ixion* as impious and shocking, 'Yet I did not take him off the stage until I had nailed him to the wheel'.

**46** Seneca, *Letters to Lucilius*

When these last verses had been uttered in a tragedy of Euripides, the whole people rose with one accord to throw out both the actor and the play until Euripides himself leapt into the middle of the stage begging them to wait and see what kind of end the admirer of money would come to. Bellerophon[2] paid in that tragedy the same penalty each man pays in his own play.

**47** Plutarch, *Dialogue on Love*

You have doubtless heard of the uproar Euripides made by the famous beginning of his *Melanippe*,
> Zeus, whoever Zeus is, for I know only by report.

---
[1] See also Valerius Maximus 3.7 ext. 1.
[2] The lines in fact come from the *Danae*, not the *Bellerophon*.

μεταλαβὼν δὲ χορὸν ἄλλον (ἐθάρρει ⟨γὰρ⟩ ὡς ἔοικε τῷ δράματι γεγραμμένῳ πανηγυρικῶς καὶ περιττῶς) ἤλλαξε τὸν στίχον ὡς νῦν γέγραπται [fr. 481 N²]·

 Ζεύς, ὡς λέκεκται τῆς ἀληθείας ὕπο.

**48 Pollux 4.111**

τῶν δὲ χορικῶν ᾀσμάτων τῶν κωμικῶν ἕν τι καὶ ἡ παράβασις, ὅταν ἃ ὁ ποιητὴς πρὸς τὸ θέατρον βούλεται λέγειν ὁ χορὸς παρελθὼν λέγῃ. ἐπιεικῶς δ' αὐτὸ ποιοῦσιν οἱ κωμῳδοποιηταί, τραγικὸν δὲ οὐκ ἔστιν· ἀλλ' Εὐριπίδης αὐτὸ πεποίηκεν ἐν πολλοῖς δράμασιν. ἐν μέν γε τῇ Δανάῃ [=N², p. 453] τὸν χορὸν τὰς γυναῖκας ὑπὲρ αὐτοῦ τι ποιήσας παράδειν, ἐκλαθόμενος ὡς ἄνδρας λέγειν ἐποίησε τῷ σχήματι τῆς λέξεως τὰς γυναῖκας. καὶ Σοφοκλῆς δὲ αὐτὸ ἐκ τῆς πρὸς ἐκεῖνον ἁμίλλης ποιεῖ σπανιάκις, ὥσπερ ἐν Ἱππόνῳ [=Radt, Soph., p. 269].

**49 Plut. *Vita Alcibiadis* 11.3, 196B**

αἱ δ' ἱπποτροφίαι [Ἀλκιβιάδου sc.] περιβόητοι μὲν ἐγένοντο καὶ τῷ πλήθει τῶν ἁρμάτων· ἑπτὰ γὰρ ἄλλος οὐδεὶς καθῆκεν Ὀλυμπίασιν ἰδιώτης οὐδὲ βασιλεύς, μόνος δ' ἐκεῖνος, καὶ τὸ νικῆσαι καὶ δεύτερον γενέσθαι καὶ τέταρτον, ὡς Θουκιδίδης φησίν [6.16], ὡς δ' Εὐριπίδης τρίτον, ὑπερβάλλει λαμπρότητι καὶ δόξῃ πᾶσαν τὴν ἐν τούτοις φιλοτιμίαν. λέγει δ' ὁ Εὐριπίδης ἐν τῷ ᾄσματι ταῦτα [*PMG* 755]·

 σὲ[1] δ' ἄγαμαι, ὦ Κλεινίου παῖ.
 καλὸν ἁ νίκα, ⟨τὸ⟩ κάλλιστον δ', ὃ μηδεὶς
 ἄλλος Ἑλλάνων ⟨ἔλαχεν⟩,
 ἅρματι πρῶτα δραμεῖν καὶ δεύτερα καὶ τρίτα(τα),
 βῆναί τ' ἀπονητὶ Διὸς στεφθέντ' ἐλαίᾳ
 κάρυκι βοᾶν παραδοῦναι.

**50 Plut. *Vita Demosth.* 1.1, 846AB**

ὁ μὲν γράψας τὸ ἐπὶ τῇ νίκῃ τῆς Ὀλυμπίασιν ἱπποδρομίας εἰς Ἀλκιβιάδην ἐγκώμιον, εἴτ' Εὐριπίδης, ὡς ὁ πολὺς κρατεῖ λόγος,

---

[1] Textum secundum Bowra exscribo

But when he got a chorus again (since he had confidence in the play, as it was written in an elevated and elaborate style) he changed the line to its present form,

> Zeus, as has been said by Truth.

## 48 Pollux, *Onomasticon*

Of comic choral songs one is the parabasis, when the chorus comes forward and says what the poet wants to say to the audience. The comic poets reasonably engage in this practice, but it is not tragic. Euripides, however, does it in many dramas. In the *Danae*, at least, when he made the women of the chorus sing something in his own behalf, he forgot and by the grammatical form that he used he made the women speak as men. Sophocles too as a result of competing with him does this rarely, as in his *Hipponöus*.

### G. *Other Poems*[1]

#### a) Victory ode for Alcibiades' Olympic victory

## 49 Plutarch, *Life of Alcibiades*

His [Alcibiades'] raising of horses became famous both for the number of his chariots (for no one else, either private individual or king, had ever entered seven chariots at Olympia, but only he) and his coming in first, second, and fourth, as Thucydides says, or first, second, and third, as Euripides says, exceeds in splendor and glory all ambition in these contests. Euripides says in the ode:

> I marvel at you, son of Cleinias: victory is splendid, but the most splendid thing, which has been the portion of no other Greek, is to be first, second, and third and to walk effortlessly, crowned with the olive-leaves of Zeus, to give the herald your name to proclaim.

## 50 Plutarch, *Life of Demosthenes*

The man who wrote the song of praise for Alcibiades for his victory at Olympia in horse-racing, whether it was Euripides, as wide-

---

[1] See also Athenaeus 2.57, 61B, citing a supposed epigram of Euripides, *EG* 478-81.

εἴθ' ἕτερός τις ἦν, ὦ Σόσσιε Σενεκίων, φησὶ χρῆναι τῷ εὐδαίμονι πρῶτον ὑπάρξαι

τὰν πόλιν εὐδόκιμον [PMG 756].

**51** Plut. *Vita Nic.* 17.4, 534D

ὁ μὲν γὰρ Εὐριπίδης μετὰ τὴν ἧτταν αὐτῶν [τὴν ἐν Συρακούσαις τῶν Ἀθηναίων sc.] καὶ τὸν ὄλεθρον γράφων ἐπικήδειον ἐποίησεν [*EG* 478-81]·

οἵδε Συρακοσίους ὀκτὼ νίκας ἐκράτησαν
ἄνδρες, ὅτ' ἦν τὰ θεῶν ἐξ ἴσου ἀμφοτέροις.

**52** Arist. *Poet.* 1460 b 32-5 [=Sophocles T 53a Radt]

πρὸς δὲ τούτοις ἐὰν ἐπιτιμᾶται ὅτι οὐκ ἀληθῆ, ἀλλ' ἴσως ⟨ὡς⟩ δεῖ, οἷον καὶ Σοφοκλῆς ἔφη αὐτὸς μὲν οἵους δεῖ ποιεῖν, Εὐριπίδην δὲ οἷοι εἰσίν, ταύτῃ λυτέον.

**53** Gnomol. Vat. 517 Sternbach, p. 190 [=*WS* 11 (1889), 228; Sophocles T 57 Radt]

Σοφοκλῆς ὁ τῶν τραγῳδιῶν ποιητὴς ἀκούσας Εὐριπίδην ἐν Μακεδονίᾳ τεθνηκέναι εἶπεν "ἀπώλετο ἡ τῶν ἐμῶν ποιημάτων ἀκόνη".

**54** Hieronymus Rhodius, fr. 35 Wehrli, ap. Athen. 13.82, 604D [=Sophocles T 75 Radt]

Ἱερώνυμος δ' ὁ Ῥόδιος ἐν τοῖς ἱστορικοῖς ὑπομνήμασίν φησιν ὅτι Σοφοκλῆς εὐπρεπῆ παῖδα ἔξω τείχους ἀπήγαγε χρησόμενος αὐτῷ. ὁ μὲν οὖν παῖς τὸ ἴδιον ἱμάτιον ἐπὶ τῇ πόᾳ ὑπέστρωσεν, τὴν δὲ τοῦ Σοφοκλέους χλανίδα περιεβάλοντο. μετ' οὖν τὴν ὁμιλίαν ὁ παῖς ἁρπάσας τὸ τοῦ Σοφοκλέους χλανίδιον ᾤχετο, καταλιπὼν τῷ Σοφοκλεῖ τὸ παιδικὸν ἱμάτιον. οἷα δὲ εἰκὸς διαλαληθέντος τοῦ

spread report maintains, or someone else, says, O Sosius Senecio, that the happy man must first have at his disposal

> his city enjoying renown.

### b) Epitaph on the Athenian dead in Syracuse

**51** Plutarch, *Life of Nicias*

For Euripides after their defeat and destruction [of the Athenians at Syracuse] composed a poem of lament:

> These men defeated the Syracusans in eight victories while the gods were impartial to both sides.[1]

## H. *Euripides and Sophocles*[2]

**52** Sophocles, quoted in Aristotle's *Poetics*

In addition, if the objection is made that [certain features] are not true, one can reply that at any rate they are perhaps as they are required to be. One should solve a *problema*[3] in the way that Sophocles said that he himself made his characters as he had to make them, Euripides the way people are.

**53** Gnomologium Vaticanum

When Sophocles, the tragic poet, heard that Euripides had died in Macedonia, he said, 'The whetstone of my poetry has perished'.

**54** Hieronymus of Rhodes quoted by Athenaeus

Hieronymus of Rhodes in his *Historical Notes* says that Sophocles led a beautiful boy outside the city-wall to enjoy him. The boy spread his own cloak on the ground, and they covered themselves with Sophocles' cloak. After their encounter, the boy snatched up Sophocles' cloak and went off, leaving Sophocles with a boy's cloak. When this story was, as one would expect, noised around, Euripides

---

[1] For the sentiment, cf. Hdt. 6.109.5.
[2] See also T 1.20, 1.34, 3.15, 100.2, and 100.5.5-7.
[3] I.e. an apparent blemish in a work of the first rank.

συμβεβηκότος Εὐριπίδης πυθόμενος καὶ ἐπιτωθάζων τὸ γεγονὸς καὶ αὐτός ποτε ἔφη τούτῳ κεχρῆσθαι τῷ παιδί, ἀλλὰ μηδὲν προσθεῖναι, τὸν δὲ Σοφοκλέα διὰ τὴν ἀκολασίαν καταφρονηθῆναι. καὶ ὁ Σοφοκλῆς ἀκούσας ἐποίησεν εἰς αὐτὸν τὸ τοιοῦτον ἐπίγραμμα [*FGE*, p. 304, *EG* 462-5], χρησάμενος τῷ περὶ τοῦ ἡλίου καὶ Βορέου λόγῳ, καί τι πρὸς μοιχείαν αὐτοῦ παραινιττόμενος·

> ἥλιος ἦν, οὐ παῖς, Εὐριπίδη, ὅς με χλιαίνων
> γυμνὸν ἐποίησεν· σοὶ δὲ φιλοῦντι †ἑταίραν†
> Βορρᾶς ὡμίλησε. σὺ δ' οὐ σοφός, ὃς τὸν Ἔρωτα,
> ἀλλοτρίαν σπείρων, λωποδύτην ἀπάγεις.

**55** Plut. *Regum et imper. apothegm.* (Archelaus 3), 177A

τοῦ δ' Εὐριπίδου τὸν καλὸν Ἀγάθωνα περιλαμβάνοντος ἐν τῷ συμποσίῳ καὶ καταφιλοῦντος ἤδη γενειῶντα, πρὸς τοὺς φίλους εἶπε [Ἀρχέλαος sc.] "Μὴ θαυμάσητε· τῶν γὰρ καλῶν καὶ τὸ μετόπωρον καλόν ἐστιν".

**56** Ael. *V. H.* 2.21

Ἥρα δέ, φασι, τοῦ αὐτοῦ Ἀγάθωνος τούτου καὶ Εὐριπίδης ὁ ποιητής, καὶ τὸν Χρύσιππον τὸ δρᾶμα αὐτῷ χαριζόμενος λέγεται διαφροντίσαι. καὶ εἰ μὲν σαφὲς τοῦτο, ἀποφήνασθαι οὐκ οἶδα, λεγόμενον δ' οὖν αὐτὸ οἶδα ἐν τοῖς μάλιστα.

**57** Plut. *An seni res publica gerenda sit* 23, 795D

οὕτω δὲ καὶ Τιμόθεον Εὐριπίδης συριττόμενον ἐπὶ τῇ καινοτομίᾳ καὶ παρανομεῖν εἰς τὴν μουσικὴν δοκοῦντα θαρρεῖν ἐκέλευσεν, ὡς ὀλίγου χρόνου τῶν θεάτρων ὑπ' αὐτῷ γενησομένων.

learned of it and twitted Sophocles, saying that he had enjoyed this same boy but had given him nothing additional, and that Sophocles had been treated contemptuously because of his licentiousness. When Sophocles heard this, he wrote the following epigram against him, making use of the fable about the Sun and the North Wind[1] and hinting additionally at Euripides' adulterous relations.

> It was the sun, Euripides, not the boy, who warmed me and caused me to strip naked. But it was the North Wind that conversed with you as you were dallying, and you are not wise, seeing that while you sow another's field you accuse Eros of being a thief.

## I. *Euripides and Agathon*

**55** Plutarch, *Sayings of Kings and Commanders*

When Euripides was embracing the fair Agathon at the drinking-party and kissing him, although he already had his beard, he [Archelaus] said, 'Do not be surprised: for of lovely things the autumn is lovely too'.[2]

**56** Aelian

Euripides the poet was in love, they say, with this same Agathon, and it is said that he composed his play *Chrysippus* as a favor to him. I am not able to say definitely whether this is true, but I know that it is very widely maintained.

## J. *Euripides and Timotheus*[3]

**57** Plutarch, *Whether an Old Man Should Engage in Public Affairs*

In like manner, when Timotheus was hissed at for his innovations and was thought to be committing crimes against music, Euripides told him to cheer up since within a short time the audiences would be at his feet.

---

[1] According to a fable, the Sun and the North Wind had a contest which of them could cause a man to strip off his cloak more quickly.
[2] The same anecdote, but with Euripides giving the punch-line, in Plut. *Amatorius* 24, 770C.
[3] See also T 4.24.

**58** Ar. *Ran.* 944, 1407-9, 1451-3 cum scholiis

εἶτ' ἀνέτρεφον [τραγῳδίαν sc.] μονῳδίαις Κηφισοφῶντα μειγνύς.

schol.: ἐδόκει δοῦλος ὢν ὁ Κηφισοφῶν συμποιεῖν αὐτῷ καὶ μάλιστα τὰ μέλη, ὃν καὶ συνεῖναι τῇ γυναικὶ αὐτοῦ κωμῳδοῦσιν.

καὶ μηκέτ' ἔμοιγε κατ' ἔπος ἀλλ' ἐς τὸν σταθμὸν
αὐτός, τὰ παιδί', ἡ γυνή, Κηφισοφῶν,
ἐμβὰς καθήσθω, ξυλλαβὼν τὰ βιβλία.

schol.: Κηφισοφῶν] καὶ διὰ τούτου δηλοῖ πάλιν σχεδόν τι τὸ συναμφότερον, ὡς Κηφισοφῶν συνεποίει τὰ δράματα καὶ τὴν γυναῖκα αὐτοῦ εἶχε.

ΔΙ(ΟΝΥΣΟΣ)
εὖ γ', ὦ Παλάμηδες, ὦ σοφωτάτη φύσις.
ταυτὶ πότερ' αὐτὸς ηὗρες ἢ Κηφισοφῶν;
ΕΥ(ΡΙΠΙΔΗΣ)
ἐγὼ μόνος· τὰς δ' ὀξίδας Κηφισοφῶν.

**59** Arist. *Rhet.* 3.15, 1416 a 28-35

ἄλλος, [τρόπος sc.] εἰ γέγονεν κρίσις, ὥσπερ Εὐριπίδης πρὸς Ὑγιαίνοντα ἐν τῇ ἀντιδόσει κατηγοροῦντα ὡς ἀσεβής, ὅς γ' ἐποίησε κελεύων ἐπιορκεῖν [*Hip.* 612]

### K. *Euripides and Cephisophon*[1]

**58** Aristophanes' *Frogs* with scholia

> Then I nourished her [Tragedy] on monodies, mixing in Cephisophon.

schol.: It was thought that Cephisophon, who was a slave, was his literary collaborator, especially in the lyric parts. The comic poets said that he also slept with Euripides' wife.

> No more line for line, but get into the scale, yourself, your children, your wife, Cephisophon, and throw in your books as well.

schol.: Cephisophon] and thereby he again almost makes plain both facts, that Cephisophon helped him write his plays and that he enjoyed his wife.

DIONYSUS
> Well done, my clever Palamedes. Is this your invention or Cephisophon's?

EURIPIDES
> Mine alone. But the vinegar-cruets were Cephisophon's.

### L. *Legal Troubles*

#### a. Suit concerning an *antidosis*[2] with Hygiaenon

**59** Aristotle, *Rhetoric*

Another [means of refutation] is if there has been a prior judgement. Euripides made this argument against Hygiainon who accused him in their *antidosis* of being impious, seeing that he wrote, encouraging perjury [*Hippolytus* 612],

---

[1] See also T 1.5, 1.29, 3.12, and 4.14-15.
[2] A legal procedure whereby a rich man who had been asked to perform a 'liturgy', a form of required public service, could request that someone else be required to perform it as being better able to pay.

ἡ γλῶσσ' ὀμώμοχ', ἡ δὲ φρὴν ἀνώμοτος.
ἔφη γὰρ αὐτὸν ἀδικεῖν τὰς ἐκ τοῦ Διονυσιακοῦ ἀγῶνος κρίσεις εἰς τὰ δικαστήρια ἄγοντα· ἐκεῖ γὰρ αὐτῶν δεδωκέναι λόγον, ἢ δώσειν εἰ βούλεται κατηγορεῖν.

**60** P. Oxy. 24.2400, saeculi p.C.n. tertii

Εὐρειπίδης Ἡρακλέα μαινόμενον ἐν Διονυσίοις ποιήσας ἐν δράματι κρίνεται ἀσεβείας.

**61** Arist. *Polit.* 5.10, 1311 b 30-4

καὶ τῆς Ἀρχελάου δ' ἐπιθέσεως Δεκάμνιχος ἡγεμὼν ἐγένετο, παροξύνων τοὺς ἐπιθεμένους πρῶτος· αἴτιον δὲ τῆς ὀργῆς ὅτι αὐτὸν ἐξέδωκε μαστιγῶσαι Εὐριπίδῃ τῷ ποιητῇ· ὁ δ' Εὐριπίδης ἐχαλέπαινεν εἰπόντος τι αὐτοῦ εἰς δυσωδίαν τοῦ στόματος.

**62** Plut. *Regum et imper. apothegm.* (Archelaus 1), 177A

Ἀρχέλαος αἰτηθεὶς παρὰ πότον ποτήριον χρυσοῦν ὑπό τινος τῶν συνήθων οὐ μὴν ἐπιεικῶν ἐκέλευσεν Εὐριπίδῃ τὸν παῖδα δοῦναι· θαυμάσαντος δὲ τοῦ ἀνθρώπου, "σὺ μὲν γάρ", εἶπεν, "αἰτεῖν, οὗτος δὲ λαμβάνειν ἄξιός ἐστι καὶ μὴ αἰτῶν".

> My tongue swore, but my mind is unsworn.

Euripides said that Hygiainon was wrong to bring judgements from the Dionysiac competitions into the courtroom. For he had already given an account of his work there, or would do so again, if Hygiainon insisted on accusing him.

### b. Accused of impiety

**60** P. Oxy. 2400, 3rd c. A.D., a list of topics for rhetorical exercise[1]

Euripides having made Heracles a madman in a play produced at the City Dionysia, is on trial for impiety.

## M. *Visit to Macedon and Death*[2]

### a. Reception by Archelaus

**61** Aristotle, *Politics*

Decamnichus was a leader of the attack against Archelaus, being the first to stimulate the fury of the attackers. The reason for his anger was that Archelaus had handed him over to Euripides the poet to be whipped. Now Euripides was annoyed that Decamnichus had made some remark about the foulness of his breath.

**62** Plutarch, *Sayings of Kings and Commanders*

When Archelaus was asked at a drinking-party for a gold cup by an ignoble familiar, he told the slave to give the cup to Euripides. And when the man expressed surprise, he said, 'You deserve to ask, but he to receive even without asking'.[3]

---

[1] See T 4.13. Since, however, in the other items in this list the action described by the aorist participle is historical while that described by the main verb is fictitious, this exercise does not actually claim to confirm Satyrus' report.
[2] See also T 1.21, 1.35, 2.8-10, 3.12-14, 4.22-3, and 5.9.
[3] The same story in Plut. *de vitioso pudore* 7, 531DE.

**63** [Ion], *FGE*, p. 158, *EG* 472-7, *A.P* 7.44

Εἰ καὶ δακρυόεις, Εὐριπίδη, εἷλέ σε πότμος,
καί σε λυκορραῖσται δεῖπνον ἔθεντο κύνες,
τὸν σκηνῆς μελίγηρυν ἀηδόνα, κόσμον Ἀθηνῶν,
τὸν σοφίῃ Μουσέων μιξάμενον χάριτα,
ἀλλ᾽ ἔμολες Πελλαῖον ὑπ᾽ ἠρίον, ὡς ἂν ὁ λάτρις
Πιερίδων ναίῃς ἀγχόθι Πιερίης.

**64** Hermesianax, fr. 7.61-8 Powell, ap. Athen. 13.71, 597B

φημὶ δὲ κἀκεῖνον τὸν ἀεὶ πεφυλαγμένον ἄνδρα
καὶ πάντων μῖσος κτώμενον ἐξ ὀνύχων[1]
πάσας ἀμφὶ γυναῖκας, ὑπὸ σκολιοῖο τυπέντα
τόξου νυκτερινὰς οὐκ ἀποθέσθ᾽ ὀδύνας·
ἀλλὰ Μακηδονίων[2] πάσας κατενίσατο λαύρας
Αἰγάων[3] μεθέπων[4] Ἀρχέλεω ταμίην,
εἰσόκε ⟨δὴ⟩ δαίμων Εὐριπίδῃ εὗρετ᾽ ὄλεθρον
Ἀρριβίου στυγνῶν ἀντιάσαντι κυνῶν.

**65** Apostol. 14.83, *Paroemiogr. Gr.* (Leutsch ii 624)

Προμέρου κύνες· τοῦτον οἰκέτην ὄντα βασιλικὸν μισῆσαι καθ᾽ ὑπερβολὴν τῶν τραγῳδιῶν τὸν ποιητὴν Εὐριπίδην ἐπαφεῖναί τε αὐτῷ κύνας ἀγρίους, οἳ τὸν Εὐριπίδην κατεθοινήσαντο.

**66** Adaeus, *GP* 11-16, *A. P.* 7.51

Οὔ σε κυνῶν γένος εἷλ᾽, Εὐριπίδη, οὐδὲ γυναικὸς
οἶστρος τὸν σκοτίης κύπριδος ἀλλότριον,
ἀλλ᾽ Ἀίδης καὶ γῆρας, ὑπαὶ Μακέτῃ δ᾽ Ἀρεθούσῃ
κεῖσαι ἑταιρείῃ τίμιος Ἀρχέλεω.
σοὶ δ᾽ οὐ τοῦτον ἐγὼ τίθεμαι τάφον, ἀλλὰ τὰ Βάκχου
βήματα καὶ σκηνὰς ἐμβάδι σειομένας.[5]

---

[1] Jacobs: ἐκ συνοχῶν codd.
[2] Lloyd-Jones: -ης codd.
[3] Bergk: αἰγείων codd.
[4] Hartung: μέθεπεν δ᾽ codd.
[5] Borthwick: πειθομένας codd.

## b. Death

**63** Anonymous poem ascribed to Ion of Chios

Even though a tearful fate was yours, Euripides, and wolf-worrying dogs made a feast of you, the honey-voiced nightingale of the stage, Athens' glory, who mixed the charm of the Muses with philosophy, still you went to a tomb in Pella so that as servant of the Pierian Muses you might dwell near Pieria.

**64** Hermesianax quoted in Athenaeus

I say that even he, the man always on his guard and full to his fingertips of hatred against all women, was struck by the crooked bow and could not put from him the pain at night. Rather he went down all the alleys of Macedonian Aegae in search of Archelaus' serving-girl until fate found death for Euripides when he met with the hateful hounds of Arrhibius.

**65** Apostolius

Hounds of Promerus: he was a slave of the king who hated the tragic poet Euripides exceedingly and set upon him fierce dogs, who made a feast of Euripides.

**66** Adaeus

It was not dogs who killed you, Euripides, or the sting of passion for a woman, since you were averse to illicit love, but Hades and old age. You lie now near Arethusa in Macedonia, honored in the companionship of Archelaus. Yet I do not consider this to be your tomb but rather the stage-sets of Dionysus and the theaters shaken by the tread of the buskin.

**67** Marmor Parium, *FGrH* 239 A 63 [=*TrGF* DID D A63]

ἀφ' οὗ Εὐριπίδης βιώσας ἔτη ⳆΔΔΓ..(?) ἐτελεύτησεν, ἔτη †ΗΔΔΔΔΓ ἄρχοντος Ἀθήνησιν Ἀντιγένους.

**68** Apollod. Athen., *FGrH* 244 F 35, ap. Diod. 13.103.4 [=Soph. T 85 Radt]

περὶ δὲ τὸν αὐτὸν χρόνον [a. 406/5] ἐτελεύτησε Σοφοκλῆς ὁ Σοφίλου, ποιητὴς τραγῳδιῶν, ἔτη βιώσας ἐνενήκοντα, νίκας δ' ἔχων ὀκτωκαίδεκα.....Ἀπολλόδωρος δ' ὁ τὴν χρονικὴν σύνταξιν πραγματευσάμενός φησι καὶ τὸν Εὐριπίδην κατὰ τὸν αὐτὸν ἐνιαυτὸν τελευτῆσαι· τινὲς δὲ λέγουσι παρ' Ἀρχελάῳ τῷ βασιλεῖ Μακεδόνων κατὰ τὴν χώραν ἐξελθόντα κυσὶ περιπεσεῖν καὶ διασπασθῆναι μικρῷ πρόσθεν τούτων τῶν χρόνων.

**69** Timaeus, *FGrH* 566 F 105, ap. Plut. *Quaest. conv.* 8.1.1, 717C [vide T 7]

ἀποθανόντος δὲ [Εὐριπίδου sc.] καθ' ἣν †ἐγεννήθη Διονύσιος ὁ πρεσβύτερος τῶν ἐν Σικελίᾳ τυράννων,[1] ἅμα τῆς τύχης, ὡς Τίμαιος ἔφη, τὸν μιμητὴν ἐξαγούσης τῶν τραγικῶν παθῶν καὶ τὸν ἀγωνιστὴν ἐπεισαγούσης.

**70** Ar. *Ach.* 393-489

ΔΙ(ΚΑΙΟΠΟΛΙΣ)
    ὥρα 'στὶν ἁρμοῖ[2] καρτερὰν ψυχὴν λαβεῖν,     393
    καί μοι βαδιστέ' ἐστὶν ὡς Εὐριπίδην.
    παῖ παῖ.

---

[1] fort. ἐγενήθη...τύραννος, nisi ex incuria Plutarchi oriundus error.
[2] Lloyd-Jones: ἀρά μοι vel ἤδη codd.

### c. Year of Death

**67** *Parian Marble*

Since Euripides the poet died at the age of 79 (?), 144[1] years, in the archonship of Antigenes (407/6).

**68** Apollodorus of Athens quoted in Diodorus

Around the same time Sophocles, son of Sophilus, the tragic poet, died at the age of ninety having won eighteen victories...Apollodorus, the man who worked on chronology, says that Euripides too died in that year. Some say that at the court of Archelaus, the king of Macedon, he went out into the countryside and happened upon dogs and was torn apart a little before this time.

**69** Timaeus quoted in Plutarch, *Table-Talk*[2]

and [Euripides] died on the day when Dionysus, the elder of the two Sicilian tyrants of that name, was born,[3] with Fate, as Timaeus says, causing the exit of the man who imitated tragic happenings and at the same time the entrance of the man to enact them.

### N. *Euripides in the Comic Poets*[4]

#### (a) Aristophanes

**70** Aristophanes, *Acharnians* 393-489

DICAEOPOLIS
> Now is the hour when I must be brave: I must go to the house of Euripides. [Knocking] Slave! Slave!

---

[1] The first of these figures is lacunose and the second incorrect (145 is the correct figure) on the stone. If 79 is the correct reading, the implied date of birth (486/5 or 487/6) agrees with T 25 rather than T 6.

[2] Continues T 7.

[3] He was not born but became tyrant in 406.

[4] See also T 1.5, 1.29-32, 1.35, 4.2, 4.12, 4.14, 4.18-19, 5.6, 9, 17, 38, 39, and 58; Aristophanes fr. 128 K.-A., Theopompus fr. 35 K.-A., Nicostratus fr. 28 K.

ΟΙΚΕΤΗΣ
    τίς οὗτος;
ΔΙ.     ἔνδον ἔστ' Εὐριπίδης;   395
ΟΙ. οὐκ ἔνδον ἔνδον ἐστίν, εἰ γνώμην ἔχεις.
ΔΙ. πῶς ἔνδον, εἶτ' οὐκ ἔνδον;
ΟΙ.     ὀρθῶς, ὦ γέρον.
 ὁ νοῦς μὲν ἔξω ξυλλέγων ἐπύλλια
 οὐκ ἔνδον, αὐτὸς δ' ἔνδον ἀναβάδην ποεῖ
 τραγῳδίαν.
ΔΙ.   ὦ τρισμακάρι' Εὐριπίδη,   400
 ὅθ' ὁ δοῦλος οὑτωσὶ σοφῶς ὑποκρίναται.
 ἐκκάλεσον αὐτόν.
ΟΙ.   ἀλλ' ἀδύνατον.
ΔΙ.     ἀλλ' ὅμως·
 οὐ γὰρ ἂν ἀπέλθοιμ'. ἀλλὰ κόψω τὴν θύραν.
 Εὐριπίδη, Εὐριπίδιον,
 ὑπάκουσον, εἴπερ πώποτ' ἀνθρώπων τινί· 405
 Δικαιόπολις καλεῖ σ' ὁ Χολλῄδης ἐγώ.
ΕΥΡΙΠΙΔΗΣ
  ἀλλ' οὐ σχολή.
ΔΙ. ἀλλ' ἐκκυκλήθητ'.
ΕΥ.   ἀλλ' ἀδύνατον.
ΔΙ.     ἀλλ' ὅμως.
ΕΥ. ἀλλ' ἐκκυκλήσομαι· καταβαίνειν δ' οὐ σχολή.
ΔΙ. Εὐριπίδη.
ΕΥ.  τί λέλακας;
ΔΙ.    ἀναβάδην ποεῖς   410
 ἐξὸν καταβάδην. οὐκ ἐτὸς χωλοὺς ποεῖς.
 ἀτὰρ τί τὰ ῥάκι' ἐκ τραγῳδίας ἔχεις,
 ἐσθῆτ' ἐλεινήν; οὐκ ἐτὸς πτωχοὺς ποεῖς.
 ἀλλ' ἀντιβολῶ πρὸς τῶν γονάτων σ', Εὐριπίδη,
 δός μοι ῥάκιόν τι τοῦ παλαιοῦ δράματος. 415
 δεῖ γάρ με λέξαι τῷ χορῷ ῥῆσιν μακράν·
 αὕτη δὲ θάνατον, ἢν κακῶς λέξω, φέρει.

SLAVE
>    Who is it?
DI. Is Euripides at home?
SL. He is at home and not at home, if you take my meaning.
DI. How at home and then not at home?
SL. In the exact sense of the word, old man. His mind, which is abroad gathering verselets, is not at home, while he himself is at home writing a tragedy with his feet up.
DI. O thrice-blest is Euripides, when his very slave plays his role so cleverly! Call him out.
SL. But it is impossible.
DI. But do it all the same. For I shall not go away. But now I shall knock on the door. Euripides, dear, sweet Euripides, hearken if ever you hearkened to mortal man. It is I, Dicaeopolis of Cholleidae, who calls you. [Euripides appears at the door.]
EURIPIDES
>    But I have no time.
DI. But roll yourself out.[1]
EU. But it is impossible.
DI. But do it all the same.
EU. Well, I will have myself rolled out. But I have no time to climb down. [The *eccyclema* rolls out the study of Euripides.]
DI. Euripides.
EU. What sayest thou?
DI. You write with your feet up when you could write with them down. No wonder the heroes you create are lame. But why are you wearing such pitiable clothing, rags from a tragedy? No wonder the heroes you create are beggars. But I beg you by your knees, Euripides, give me a rag from that old play of yours. For I must make a long speech to the Chorus, and the result of it will be death for me if I fail to be eloquent.

---

[1] I.e. Euripides is asked to make use of the *eccyclema*, a stage-machine that rolled out a platform representing the inside of the house.

| | | |
|---|---|---|
| ΕΥ. | τὰ ποῖα τρύχη; μῶν ἐν οἷς Οἰνεὺς ὁδὶ | |
| | ὁ δύσποτμος γεραιὸς ἠγωνίζετο; | |
| ΔΙ. | οὐκ Οἰνέως ἦν, ἀλλ' ἔτ' ἀθλιωτέρου. | 420 |
| ΕΥ. | τὰ τοῦ τυφλοῦ Φοίνικος; | |
| ΔΙ. | οὐ Φοίνικος, οὔ, | |
| | ἀλλ' ἕτερος ἦν Φοίνικος ἀθλιώτερος. | |
| ΕΥ. | ποίας ποθ' ἀνὴρ λακίδας αἰτεῖται πέπλων; | |
| | ἀλλ' ἦ Φιλοκτήτου τὰ τοῦ πτωχοῦ λέγεις; | |
| ΔΙ. | οὔκ, ἀλλὰ τούτου πολὺ πολὺ πτωχιστέρου. | 425 |
| ΕΥ. | ἀλλ' ἦ τὰ δυσπινῆ θέλεις πεπλώματα, | |
| | ἃ Βελλεροφόντης εἶχ' ὁ χωλὸς οὑτοσί; | |
| ΔΙ. | οὐ Βελλεροφόντης· ἀλλὰ κἀκεῖνος μὲν ἦν | |
| | χωλὸς προσαιτῶν στωμύλος δεινὸς λέγειν. | |
| ΕΥ. | οἶδ' ἄνδρα, Μυσὸν Τήλεφον. | |
| ΔΙ. | ναί, Τήλεφον· | 430 |
| | τούτου δὸς ἀντιβολῶ σέ μοι τὰ σπάργανα. | |
| ΕΥ. | ὦ παῖ, δὸς αὐτῷ Τηλέφου ῥακώματα. | |
| | κεῖται δ' ἄνωθεν τῶν Θυεστείων ῥακῶν | |
| | μεταξὺ τῶν Ἰνοῦς. ἰδοὺ ταυτὶ λαβέ. | |
| ΔΙ. | ὦ Ζεῦ διόπτα καὶ κατόπτα πανταχῇ | 435 |
| | [ἐνσκευάσασθαί μ' οἷον ἀθλιώτατον].[1] | |
| | Εὐριπίδη, 'πειδήπερ ἐχαρίσω ταδί, | |
| | κἀκεῖνά μοι δὸς τἀκόλουθα τῶν ῥακῶν, | |
| | τὸ πιλίδιον περὶ τὴν κεφαλὴν τὸ Μύσιον. | |
| | δεῖ γάρ με δόξαι πτωχὸν εἶναι τήμερον, | 440 |
| | εἶναι μὲν ὅσπερ εἰμί, φαίνεσθαι δὲ μή· | |
| | τοὺς μὲν θεατὰς εἰδέναι μ' ὅς εἰμ' ἐγώ, | |
| | τοὺς δ' αὖ χορευτὰς ἠλιθίους παρεστάναι, | |
| | ὅπως ἂν αὐτοὺς ῥηματίοις σκιμαλίσω. | |
| ΕΥ. | δώσω· πυκνῇ γὰρ λεπτὰ μηχανᾷ φρενί. | 445 |
| ΔΙ. | εὐδαιμονοίης, Τηλέφῳ δ' ἁγὼ φρονῶ. | |
| | εὖ γ'· οἷον ἤδη ῥηματίων ἐμπίμπλαμαι. | |
| | ἀτὰρ δέομαί γε πτωχικοῦ βακτηρίου. | |
| ΕΥ. | τουτὶ λαβὼν ἄπελθε λαΐνων σταθμῶν. | |
| ΔΙ. | ὦ θύμ'—ὁρᾷς γὰρ ὡς ἀπωθοῦμαι δόμων | 450 |
| | πολλῶν δεόμενος σκευαρίων—νῦν δὴ γενοῦ | |

---

[1] del. Dobree (=384)

EU. What rags do you mean? Those in which Oeneus here, hapless old man, contended for the prize? [He holds up a ragged costume.]
DI. Not Oeneus' rags: someone even more wretched.
EU. Was it blind old Phoenix?
DI. Not Phoenix, no. But another more wretched than Phoenix.
EU. Which are the tatters that this wight requires? Mean you the rags of beggar Philoctetes?
DI. No. One far, far more beggarish than he.
EU. Perhaps thou mean'st the wretched garments worn by lame Bellerophon—right over here. [Holds up another ragged costume.]
DI. Not Bellerophon. But like him he was lame, a beggar, glib and eloquent.
EU. I know the man: 'tis Telephus the Mysian.
DI. Yes, Telephus. *His* clothes, I beg of you, give me.
EU. Slave, give this man the rags of Telephus. You'll find them above those of Thyestes and below those of Ino. Here, take them. [Gives him the costume.]
DI. [looking through the holes in the garment] O Zeus, that see'st through and spyest all [costume me out as wretched as can be]! Euripides, since you have granted me this, give me also what goes with the rags, the little Mysian cap about the head: 'For I must seem a beggar'—on this date—'and be myself but not appear myself.' The audience must know who I am but the Chorus must stand around like fools so that with my little speechlets I may flip them the bird.
EU. Done, for your clever mind has subtle thoughts. [Gives him the cap.]
DI. Blessings on you! And on Telephus, what I have in mind. [Puts on the clothes.] Bravo! How I am filled with little speeches already! But I need still a beggar's staff.
EU. This thing—take it and leave my halls of granite hewn. [Gives him the staff.]
DI. Heart, see'st thou how they thrust me from the house, in need of many props. Now you must be a wheedling and in-

|     |     |     |
| --- | --- | --- |
|     | γλίσχρος προσαιτῶν λιπαρῶν. Εὐριπίδη, |     |
|     | δός μοι σπυρίδιον διακεκαυμένον λύχνῳ. |     |
| ΕΥ. | τί δ' ὦ τάλας σε τοῦδ' ἔχει πλέκους χρέος; |     |
| ΔΙ. | χρέος μὲν οὐδέν, βούλομαι δ' ὅμως λαβεῖν. | 455 |
| ΕΥ. | λυπηρὸς ἴσθ' ὧν κἀποχώρησον δόμων. |     |
| ΔΙ. | φεῦ. |     |
|     | εὐδαιμονοίης, ὥσπερ ἡ μήτηρ ποτέ. |     |
| ΕΥ. | ἄπελθέ νύν μοι. |     |
| ΔΙ. | μἀλλά μοι δὸς ἓν μόνον, |     |
|     | κοτυλίσκιον τὸ χεῖλος ἀποκεκρουμένον. |     |
| ΕΥ. | φθείρου λαβὼν τόδ'· ἴσθ' ὀχληρὸς ὢν δόμοις. | 460 |
| ΔΙ. | οὔπω μὰ Δί'· οἶσ'[1] οἷ' αὐτὸς ἐργάζει κακά. |     |
|     | ἀλλ', ὦ γλυκύτατ' Εὐριπίδη, τουτὶ μόνον, |     |
|     | δός μοι χυτρίδιον σφογγίῳ βεβυσμένον. |     |
| ΕΥ. | ἄνθρωπ', ἀφαιρήσει με τὴν τραγῳδίαν. |     |
|     | ἄπελθε ταυτηνὶ λαβών. |     |
| ΔΙ. | ἀπέρχομαι. | 465 |
|     | καίτοι τί δράσω; δεῖ γὰρ ἑνὸς οὗ μὴ τυχὼν |     |
|     | ἀπόλωλ'. ἄκουσον, ὦ γλυκύτατ' Εὐριπίδη· |     |
|     | τουτὶ λαβὼν ἄπειμι κοὐ πρόσειμ' ἔτι· |     |
|     | εἰς τὸ σπυρίδιον ἰσχνά μοι φυλλεῖα δός. |     |
| ΕΥ. | ἀπολεῖς μ'. ἰδού σοι. φροῦδά μοι τὰ δράματα. | 470 |
| ΔΙ. | ἀλλ' οὐκέτ', ἀλλ' ἄπειμι. καὶ γάρ εἰμ' ἄγαν |     |
|     | ὀχληρός, οὐ δοκῶν με κοιράνους στυγεῖν. |     |
|     | οἴμοι κακοδαίμων, ὡς ἀπόλωλ'. ἐπελαθόμην |     |
|     | ἐν ᾧπέρ ἐστι πάντα μοι τὰ πράγματα. |     |
|     | Εὐριπίδιον ὦ γλυκύτατον καὶ φίλτατον, | 475 |
|     | κάκιστ' ἀπολοίμην, εἴ τί σ' αἰτήσαιμ' ἔτι, |     |
|     | πλὴν ἓν μόνον, τουτὶ μόνον, τουτὶ μόνον· |     |
|     | σκάνδικά μοι δὸς μητρόθεν δεδεγμένος. |     |
| ΕΥ. | ἁνὴρ ὑβρίζει· κλῇε πηκτὰ δωμάτων. |     |
| ΔΙ. | ὦ θύμ', ἄνευ σκάνδικος ἐμπορευτέα. | 480 |
|     | ἆρ' οἶσθ' ὅσον τὸν ἀγῶν' ἀγωνιεῖ τάχα, |     |
|     | μέλλων ὑπὲρ Λακεδαιμονίων ἀνδρῶν λέγειν; |     |
|     | πρόβαινέ νυν, ὦ θυμέ· γραμμὴ δ' αὑτηί. |     |
|     | ἕστηκας; οὐκ εἶ καταπιὼν Εὐριπίδην; |     |

---

[1] scripsi: οἶσθ' vel οἶδ' codd.

|      | sistent beggar. Euripides, give me a little wicker-basket with a lamp-burn on it. |
| ---- | ---- |
| EU.  | What need, unhappy man, of wicker-work? |
| DI.  | No need, but nonetheless I want to have it. |
| EU.  | Know that you vex me, from these halls be gone! [Gives him the basket.] |
| DI.  | Well, well! Happiness attend you, just as it did your mother! |
| EU.  | Please depart then. |
| DI.  | Nay, but give me one thing more, a little cup with its lip broken off. |
| EU.  | Take it and clear off. Know you vex the house. [Gives him the cup.] |
| DI.  | Not yet, by Zeus: endure the bane you yourself inflict! But, dear sweet Euripides, give me this one thing more, a little pot stuffed with a sponge. |
| EU.  | Creature, you'll rob me of my tragic art. Take it and go. [Gives him the pot.] |
| DI.  | I go. And yet what am I to do? For I lack the one thing that is my death if I do not get it. Hear me, dear sweet Euripides; if I get *this*, I will depart and come no more. For my basket give me some withered leaves. |
| EU.  | You will be my death. Here you are. [Gives him leaves.] My plays are now all gone. |
| DI.  | I shall trouble you no more but go. 'For I am vexatious to the house, thinking the royal family hates me not.' O alas! I am utterly undone! For I have forgot 'the thing in which my fortunes are bound up'. Euripides, o dearest and sweetest, ruin take me if I ever ask you for another thing, except for this one, this single, this only thing: give me some chervil from your mother.[1] |
| EU.  | The man insults me! Bolt palace-portal fast. [Euripides wheels inside on the *eccylema*.] |
| DI.  | O heart, I must fare forth without my chervil! Do you know how great a struggle you must soon wage since you intend to speak on behalf of the Spartans? March forward, then, my heart. There is the finish-line. Do you hesitate? Won't |

---

[1] Cf. T 1.1, 1.32, and 76.387.

ἐπήνεσ'· ἄγε νυν, ὦ τάλαινα καρδία, 485
ἄπελθ' ἐκεῖσε, κᾆτα τὴν κεφαλὴν ἐκεῖ
παράσχες εἰποῦσ' ἅττ' ἂν αὐτῇ σοὶ δοκῇ.
τόλμησον, ἴθι, χώρησον· ἄγαμαι καρδίας. 488

**71 id. Equ. 11-20**

ΟΙ(ΚΕΤΗΣ) Α
 τί κινυρόμεθ' ἄλλως; οὐκ ἐχρῆν ζητεῖν τινα 11
 σωτηρίαν νῷν, ἀλλὰ μὴ κλάειν ἔτι;
ΟΙ(ΚΕΤΗΣ) Β
 τίς οὖν γένοιτ' ἄν; λέγε σύ.
ΟΙ^Α.         σὺ μὲν οὖν μοι λέγε,
 ἵνα μὴ μάχωμαι.
ΟΙ^Β.       μὰ τὸν Ἀπόλλω 'γὼ μὲν οὔ.
 ἀλλ' εἰπὲ θαρρῶν, εἶτα κἀγώ σοι φράσω. 15
ΟΙ^Α.  "πῶς ἂν σύ μοι λέξειας ἁμὲ χρὴ λέγειν;"
ΟΙ^Β.  ἀλλ' οὐκ ἔνι μοι τὸ θρέττε. πῶς ἂν οὖν ποτε
 εἴποιμ' ἂν αὐτὸ δῆτα κομψευριπικῶς;
ΟΙ^Α.  μή μοί γε, μὴ 'μοί, μὴ διασκανδικίσῃς.
 ἀλλ' εὑρέ τιν' ἀπόκινον ἀπὸ τοῦ δεσπότου. 20

**72 id. Nub. 1364-78**

ΣΤ(ΡΕΨΙΑΔΗΣ)
 ....
 ἔπειτα δ' ἐκέλευσ' αὐτὸν ἀλλὰ μυρρίνην λαβόντα
 τῶν Αἰσχύλου λέξαι τί μοι· κᾆθ' οὗτος εὐθὺς εἶπεν·
 "ἐγὼ γὰρ Αἰσχύλον νομίζω πρῶτον ἐν ποηταῖς, 1366
 ψόφου πλέων ἀξύστατον στόμφακα κρημνοποιόν;"
 κἀνταῦθα πῶς οἴεσθέ μου τὴν καρδίαν ὀρεχθεῖν;
 ὅμως δὲ τὸν θυμὸν δακὼν ἔφην· "σὺ δ' ἀλλὰ τούτων
 λέξον τι τῶν νεωτέρων, ἅττ' ἐστὶ τὰ σοφὰ ταῦτα". 1370
 ὁ δ' εὐθὺς ᾖσ' Εὐριπίδου ῥῆσίν τιν', ὡς ἐκίνει
 ἀδελφός, ὠλεξίκακε, τὴν ὁμομητρίαν ἀδελφήν.

you drink down Euripides and go? [Starts to move.] Bravo! Come now, my wretched heart, depart to that place and lay your head on the block when you have said what you deem best. Be daring, go, proceed. I admire your spirit.

**71** Aristophanes, *Knights*[1]

FIRST SLAVE

Why do we utter useless laments? Ought we not rather to be looking for some means of safety for ourselves rather than continuing to cry?

SECOND SLAVE

What means of safety could there be? You tell me.

F.S. No, rather you must tell me, to avoid a fight.

S.S. No, by Apollo, not I. But pluck up your courage and tell me, then I shall tell you.

F.S. 'O would that thou could'st say what I must say!'[2]

S.S. But I don't have the guts. How could I express it in a clever Euripidean fashion?

F.S. Do not, I beg you, do not, I pray, be-chervil me. But find some way of moving out from master.

**72** Aristophanes, *Clouds*

STREPSIADES

Then I told him, 'Well, take up a myrtle branch and say something of Aeschylus for me'. And he said straight off, 'What, am I to consider Aeschylus the best among the poets, Aeschylus, full of noise, an uncouth mouther of bombast, poet of mountain-high words?' How do you think my heart quivered at that? Yet I bit back my anger and said, 'Well then, recite something from one of these newer poets, this clever stuff you mention'. He immediately sang a long speech by Euripides, how a brother—heavens above—was banging his sister by the same mother.[3] I could no longer

---

[1] For a defense of the text printed here, see K. J. Dover, *Greek and the Greeks* (Oxford, 1987), i 307-10.
[2] *Hippolytus* 345.
[3] An allusion to the *Aeolus*.

κἀγὼ οὐκέτ' ἐξηνεσχόμην, ἀλλ' εὐθέως ἀράττω
πολλοῖς κακοῖς κᾀσχροῖσι· κᾆτ' ἐντεῦθεν, οἷον εἰκός,
ἔπος πρὸς ἔπος ἠρειδόμεσθ'· εἶθ' οὗτος ἐπαναπηδᾷ,
κἄπειτ' ἔφλα με κἀσπόδει κἄπνιγε κἀπέθλιβεν.    1376

ΦΕ(ΙΔΙΠΠΙΔΗΣ)
    οὔκουν δικαίως, ὅστις οὐκ Εὐριπίδην ἐπαινεῖς
    σοφώτατον;
ΣΤ.              σοφώτατόν γ' ἐκεῖνον, ὦ—τί σ' εἴπω;    1378

**73** id. *Vesp.* 54-61 et 1412-14

ΞΑ(ΝΘΙΑΣ)
    φέρε νυν κατείπω τοῖς θεαταῖς τὸν λόγον,
    ὀλίγ' ἄτθ' ὑπειπὼν πρῶτον αὐτοῖσιν ταδί,    55
    μηδὲν παρ' ἡμῶν προσδοκᾶν λίαν μέγα,
    μηδ' αὖ γέλωτα Μεγαρόθεν κεκλεμμένον.
    ἡμῖν γὰρ οὐκ ἔστ' οὔτε κάρυ' ἐκ φορμίδος
    δούλω διαρριπτοῦντε τοῖς θεωμένοις,
    οὔθ' Ἡρακλῆς τὸ δεῖπνον ἐξαπατώμενος,    60
    οὐδ' αὖθις ἀνασελγαινόμενος Εὐριπίδης.

..............

ΦΙ(ΛΟΚΛΕΩΝ)
        καὶ σὺ δή μοι, Χαιρεφῶν,    1412
    γυναικὶ κλητεύεις ἐοικὼς θαψίνῃ
    Ἰνοῖ κρεμαμένῃ πρὸς ποδῶν Εὐριπίδου;

**74** id. *Pax* 146-8 et 528-34

ΠΑ(ΙΔΙΟΝ ΤΡΥΓΑΙΟΥ)
    ἐκεῖνο τήρει, μὴ σφαλεὶς καταρρυῇς    146
    ἐντεῦθεν, εἶτα χωλὸς ὢν Εὐριπίδῃ
    λόγον παράσχῃς καὶ τραγῳδία γένῃ.

..............

contain myself and I berated him at once with many foul insults. And then, as you might expect, we were wrangling speech with speech. Then up he leaped and knocked, beat, choked, and whacked me.

PHEIDIPPIDES
And wasn't I justified, too, since you don't praise Euripides, the wisest man alive?

ST. Him wisest, you, you—unspeakable wretch!

**73** Aristophanes, *Wasps*

XANTHIAS
[addressing the audience] Come now, let me explain this story to the audience, making a few preliminary remarks, telling them not to expect anything too grand from us, nor, on the other hand, a joke stolen from Megara. We don't have two slaves scattering nuts from a basket among the spectators, nor do we have Heracles being cheated of his dinner, nor Euripides being abusively treated[1] yet again.

............

PHILOCLEON
And are you, Chaerephon, really acting as witness for a woman, when you look like a sallow version of Ino hanging onto the feet of—Euripides.[2]

**74** Aristophanes, *Peace*

TRYGAEUS' SON
Watch out that you don't slip and fall down from there and then when you are lame provide Euripides with a plot and become a tragedy.[3]

............

---

[1] This is not a word Aristophanes would use of his own treatment. It implies, therefore, that Euripides was a target of other comic poets, at whose hands he may have fared worse than he had to date from Aristophanes.

[2] Presumably, in Euripides' *Ino* the heroine throws herself at the feet of her husband Athamas.

[3] Trygaeus is about to fly up to heaven on a dung-beetle. Euripides' Bellerophon, who had ridden Pegasus, fell off and became lame.

ΤΡ(ΥΓΑΙΟΣ)
  ἀπέπτυσ' ἐχθροῦ φωτὸς ἔχθιστον πλέκος.  528
  τοῦ μὲν γὰρ ὄζει κρομμυοξυρεγμίας,
  ταύτης δ' †ὀπώρας, ὑποδοχῆς, Διονυσίων,  530
  αὐλῶν, τραγῳδῶν, Σοφοκλέους μελῶν, κιχλῶν,
  ἐπυλλίων Εὐριπίδου—
ΕΡ(ΜΗΣ)
      κλαύσᾶρα σὺ
  ταύτης καταψευδόμενος· οὐ γὰρ ἥδεται
  αὕτη ποητῇ ῥηματίων δικανικῶν.  534

**75** id. *Lys.* 283-4 et 368-9

Χ(ΟΡΟΣ) ΓΕ(ΡΟΝΤΩΝ)
  τασδὶ δὲ τὰς Εὐριπίδῃ θεοῖς τε πᾶσιν ἐχθρὰς  283
  ἐγὼ οὐκ ἄρα σχήσω παρὼν τολμήματος τοσούτου;
..............
Χ<sup>ΓΕ</sup>. οὐκ ἔστ' ἀνὴρ Εὐριπίδου σοφώτερος ποητής·  368
  οὐδὲν γὰρ ὧδε θρέμμ' ἀναιδές ἐστιν ὡς γυναῖκες.

**76** id. *Thesmo.* 3-21, 76-94, 269-76, 331-51, 373-431, 443-56

ΚΗΔΕΣΤΗΣ
....
  οἷόν τε, πρὶν τὸν σπλῆνα κομιδῇ μ' ἐκβαλεῖν,  3
  παρὰ σοῦ πυθέσθαι ποῖ μ' ἄγεις, ὠὐριπίδη;
ΕΥΡΠΙΙΔΗΣ
  ἀλλ' οὐκ ἀκούειν δεῖ σε πάνθ' ὅσ' αὐτίκα  5
  ὄψει παρεστώς.
ΚΗ.     πῶς λέγεις; αὖθις φράσον.
  οὐ δεῖ μ' ἀκούειν;
ΕΥ.      οὐχ ἅ γ' ἂν μέλλῃς ὁρᾶν.
ΚΗ. οὐδ' ἄρ' ὁρᾶν δεῖ μ';
ΕΥ.      οὐχ ἅ γ' ἂν ἀκούειν δέῃ.
ΚΗ. πῶς μοι παραινεῖς; δεξιῶς μέντοι λέγεις.
  οὐ φῂς σὺ χρῆναί μ' οὔτ' ἀκούειν οὔθ' ὁρᾶν;  10
ΕΥ. χωρὶς γὰρ αὐτοῖν ἑκατέρου 'στὶν ἡ φύσις.
ΚΗ. τοῦ μήτ' ἀκούειν μήθ' ὁρᾶν;
ΕΥ.      εὖ ἴσθ' ὅτι.

**TRYGAEUS**
    'I loathe a hated man's most hateful basket.' A kit-bag smells of the belch of onions and vinegar, whereas she [the goddess Peace] smells of harvest, hospitality, the Dionysia, flutes, tragic performances, the lyrics of Sophocles, roast thrush, and speechlets by Euripides—

**HERMES**
    You'll catch it, telling lies about her. *She* doesn't like the poet of law-court speeches.

**75** Aristophanes, *Lysistrata*

**CHORUS OF OLD MEN**
    ...Shall I not then stop these women, hated by Euripides and by all the gods, from such an act of daring since I am here?

..................

CH.     There is no poet wiser than Euripides, for there is no more shameless creature on earth than women.

**76** Aristophanes, *Women at the Thesmophoria*

**KINSMAN**
    ...Is it possible, before I lose my liver, to learn from you where you are taking me, Euripides?

**EURIPIDES**
    But you ought not to hear all the things that you will soon see in person.

KIN.   How's that? Say it again. I ought not to hear?
EU.    Not at any rate what you are going to see.
KIN.   And I ought not to see?
EU.    Not at any rate what you ought to hear.
KIN.   What advice is this you are giving me? My, how cleverly you speak. You say I ought neither to see nor to hear?
EU.    Yes, for the nature of each of them is separate.
KIN.   Not seeing and not hearing?
EU.    Of course.

KH.  πῶς χωρίς;
EY.  οὕτω ταῦτα διεκρίθη τότε.
αἰθὴρ γὰρ ὅτε τὰ πρῶτα διεχωρίζετο
καὶ ζῷ' ἐν αὑτῷ ξυνετέκνου κινούμενα, 15
ᾧ μὲν βλέπειν χρὴ πρῶτ' ἐμηχανήσατο
ὀφθαλμὸν ἀντίμιμον ἡλίου τροχῷ,
ἀκοῇ δὲ χοάνην ὦτα διετετρήνατο.
KH.  διὰ τὴν χοάνην οὖν μήτ' ἀκούω μήθ' ὁρῶ;
νὴ τὸν Δί' ἥδομαί γε τουτὶ προσμαθών. 20
οἷόν γέ πού 'στιν ἡ σοφῶν ξυνουσία.[1]

.................
EY.  τῇδε θἠμέρᾳ κριθήσεται 76
εἴτ' ἔστ' ἔτι ζῶν εἴτ' ἀπόλωλ' Εὐριπίδης.
KH.  καὶ πῶς; ἐπεὶ νῦν γ' οὔτε τὰ δικαστήρια
μέλλει δικάζειν οὔτε βουλῆς ἐσθ' ἕδρα,
ἐπείπερ ἐστὶ Θεσμοφορίων ἡ μέση. 80
EY.  τοῦτ' αὐτὸ γάρ τοι κἀπολεῖν με προσδοκῶ.
αἱ γὰρ γυναῖκες ἐπιβεβουλεύκασί μοι
κἀν Θεσμοφόροιν μέλλουσι περί μου τήμερον
ἐκκλησιάζειν ἐπ' ὀλέθρῳ.
KH.                                        τιὴ τί δή;
EY.  ὁτιὴ τραγῳδῶ καὶ κακῶς αὐτὰς λέγω. 85
KH.  νὴ τὸν Ποσειδῶ καὶ δίκαιά ⟨γ'⟩ ἂν πάθοις.
ἀτὰρ τίν' ἐκ τούτων σὺ μηχανὴν ἔχεις;
EY.  Ἀγάθωνα πεῖσαι τὸν τραγῳδοδιδάσκαλον
εἰς Θεσμοφόροιν ἐλθεῖν.
KH.                                        τί δράσοντ'; εἰπέ μοι.
EY.  ἐκκλησιάσοντ' ἐν ταῖς γυναιξὶ χἂν δέῃ 90
λέξονθ' ὑπὲρ ἐμοῦ.
KH.                                πότερα φανερῶς ἢ λάθρᾳ;
EY.  λάθρᾳ, στολὴν γυναικὸς ἠμφιεσμένον.
KH.  τὸ πρᾶγμα κομψὸν καὶ σφόδρ' ἐκ τοῦ σοῦ τρόπου·
τοῦ γὰρ τεχνάζειν ἡμέτερος ὁ πυραμοῦς. 94

.................
EY.  βάδιζε τοίνυν.
KH.                          μὰ τὸν Ἀπόλλω οὔκ, ἤν γε μὴ 269

---

[1] nescioquis apud Blaydes: αἱ σοφαὶ συνουσίαι codd.

KIN. How are they separate?
EU. That is the way they were separated long ago. For when the Ether began to separate for the first time and gave birth to the creatures that move in her, she first devised the eye for seeing, in imitation of the sun's orb, and for hearing she bored out the funnel known as the ear.[1]
KIN. So because of this funnel I am neither to see nor hear? By Zeus, I am delighted to learn these new things. What a thing it is to spend time with intellectuals!

..............

EU. On this day it will be decided whether Euripides still lives or is done for.
KIN. How is that? Today no law court is going to sit in judgement and there is no session of the Council, since this is the middle day of the Thesmophoria.
EU. This is the very thing I expect will be my undoing. The women have formed a conspiracy against me, and at the Thesmophoria they mean to hold an assembly about me today, to destroy me.
KIN. But why is that?
EU. Because I write tragedies and speak ill of them.
KIN. Yes, by Poseidon, and serves you right. But what plan do you have to counter this?
EU. I plan to persuade Agathon, the tragic poet, to go to the Thesmophoria.
KIN. For what purpose? Tell me.
EU. To join the assembly of women and to say what is necessary in my defense.
KIN. Openly or in secret?
EU. In secret, dressed in women's clothing.
KIN. The plan is clever and quite after your manner. Where clever devices are concerned, our family takes the cake.

..............

EU. March then.
KIN. By Apollo, no, unless you swear to me—

---

[1] A parody of *Melanippe the Wise*, fr. 484 N$^2$.

|        | ὀμόσῃς ἐμοί— |     |
|--------|--------------|-----|
| ΕΥ.    | τί χρῆμα;    |     |
| ΚΗ.    | συσσώσειν ἐμὲ | 270 |
|        | πάσαις τέχναις, ἤν μοί τι περιπίπτῃ κακόν. | |
| ΕΥ.    | ὄμνυμι τοίνυν αἰθέρ', οἴκησιν Διός. | |
| ΚΗ.    | τί μᾶλλον ἢ τὴν Ἱπποκράτους ξυνοικίαν; | |
| ΕΥ.    | ὄμνυμι τοίνυν πάντας ἄρδην τοὺς θεούς. | |
| ΚΗ.    | μέμνησο τοίνυν ταῦθ', ὅτι ἡ φρὴν ὤμοσεν, | 275 |
|        | ἡ γλῶττα δ' οὐκ ὀμώμοκ', οὐδ' ὤρκωσ' ἐγώ. | |

..................

**ΚΗΡΥΚΑΙΝΑ**
    εὔχεσθε τοῖς θεοῖσι τοῖς Ὀλυμπίοις
    καὶ ταῖς Ὀλυμπίαισι, καὶ τοῖς Πυθίοις
    καὶ ταῖσι Πυθίαισι, καὶ τοῖς Δηλίοις
    καὶ ταῖσι Δηλίαισι, τοῖς τ' ἄλλοις θεοῖς.
    εἴ τις ἐπιβουλεύει τι τῷ δήμῳ κακὸν    335
    τῷ τῶν γυναικῶν ἢ 'πικηρυκεύεται
    Εὐριπίδῃ Μήδοις ⟨τ'⟩ ἐπὶ βλάβῃ τινὶ
    τῇ τῶν γυναικῶν, ἢ τυραννεῖν ἐπινοεῖ,
    ἢ τὸν τύραννον συγκατάγειν, ἢ παιδίον
    ὑποβαλλομένης κατεῖπεν, ἢ δούλη τινὸς    340
    προαγωγὸς οὖσ' ἐνετρύλισεν τῷ δεσπότῃ,
    ἢ πεμπομένη τις ἀγγελίας ψευδεῖς φέρει,
    ἢ μοιχὸς εἴ τις ἐξαπατᾷ ψευδῆ λέγων
    καὶ μὴ δίδωσιν ἃν ὑπόσχηταί ποτε,
    ἢ δῶρά τις δίδωσι μοιχῷ γραῦς γυνή,    345
    ἢ καὶ δέχεται προδιδοῦσ' ἑταίρα τὸν φίλον,
    κεἴ τις κάπηλος ἢ καπηλὶς τοῦ χοῶς
    ἢ τῶν κοτυλῶν τὸ νόμισμα διαλυμαίνεται,
    κακῶς ἀπολέσθαι τοῦτον αὐτὸν κᾠκίαν
    ἀρᾶσθε, ταῖς δ' ἄλλαισιν ἡμῖν τοὺς θεοὺς    350
    εὔχεσθε πάσαις πολλὰ δοῦναι κἀγαθά.

..................

| ΚΗ. | ἄκουε πᾶσ'. ἔδοξε τῇ βουλῇ τάδε | 372 |
|-----|-------------------------------------|-----|
|     | τῇ τῶν γυναικῶν· Τιμόκλει' ἐπεστάτει, | |
|     | Λύσιλλ' ἐγραμμάτευεν, εἶπε Σωστράτη· | |
|     | ἐκκλησίαν ποιεῖν ἕωθεν τῇ μέσῃ | 375 |
|     | τῶν Θεσμοφορίων, ᾗ μάλισθ' ἡμῖν σχολή, | |

EU.  Swear what?
KIN. that you will come to my rescue with all the skill you have if I get into any trouble.
EU.  I swear then by Ether, the abode of Zeus.[1]
KIN. Why by that rather than Hippocrates' apartment-house?
EU.  I swear then by all the gods together.
KIN. Remember then that it was your mind that swore, and your tongue did not, nor did I put it under oath.[2]

...............

HERALDESS
Pray to all the gods and goddesses of Olympia, the gods and goddesses of Pytho, the gods and goddesses of Delos, and the other gods. If anyone is plotting harm to the community of women or parleying with Euripides or with the Medes to the hurt of the women; if anyone intends to make himself tyrant or to help bring a tyrant in; if anyone has snitched when a woman is palming off a baby as her own, or when acting as go-between for her mistress blabs to master, or being sent on an errand brings back false messages; if any lover fools women with falsehoods and fails to deliver the gifts he promised to give; if any old hag bribes a lover or any *hetaira* betrays her boy-friend and accepts gifts, if any barkeep, male or female, should give short measure in pint-pot or gallon-jar, pray that he may perish painfully, himself and his household, and that to all the rest of us women the gods may grant many blessings.

...............

HER. Attention all. A resolution of the Council of Women, Timocleia presiding, Lysilla as clerk, on the motion of Sostrate: 'That an assembly shall be held at daybreak on the middle day of the Thesmophoria, when we have the most leisure,

---

[1] Fr. 487 of Euripides' *Melanippe the Wise*.
[2] Cf. *Hippolytus* 612.

καὶ χρηματίζειν πρῶτα περὶ Εὐριπίδου,
ὅ τι χρὴ παθεῖν ἐκεῖνον· ἀδικεῖν γὰρ δοκεῖ
ἡμῖν ἁπάσαις. τίς ἀγορεύειν βούλεται;
ΓΥΝΗ Α
ἐγώ.
ΚΗ.      περίθου νυν τόνδε πρῶτον πρὶν λέγειν.         380
ΧΟ(ΡΟΣ)
σίγα σιώπα, πρόσεχε τὸν νοῦν· χρέμπτεται γὰρ ἤδη
ὅπερ ποοῦσ' οἱ ῥήτορες. μακρὰν ἔοικε λέξειν.
ΓΥ<sup>Α</sup>. φιλοτιμίᾳ μὲν οὐδεμιᾷ μὰ τὼ θεὼ
λέξουσ' ἀνέστην, ὦ γυναῖκες· ἀλλὰ γὰρ
βαρέως φέρω τάλαινα πολὺν ἤδη χρόνον           385
προπηλακιζομένας ὁρῶσ' ἡμᾶς ὑπὸ
Εὐριπίδου τοῦ τῆς λαχανοπωλητρίας
καὶ πολλὰ καὶ παντοῖ' ἀκουούσας κακά.
τί γὰρ οὗτος ἡμᾶς οὐκ ἐπισμῇ τῶν κακῶν;
ποῦ δ' οὐχὶ διαβέβληχ', ὅπουπερ ἔμβραχυ           390
εἰσὶν θεαταὶ καὶ τραγῳδοὶ καὶ χοροί,
τὰς μοιχοτρόπους, τὰς ἀνδρεραστρίας καλῶν,
τὰς οἰνοπότιδας, τὰς προδότιδας, τὰς λάλους,
τὰς οὐδὲν ὑγιές, τὰς μέγ' ἀνδράσιν κακόν;
ὥστ' εὐθὺς εἰσιόντες ἀπὸ τῶν ἰκρίων               395
ὑποβλέπουσ' ἡμᾶς σκοποῦνταί τ' εὐθέως
μὴ μοιχὸς ἔνδον ᾖ τις ἀποκεκρυμμένος.
δρᾶσαι δ' ἔθ' ἡμῖν οὐδὲν ὧνπερ καὶ πρὸ τοῦ
ἔξεστι· τοιαῦθ' οὗτος ἐδίδαξεν κακὰ
τοὺς ἄνδρας ἡμῶν· ὥστ' ἐάν τίς ⟨τινα⟩ πλέκῃ         400
γυνὴ στέφανον, ἐρᾶν δοκεῖ· κἂν ἐκβάλῃ
σκεῦός τι κατὰ τὴν οἰκίαν πλανωμένη,
ἀνὴρ ἐρωτᾷ, "τῷ κατέαγεν ἡ χύτρα;
οὐκ ἔσθ' ὅπως οὐ τῷ Κορινθίῳ ξένῳ".
κάμνει κόρη τις, εὐθὺς ἀδελφὸς λέγει,             405
"τὸ χρῶμα τοῦτό μ' οὐκ ἀρέσκει τῆς κόρης".
εἶεν· γυνή τις ὑποβαλέσθαι βούλεται
ἀποροῦσα παίδων, οὐδὲ τοῦτ' ἔστιν λαθεῖν.
ἄνδρες γὰρ ἤδη παρακάθηνται πλησίον·
πρὸς τοὺς γέροντάς θ' οἳ πρὸ τοῦ τὰς μείρακας       410
ἤγοντο, διαβέβληκεν, ὥστ' οὐδεὶς γέρων

and the subject of Euripides shall be discussed, namely, what should be done to him. For all of us women think him guilty'. Who wishes to speak?

FIRST WOMAN
I do.

HER. [Giving her a speaker's garland] Put this on before you speak.

CHORUS
Silence and order, your attention please. She is clearing her throat now, the way public speakers do. It seems she is going to make a long speech.

F.W. I have not gotten up to speak from any ambition for honor, I swear by Demeter and Kore. But in fact I have been vexed for a long time now at seeing us insulted by Euripides, the vegetable-seller's son, and having all kinds of bad tales told of us. What evil does he not smear us with? Where has he not traduced us, provided only he has an audience and actors and choruses, calling us adulterous in our ways, lecherous, wine-tipplers, traitoresses, garrulous, no good at all, and a great trouble to men? The result is that as soon as they come in from the theater, they look suspiciously at us and at once look around to see if there is a lover hidden inside. And now we can no longer do any of the things we used to do, such are the tricks this man has taught our husbands about. And so if a woman is weaving a garland, she is thought to be in love. And if a woman walking about the house drops a pot, her husband asks, 'For whose sake was this jar broken? Undoubtedly for "the guest from Corinth."'[1] Suppose some girl isn't well: at once her brother says, 'I don't like the color I see in this girl'. Or, suppose a woman who has no children wants to pass off another child as her own. Even this she can't get away with. For the men are already sitting nearby. And he has slandered us also to the old men who used to marry young girls, so that no old man is willing to

---

[1] A reference to the words of Sthenoboea, Euripides fr. 664 N$^2$.

γαμεῖν ἐθέλει γυναῖκα διὰ τοὔπος τοδί,
"δέσποινα γὰρ γέροντι νυμφίῳ γυνή".
εἶτα διὰ τοῦτον ταῖς γυναικωνίτισιν
σφραγῖδας ἐπιβάλλουσιν ἤδη καὶ μοχλοὺς 415
τηροῦντες ἡμᾶς, καὶ προσέτι Μολοττικοὺς
τρέφουσι μορμολυκεῖα τοῖς μοιχοῖς κύνας.
καὶ ταῦτα μὲν ξυγγνώσθ᾽· ἃ δ᾽ ἦν ἡμῖν πρὸ τοῦ
αὐταῖς ταμιεῦσαι καὶ προαιρούσαις λαθεῖν[1]
ἄλφιτον ἔλαιον οἶνον, οὐδὲ ταῦτ᾽ ἔτι 420
ἔξεστιν. οἱ γὰρ ἄνδρες ἤδη κλειδία
αὐτοὶ φοροῦσι κρυπτά, κακοηθέστατα
Λακωνίκ᾽ ἄττα, τρεῖς ἔχοντα γομφίους.
πρὸ τοῦ μὲν οὖν ἦν ἀλλ᾽ ὑποῖξαι τὴν θύραν
ποιησαμέναισι δακτύλιον τριωβόλου, 425
νῦν δ᾽ οὗτος αὐτοὺς ᾠκότριψ Εὐριπίδης
ἐδίδαξε θριπήδεστ᾽ ἔχειν σφραγίδια
ἐξαψαμένους. νῦν οὖν ἐμοὶ τούτῳ δοκεῖ
ὄλεθρόν τιν᾽ ἡμᾶς κυρκανᾶν ἀμωσγέπως,
ἢ φαρμάκοισιν ἢ μιᾷ γέ τῳ τέχνῃ 430
ὅπως ἀπολεῖται. ταῦτ᾽ ἐγὼ φανερῶς λέγω·
τὰ δ᾽ ἄλλα μετὰ τῆς γραμματέως συγγράψομαι. 432

..................

ΓΥΝΗ Β

ὀλίγων ἕνεκα καὐτὴ παρῆλθον ῥημάτων. 443
τὰ μὲν γὰρ ἄλλ᾽ αὕτη κατηγόρηκεν εὖ·
ἃ δ᾽ ἐγὼ πέπονθα, ταῦτα λέξαι βούλομαι. 445
ἐμοὶ γὰρ ἀνὴρ ἀπέθανεν μὲν ἐν Κύπρῳ
παιδάρια πέντε καταλιπών, ἁγὼ μόλις
στεφανηπλοκοῦσ᾽ ἔβοσκον ἐν ταῖς μυρρίναις.
τέως μὲν οὖν ἀλλ᾽ ἡμικάκως ἐβοσκόμην·
νῦν δ᾽ οὗτος ἐν ταῖσιν τραγῳδίαις ποῶν 450
τοὺς ἄνδρας ἀναπέπεικεν οὐκ εἶναι θεούς·
ὥστ᾽ οὐκέτ᾽ ἐμπολῶμεν οὐδ᾽ εἰς ἥμισυ.
νῦν οὖν ἁπάσαισιν παραινῶ καὶ λέγω
τοῦτον κολάσαι τὸν ἄνδρα πολλῶν οὕνεκα·
ἄγρια γὰρ ἡμᾶς, ὦ γυναῖκες, δρᾷ κακά, 455

---

[1] Scaliger: λαβεῖν codd.

marry on account of the line 'An old bridegroom does not take a wife but a ruler'.[1] And because of him they put seals and bolts on the doors of the women's quarters to guard us, and furthermore they keep Molossian hounds to scare away our lovers. These things we could forgive. But the things we used to be able to ration out ourselves and take a bit of beforehand on the sly, barley, oil, wine, these things we can no longer get. Our husbands now carry the keys themselves, secret, nasty, Spartan things with three teeth. Previously one could open the door secretly by having a ring made for three obols to seal it up again. But now this slave Euripides taught them to wear worm-eaten seals around their necks. So now I propose that we cook up harm for him in some way or other, either by poisons or by some other device. I will make my other suggestions with the help of the secretary in my written bill.

..................

SECOND WOMAN

I for my part have come forward to make only a short speech. The first speaker has made all her indictments well. I wish to tell my own experience. My husband was killed in action in Cyprus, leaving five children behind. I was barely able to feed them by plaiting crowns of myrtle and selling them in the market. For a while, then, I was able, though half-badly, to keep them alive. But now *he* by his tragic poetry has persuaded the men that there are no gods, and as a result I don't sell even half of what I sold before. Now therefore my counsel and proposal to all you women is to punish this man and for more than one reason. Wild are the wrongs he commits against us, since he himself was raised

---

[1] Fr. 804.3 (*Phoenix*).

ἅτ' ἐν ἀγρίοισι τοῖς λαχάνοις αὐτὸς τραφείς.

**77** id. *Ran.* 52-107, 757-811, 830-70, 885-94, 936-7, 971-9, 1043-73, 1078-88, 1467-99

ΔΙ(ΟΝΥΣΟΣ)
   καὶ δῆτ' ἐπὶ τῆς νεὼς ἀναγιγνώσκοντί μοι    52
   τὴν 'Ανδρομέδαν πρὸς ἐμαυτὸν ἐξαίφνης πόθος
   τὴν καρδίαν ἐπάταξε πῶς οἴει σφόδρα.
ΗΡ(ΑΚΛΗΣ)
   πόθος; πόσος τις;
ΔΙ.        σμικρός, ἡλίκος Μόλων.    55
ΗΡ.   γυναικός;
ΔΙ.       οὐ δῆτ'.
ΗΡ.          ἀλλὰ παιδός;
ΔΙ.             οὐδαμῶς.
ΗΡ.   ἀλλ' ἀνδρός;
ΔΙ.        ἀπαπαῖ.
ΗΡ.             ξυνεγένου τῷ Κλεισθένει;
ΔΙ.   μὴ σκῶπτέ μ', ὠδέλφ'· οὐ γὰρ ἀλλ' ἔχω κακῶς·
   τοιοῦτος ἵμερός με διαλυμαίνεται.
ΗΡ.   ποῖός τις ὠδελφίδιον;
ΔΙ.          οὐκ ἔχω φράσαι.    60
   ὅμως γε μέντοι σοι δι' αἰνιγμῶν ἐρῶ.
   ἤδη ποτ' ἐπεθύμησας ἐξαίφνης ἔτνους;
ΗΡ.   ἔτνους; βαβαιάξ, μυριάκις γ' ἐν τῷ βίῳ.
ΔΙ.   ἆρ' ἐκδιδάσκω τὸ σαφὲς ἢ πέρα φράσω;
ΗΡ.   μὴ δῆτα περὶ ἔτνους γε· πάνυ γὰρ μανθάνω.    65
ΔΙ.   τοιουτοσὶ τοίνυν με δαρδάπτει πόθος
   Εὐριπίδου.
ΗΡ.       καὶ ταῦτα τοῦ τεθνηκότος;
ΔΙ.   κοὐδείς γέ μ' ἂν πείσειεν ἀνθρώπων τὸ μὴ οὐκ
   ἐλθεῖν ἐπ' ἐκεῖνον.
ΗΡ.         πότερον εἰς Ἅιδου κάτω;
ΔΙ.   καὶ νὴ Δί' εἴ τί γ' ἔστιν ἔτι κατωτέρω.    70

amidst wild vegetables.

**77** Aristophanes, *Frogs*

DIONYSUS
    And then when I was reading the *Andromeda* aloud to myself on board ship, all of a sudden a longing knocked upon my heart, you can't think how violently.
HERACLES
    A longing? About how big?
DI.    A small one, about the size of Molon.
HER.    For a woman?
DI.    No indeed.
HER.    For a boy then?
DI.    Not at all.
HER.    For a man then?
DI.    Oh my goodness yes.
HER.    Did you have your Cleisthenes[1] then?
DI.    Don't mock me, brother: I'm really in a bad way, 'such is the longing that my soul doth rend'.
HER.    Dear brother, what kind of longing?
DI.    I can't say. But I will tell you in riddles. Have you ever conceived a desire for pea-soup?
HER.    Pea soup? Mercy me, countless times in my life!
DI.    Am I giving you a clear idea, or shall I keep talking?
HER.    Where the pea-soup is concerned, you need say no more. I understand completely.
DI.    Well, that is the kind of desire that gnaws at me—for Euripides.
HER.    What, and him being dead at that?
DI.    Yes, and no mortal man shall dissuade me from going after him.
HER.    You mean down to Hades?
DI.    Yes, by Zeus, and even to any place farther down, if it exists.

---

[1] A comic target of Aristophanes for twenty years, Cleisthenes was pilloried as a eunuch and then as a passive homosexual, probably for no better reason than his lack of a good beard: see K. J. Dover, *Greek Homosexuality* (London, 1978), pp. 144-5.

HP. τί βουλόμενος;
ΔΙ. δέομαι ποητοῦ δεξιοῦ.
οἱ μὲν γὰρ οὐκέτ' εἰσίν, οἱ δ' ὄντες κακοί.
HP. τί δ'; οὐκ Ἰοφῶν ζῇ;
ΔΙ. τοῦτο γάρ τοι καὶ μόνον
ἔτ' ἐστὶ λοιπὸν ἀγαθόν, εἰ καὶ τοῦτ' ἄρα·
οὐ γὰρ σάφ' οἶδ' οὐδ' αὐτὸ τοῦθ' ὅπως ἔχει. 75
HP. εἶτ' οὐ Σοφοκλέα πρότερον ἀντ' Εὐριπίδου
μέλλεις ἀνάγειν, εἴπερ ⟨γ'⟩ ἐκεῖθεν δεῖ σ' ἄγειν;
ΔΙ. οὔ, πρίν γ' ἂν Ἰοφῶντ', ἀπολαβὼν αὐτὸν μόνον,
ἄνευ Σοφοκλέους ὅ τι ποεῖ κωδωνίσω.
κἄλλως ὁ μέν γ' Εὐριπίδης πανοῦργος ὢν 80
κἂν ξυναποδρᾶναι δεῦρ' ἐπιχειρήσειέ μοι·
ὁ δ' εὔκολος μὲν ἐνθάδ', εὔκολος δ' ἐκεῖ.
HP. Ἀγάθων δὲ ποῦ 'στιν;
ΔΙ. ἀπολιπών μ' ἀποίχεται,
ἀγαθὸς ποητὴς καὶ ποθεινὸς τοῖς φίλοις.
HP. ποῖ γῆς ὁ τλήμων;
ΔΙ. ἐς Μακάρων εὐωχίαν. 85
HP. ὁ δὲ Ξενοκλέης;
ΔΙ. ἐξόλοιτο νὴ Δία.
HP. Πυθάγγελος δέ;
ΞΑ(ΝΘΙΑΣ)
περὶ ἐμοῦ δ' οὐδεὶς λόγος
ἐπιτριβομένου τὸν ὦμον οὑτωσὶ σφόδρα.
HP. οὔκουν ἕτερ' ἔστ' ἐνταῦθα μειρακύλλια
τραγῳδίας ποιοῦντα πλεῖν ἢ μυρία, 90
Εὐριπίδου πλεῖν ἢ σταδίῳ λαλίστερα;
ΔΙ. ἐπιφυλλίδες ταῦτ' ἐστὶ καὶ στωμύλματα,
χελιδόνων μουσεῖα, λωβηταὶ τέχνης,
ἃ φροῦδα θᾶττον, ἢν μόνον χορὸν λάβῃ,
ἅπαξ προσουρήσαντα τῇ τραγῳδίᾳ. 95
γόνιμον δὲ ποιητὴν ἂν οὐχ εὕροις ἔτι
ζητῶν ἄν, ὅστις ῥῆμα γενναῖον λάκοι.
HP. πῶς γόνιμον;

HER. What ever for?
DI. I need a clever poet. For some of the poets are dead, and the ones still alive are bad.
HER. What? Isn't Iophon[1] living?
DI. That, you know, is the only good thing still left to me, if indeed I have that. For I am not entirely clear how things stand on this point.
HER. But won't you bring up Sophocles first instead of Euripides, if you need to draw from that region?
DI. No, not until I take Iophon all alone by himself and test what poetry he writes without Sophocles. And furthermore, Euripides, who sticks at nothing, might even try to escape to the upper world for me, whereas Sophocles, who was even-tempered in life, is even-tempered among the dead.
HER. But where is Agathon?
DI. He has left me and gone off, a good poet and much missed by his friends.
HER. Where in the world has the poor wretch gone?
DI. To the feast of the blessed.[2]
HER. And Xenocles?
DI. He can go hang!
HER. And Pythangelus?
XANTHIAS
And not a word about me, though my shoulder is being rubbed so sore.
HER. Well, aren't there in Athens some other young lads, more than ten thousand of them, who write tragedies and are more talkative than Euripides by a good furlong?
DI. These are small grapes not worth the harvesting, mere chatterers, a chorus of twittering swallows, a disgrace to their art. If they are granted a chorus once, they disappear on the double, after having pee'd a single time on Tragedy. But what you will no longer find, even if you look for it, is a truly fertile poet, one who can utter a noble line.
HER. Fertile? What do you mean?

---

[1] Sophocles' son.
[2] There is in μακάρων, 'the blessed', a suggestion of Μακεδόνων, 'Macedonians'. Agathon, like Euripides, accepted the hospitality of Archelaus, the Macedonian king.

ΔΙ.	ὡδὶ γόνιμον, ὅστις φθέγξεται
τοιουτονί τι παρακεκινδυνευμένον,
"αἰθέρα Διὸς δωμάτιον" ἢ "χρόνου πόδα"	100
ἢ "φρένα μὲν οὐκ ἐθέλουσαν ὀμόσαι καθ' ἱερῶν,
γλῶτταν δ' ἐπιορκήσασαν ἰδίᾳ τῆς φρενός".
ΗΡ.	σὲ δὲ ταῦτ' ἀρέσκει;
ΔΙ.	μάλλὰ πλεῖν ἢ μαίνομαι.
ΗΡ.	ἦ μὴν κόβαλά γ' ἐστίν, ὡς καὶ σοὶ δοκεῖ.
ΔΙ.	μὴ τὸν ἐμὸν οἴκει νοῦν· ἔχεις γὰρ οἰκίαν.	105
ΗΡ.	καὶ μὴν ἀτεχνῶς γε παμπόνηρα φαίνεται.
ΔΙ.	δειπνεῖν με δίδασκε.	107

...............
ΞΑ.

.....
τίς οὗτος οὕνδον ἐστὶ θόρυβος καὶ βοὴ	757
χὠ λοιδορησμός;
ΟΙ(ΚΕΤΗΣ)
Αἰσχύλου κεὐριπίδου.
ΞΑ.	ἆ.
ΟΙ.	πρᾶγμα πρᾶγμα μέγα κεκίνηται, μέγα
ἐν τοῖς νεκροῖσι καὶ στάσις πολλὴ πάνυ.	760
ΞΑ.	ἐκ τοῦ;
ΟΙ.	νόμος τις ἐνθάδ' ἐστὶ κείμενος
ἀπὸ τῶν τεχνῶν ὅσαι μεγάλαι καὶ δεξιαί,
τὸν ἄριστον ὄντα τῶν ἑαυτοῦ ξυντέχνων
σίτησιν αὐτὸν ἐν πρυτανείῳ λαμβάνειν
θρόνον τε τοῦ Πλούτωνος ἑξῆς—
ΞΑ.	μανθάνω.	765
ΟΙ.	ἕως ἀφίκοιτο τὴν τέχνην σοφώτερος
ἕτερός τις αὐτοῦ· τότε δὲ παραχωρεῖν ἔδει.
ΞΑ.	τί δῆτα τουτὶ τεθορύβηκεν Αἰσχύλον;
ΟΙ.	ἐκεῖνος εἶχε τὸν τραγῳδικὸν θρόνον,
ὡς ὢν κράτιστος τὴν τέχνην.
ΞΑ.	νυνὶ δὲ τίς;	770
ΟΙ.	ὅτε δὴ κατῆλθ' Εὐριπίδης, ἐπεδείκνυτο
τοῖς λωποδύταις καὶ τοῖσι βαλλαντιοτόμοις
καὶ τοῖσι πατραλοίαισι καὶ τοιχωρύχοις,
ὅπερ ἔστ' ἐν Ἅιδου πλῆθος, οἱ δ' ἀκροώμενοι

| | |
|---|---|
| DI. | Fertile like this, someone who will utter something bold and venturesome along these lines: 'Ether the bungalow of Zeus' or 'the foot of Time' or 'the heart refusing to swear an oath by the sacred victims while the tongue commits perjury without its knowledge'.[1] |
| HER. | You *like* that? |
| DI. | Like it? I'm crazy about it. |
| HER. | But it's utter humbug, and you think so too. |
| DI. | Don't manage my views: you have your own to live in. |
| HER. | I will say more: it is complete and manifest villainy. |
| DI. | Give me lessons in *dining*. |

..............

| | |
|---|---|
| XA. | ...What is this noise, shouting, and abuse indoors? |
| PLUTO'S SLAVE | Comes from Aeschylus and Euripides. |
| XA. | Ah. |
| SL. | Some great action is stirring among the dead and some high division. |
| XA. | What is the cause? |
| SL. | There is a law in force here that in all the arts that are great and skilful, the man who bests his fellow artists receives free meals in the *prytaneion* and a seat next to Pluto— |
| XA. | I see. |
| SL. | until someone else comes more skilled in the art than he is. Then he must give way. |
| XA. | How has this gotten Aeschylus in a tizzy? |
| SL. | He had the tragic chair as being the best in his art. |
| XA. | And who has it now? |
| SL. | Well, when Euripides came down to Hades, he began to show off his art to the footpads, cutpurses, parricides, and burglars, who make up the majority in Hades. And these, hearing his counter-arguments, twistings, and turnings, went |

---

[1] Cf. Euripides, fr. 487 and 42 and *Hippolytus* 612.

|      |                                                                              |     |
|------|------------------------------------------------------------------------------|-----|
|      | τῶν ἀντιλογιῶν καὶ λυγισμῶν καὶ στροφῶν                                      | 775 |
|      | ὑπερεμάνησαν κἀνόμισαν σοφώτατον·                                            |     |
|      | κᾆπειτ' ἐπαρθεὶς ἀντελάβετο τοῦ θρόνου,                                      |     |
|      | ἵν' Αἰσχύλος καθῆστο.                                                         |     |
| ΞΑ.  | κοὐκ ἐβάλλετο;                                                               |     |
| ΟΙ.  | μὰ Δί' ἀλλ' ὁ δῆμος ἀνεβόα κρίσιν ποεῖν                                      |     |
|      | ὁπότερος εἴη τὴν τέχνην σοφώτερος.                                           | 780 |
| ΞΑ.  | ὁ τῶν πανούργων;                                                             |     |
| ΟΙ.  | νὴ Δί', οὐράνιόν γ' ὅσον.                                                    |     |
| ΞΑ.  | μετ' Αἰσχύλου δ' οὐκ ἦσαν ἕτεροι σύμμαχοι;                                   |     |
| ΟΙ.  | ὀλίγον τὸ χρηστόν ἐστιν, ὥσπερ ἐνθάδε.                                       |     |
| ΞΑ.  | τί δῆθ' ὁ Πλούτων δρᾶν παρασκευάζεται;                                       |     |
| ΟΙ.  | ἀγῶνα ποιεῖν αὐτίκα μάλα καὶ κρίσιν                                          | 785 |
|      | κἄλεγχον αὐτοῖν τῆς τέχνης.                                                   |     |
| ΞΑ.  | κᾆπειτα πῶς                                                                   |     |
|      | οὐ καὶ Σοφοκλέης ἀντελάβετο τοῦ θρόνου;                                       |     |
| ΟΙ.  | μὰ Δί' οὐκ ἐκεῖνος, ἀλλ' ἔκυσε μὲν Αἰσχύλον,                                 |     |
|      | ὅτε δὴ κατῆλθε, κἀνέβαλε τὴν δεξιάν                                           |     |
|      | κἄνεικος ὑπεχώρησεν αὐτῷ τοῦ θρόνου·                                         | 790 |
|      | νυνὶ δ' ἔμελλεν, ὡς ἔφη Κλειδημίδης,                                          |     |
|      | ἔφεδρος καθεδεῖσθαι· κἂν μὲν Αἰσχύλος κρατῇ,                                 |     |
|      | ἕξειν κατὰ χώραν· εἰ δὲ μή, περὶ τῆς τέχνης                                  |     |
|      | διαγωνιεῖσθ' ἔφασκε πρός γ' Εὐριπίδην.                                        |     |
| ΞΑ.  | τὸ χρῆμ' ἄρ' ἔσται;                                                          |     |
| ΟΙ.  | νὴ Δί' ὀλίγον ὕστερον.                                                        | 795 |
|      | κἀνταῦθα δὴ τὰ δεινὰ κινηθήσεται.                                             |     |
|      | καὶ γὰρ ταλάντῳ μουσικὴ σταθμήσεται—                                         |     |
| ΞΑ.  | τί δέ; μειαγωγήσουσι τὴν τραγῳδίαν;                                          |     |
| ΟΙ.  | καὶ κανόνας ἐξοίσουσι καὶ πήχεις ἐπῶν                                        |     |
|      | καὶ πλαίσια ξύμπτυκτα—                                                       |     |
| ΞΑ.  | πλινθεύσουσι γάρ;                                                            | 800 |
| ΟΙ.  | καὶ διαμέτρους καὶ σφῆνας. ὁ γὰρ Εὐριπίδης                                  |     |
|      | κατ' ἔπος βασανιεῖν φησι τὰς τραγῳδίας.                                      |     |
| ΞΑ.  | ἦ που βαρέως οἶμαι τὸν Αἰσχύλον φέρειν.                                      |     |
| ΟΙ.  | ἔβλεψε γοῦν ταυρηδὸν ἐγκύψας κάτω.                                           |     |
| ΞΑ.  | κρινεῖ δὲ δὴ τίς ταῦτα;                                                      |     |

|     | |
| --- | --- |
|     | quite crazy for him and thought him very clever. And then he was encouraged and laid claim to the chair where Aeschylus sat. |
| XA. | Didn't they throw things at him? |
| SL. | No, by Zeus: the crowd shouted out that they should hold a contest to see which of them was the better in the art. |
| XA. | The crowd of knaves? |
| SL. | Yes, by Zeus, shouted to high heaven. |
| XA. | But were there not others who sided with Aeschylus? |
| SL. | The better element is in the minority—just as it is here. [He points towards the audience.] |
| XA. | Well, what is Pluto intending to do about it? |
| SL. | He means to hold a contest to judge and test them in their craft. |
| XA. | Then how is it that Sophocles is not laying claim to the chair? |
| SL. | He would never do that, by Zeus. When he finally arrived, he kissed Aeschylus and gave him his hand and without a quarrel conceded the chair to him. And just now he announced his intention, in Cleidemides' words, to sit by as odd-man-out, and if Aeschylus wins, to keep to his place, but otherwise, to fight to the finish with Euripides for pre-eminence in the art. |
| XA. | And will this event really take place, then? |
| SL. | Yes, by Zeus, in a very short time, and on this very spot the wonders will be set in motion. For Art will be weighed up on a scale— |
| XA. | What? Will they treat tragedy like a sacrificial lamb? |
| SL. | and they will bring out measuring-sticks and cubit-rods to measure their speech and collapsible frames— |
| XA. | What? Are they going to make bricks? |
| SL. | and mitre-squares and wedges. For Euripides says that he is going to put the tragedies to the rack word by word. |
| XA. | I suppose Aeschylus isn't taking this any too well. |
| SL. | At any rate, he bends himself double and glowers like a bull. |
| XA. | But who is going to *judge* this contest? |

ΟΙ. τοῦτ' ἦν δύσκολον· 805
σοφῶν γὰρ ἀνδρῶν ἀπορίαν ηὑρισκέτην.
οὔτε γὰρ Ἀθηναίοισι συνέβαιν' Αἰσχύλος—
ΞΑ. πολλοὺς ἴσως ἐνόμιζε τοὺς τοιχωρύχους.
ΟΙ. ληρόν τε τἄλλ' ἡγεῖτο τοῦ γνῶναι πέρι
φύσεις ποιητῶν· εἶτα τῷ σῷ δεσπότῃ 810
ἐπέτρεψαν, ὁτιὴ τῆς τέχνης ἔμπειρος ἦν.

..................
ΕΥΡΙΠΙΔΗΣ
οὐκ ἂν μεθείμην τοῦ θρόνου, μὴ νουθέτει. 830
κρείττων γὰρ εἶναί φημι τούτου τὴν τέχνην.
ΔΙ. Αἰσχύλε, τί σιγᾷς; αἰσθάνει γὰρ τοῦ λόγου.
ΕΥ. ἀποσεμνυνεῖται πρῶτον, ἅπερ ἑκάστοτε
ἐν ταῖς τραγῳδίαισιν ἐτερατεύετο.
ΔΙ. ὦ δαιμόνι' ἀνδρῶν μὴ μεγάλα λίαν λέγε. 835
ΕΥ. ἐγᾦδα τοῦτον καὶ διέσκεμμαι πάλαι,
ἄνθρωπον ἀγριοποιόν, αὐθαδόστομον,
ἔχοντ' ἀχάλινον, ἀκρατὲς, ἀπύλωτον στόμα,
ἀπεριλάλητον, κομποφακελορρήμονα.
ΑΙΣΧΥΛΟΣ
ἄληθες, ὦ παῖ τῆς ἀρουραίας θεοῦ; 840
σὺ δή με ταῦτ', ὦ στωμυλιοσυλλεκτάδη
καὶ πτωχοποιὲ καὶ ῥακιοσυρραπτάδη;
ἀλλ' οὔ τι χαίρων αὔτ' ἐρεῖς.
ΔΙ. παῦ' Αἰσχύλε,
καὶ μὴ πρὸς ὀργὴν σπλάγχνα θερμήνῃς κότῳ.
ΑΙ. οὐ δῆτα, πρίν γ' ἂν τοῦτον ἀποφήνω σαφῶς 845
τὸν χωλοποιὸν οἷος ὢν θρασύνεται.
ΔΙ. ἄρν', ἄρνα μέλανα, παῖδες, ἐξενέγκατε·
τυφὼς γὰρ ἐκβαίνειν παρασκευάζεται.
ΑΙ. ὦ Κρητικὰς μὲν συλλέγων μονῳδίας,
γάμους δ' ἀνοσίους ἐσφέρων ἐς τὴν τέχνην— 850

SL.   That was difficult. For the poets found there was a dearth of clever men. On the one hand Aeschylus did not get on with Athenians—
XA.   Perhaps he thought the burglars were the majority.
SL.   and he thought the rest of humanity were fools when it came to discerning the nature of poets. And so they entrusted the judgement to your master because he was knowledgeable in the art.

..................

EURIPIDES
   [to Dionysus] I won't relinquish my claim to the chair, spare me your admonitions. For I contend that I am this man's superior in the tragic art.
DI.   Aeschylus, why are you silent? Don't you hear what he is saying?
EU.   He'll open with a show of haughty demeanor, which is what he does every time in his tragedies to awe the audience.
DI.   My dear, good fellow, no high-and-mighty words, please!
EU.   I know this man and have observed him for a long time: he is a poet of boors, self-willed of speech, with a mouth that prates unchecked, unbated, unbarred. His talk lacks finesse and is all pompous and polysyllabic.

AESCHYLUS
   So that's your story, is it, son of the goddess agrarian?[1] Do *you* speak thus of *me*, you collector of chatter, poet of beggars, playwright of rags stitched together? You will not get away with saying this.
DI.   Stop, Aeschylus, and do not angrily heat your heart with spite.
AE.   I shall not stop, at least until I have shown clearly what sort of character this poet of cripples brazenly displays.
DI.   Bring out a black lamb, slaves, for a whirlwind is about to arise.
AE.   You collector of Cretan monodies,[2] importer into our sacred art of unions unholy—

---

[1] An allusion to Euripides' mother, said to have sold vegetables.
[2] An allusion to the sexual immorality of Pasiphae, Aerope, and Phaedra, who all came from Crete.

| | | |
|---|---|---|
| ΔΙ. | ἐπίσχες οὗτος, ὦ πολυτίμητ' Αἰσχύλε. | |
| | ἀπὸ τῶν χαλαζῶν δ', ὦ πόνηρ' Εὐριπίδη, | |
| | ἄναγε σεαυτὸν ἐκποδών, εἰ σωφρονεῖς, | |
| | ἵνα μὴ κεφαλαίῳ τὸν κρόταφόν σου ῥήματι | |
| | θενὼν ὑπ' ὀργῆς ἐκχέῃ τὸν Τήλεφον. | 855 |
| | σὺ δὲ μὴ πρὸς ὀργήν, Αἰσχύλ', ἀλλὰ πραόνως | |
| | ἔλεγχ', ἐλέγχου· λοιδορεῖσθαι δ' οὐ πρέπει | |
| | ἄνδρας ποητὰς ὥσπερ ἀρτοπώλιδας. | |
| | σὺ δ' εὐθὺς ὥσπερ πρῖνος ἐμπρησθεὶς βοᾷς. | |
| ΕΥ. | ἕτοιμός εἰμ' ἔγωγε, κοὐκ ἀναδύομαι, | 860 |
| | δάκνειν, δάκνεσθαι πρότερος, εἰ τούτῳ δοκεῖ, | |
| | τἄπη, τὰ μέλη, τὰ νεῦρα τῆς τραγῳδίας, | |
| | καὶ νὴ Δία τὸν Πηλέα γε καὶ τὸν Αἴολον | |
| | καὶ τὸν Μελέαγρον κἄτι μάλα τὸν Τήλεφον. | |
| ΔΙ. | σὺ δὲ ⟨δὴ⟩ τί βουλεύει ποεῖν; λέγ', Αἰσχύλε. | 865 |
| ΑΙ. | ἐβουλόμην μὲν οὐκ ἐρίζειν ἐνθάδε· | |
| | οὐκ ἐξ ἴσου γάρ ἐστιν ἀγὼν νῷν. | |
| ΔΙ. | τί δαί; | |
| ΑΙ. | ὅτι ἡ πόησις οὐχὶ συντέθνηκέ μοι, | |
| | τούτῳ δὲ συντέθνηκεν, ὥσθ' ἕξει λέγειν. | |
| | ὅμως δ' ἐπειδὴ σοὶ δοκεῖ, δρᾶν ταῦτα χρή. | 870 |

...............

| | | |
|---|---|---|
| ΔΙ. | εὔχεσθε δὴ καὶ σφώ τι πρὶν τἄπη λέγειν. | 885 |
| ΑΙ. | Δήμητερ ἡ θρέψασα τὴν ἐμὴν φρένα, | |
| | εἶναί με τῶν σῶν ἄξιον μυστηρίων. | |
| ΔΙ. | ἐπίθες λαβὼν δὴ καὶ σὺ λιβανωτόν. | |
| ΕΥ. | καλῶς· | |
| | ἕτεροι γάρ εἰσιν οἷσιν εὔχομαι θεοῖς. | |
| ΔΙ. | ἴδιοί τινές σου, κόμμα καινόν; | |
| ΕΥ. | καὶ μάλα. | 890 |
| ΔΙ. | ἴθι δὴ προσεύχου τοῖσιν ἰδιώταις θεοῖς. | |
| ΕΥ. | αἰθήρ, ἐμὸν βόσκημα, καὶ γλώττης στρόφιγξ | |
| | καὶ ξύνεσι καὶ μυκτῆρες ὀσφραντήριοι, | |
| | ὀρθῶς μ' ἐλέγχειν ὧν ἂν ἅπτωμαι λόγων. | 894 |

...............

DI. You there, highly esteemed Aeschylus, hold off! And you, poor Euripides, take shelter from the hail-storm if you are sensible, so that he may not strike you in anger on the temples with a crowning pediment of a phrase and knock the *Telephus* clear out of you! As for you Aeschylus, you should trade refutations not in anger but mildly. Poets ought not to engage in insult like bread-wives. But you start off shrieking like the noise of a holm-oak in full blaze.

EU. I am ready, I do not shrink from it, to be the first to bite and, if he thinks it best, to be bitten in the diction, the songs, the nerves and sinews of my tragedy, and yes by Zeus, to have this done to my *Peleus,* my *Aeolus,* my *Meleager,* and yes, my *Telephus.*

DI. And you, Aeschylus, tell us, what do you plan to do?

AE. I should have preferred not to engage in wrangling here since we are not competing on equal terms.

DI. Why is that?

AE. Because my poetry has not died with me,[1] while his has, and so he will be able to recite it. Nevertheless, since this is what you think best, this is what we must do.

...............

DI. You two must also make a prayer before reciting your verse.

AE. Demeter, who hast nourished my spirit, grant me to be worthy of your mysteries.

DI. You too, Euripides, should take some incense and put it on the flame.

EU. Thank you but no. For it is a different set of gods that I pray to.

DI. Your own private ones, some new coinage?

EU. Yes indeed.

DI. Come, then, and pray to your private gods.

EU. Ether, that art my nourishment, and Pivot of the Tongue, and Reason, and Nostrils keen of scent, may I correctly refute all the arguments I touch!

...............

---

[1] The Athenians, shortly after Aeschylus' death, decreed that anyone wanting to revive his tragedies at the festivals would be allowed to do so. See Quintilian 10.1.66.

ΑΙ. σὺ δ', ὦ θεοῖσιν ἐχθρέ, ποῖ' ἄττ' ἐστὶν ἄττ' ἐποίεις; 936
ΕΥ. οὐχ ἱππαλεκτρυόνας μὰ Δί' οὐδὲ τραγελάφους, ἅπερ σύ,
ἃν τοῖσι παραπετάσμασιν τοῖς Μηδικοῖς γράφουσιν·
ἀλλ' ὡς παρέλαβον τὴν τέχνην παρὰ σοῦ τὸ πρῶτον εὐθὺς
οἰδοῦσαν ὑπὸ κομπασμάτων καὶ ῥημάτων ἐπαχθῶν, 940
ἴσχνανα μὲν πρώτιστον αὐτὴν καὶ τὸ βάρος ἀφεῖλον
ἐπυλλίοις καὶ περιπάτοις καὶ τευτλίοισι λευκοῖς,
χυλὸν διδοὺς στωμυλμάτων ἀπὸ βιβλίων ἀπηθῶν·
εἶτ' ἀνέτρεφον μονῳδίαις Κηφισοφῶντα μειγνύς.
εἶτ' οὐκ ἐλήρουν ὅ τι τύχοιμ' οὐδ' ἐμπεσὼν ἔφυρον, 945
ἀλλ' οὑξιὼν πρώτιστα μέν μοι τὸ γένος εἶπ' ἂν εὐθὺς
τοῦ δράματος.
ΔΙ. κρεῖττον γὰρ ἦν σοι νὴ Δί' ἢ τὸ σαυτοῦ.
ΕΥ. ἔπειτα' ἀπὸ τῶν πρώτων ἐπῶν οὐδένα[1] παρῆκ' ἂν ἀργόν,
ἀλλ' ἔλεγεν ἡ γυνή τέ μοι χὠ δοῦλος οὐδὲν ἧτττον,
χὠ δεσπότης χἠ παρθένος χἠ γραῦς ἄν.
ΑΙ. εἶτα δῆτα 950
οὐκ ἀποθανεῖν σε ταῦτ' ἐχρῆν τολμῶντα;
ΕΥ. μὰ τὸν Ἀπόλλω·
δημοκρατικὸν γὰρ αὔτ' ἔδρων.
ΔΙ. τοῦτο μὲν ἔασον, ὦ τᾶν.
οὐ σοὶ γάρ ἐστι περίπατος κάλλιστα περί γε τούτου.
ΕΥ. ἔπειτα τουτουσὶ λαλεῖν ἐδίδαξα—
ΑΙ. φημὶ κἀγώ·
ὡς πρὶν διδάξαι γ' ὤφελες μέσος διαρραγῆναι. 955
ΕΥ. λεπτῶν τε κανόνας εἰσβολῶν[2] ἐπῶν τε γωνιασμούς,
νοεῖν, ὁρᾶν, ξυνιέναι, στρέφειν ἐρᾶν, τεχνάζειν,
κάχ' ὑποτοπεῖσθαι, περινοεῖν ἅπαντα—
ΑΙ. φημὶ κἀγώ.
ΕΥ. οἰκεῖα πράγματ' εἰσάγων, οἷς χρώμεθ', οἷς ξύνεσμεν,
ἐξ ὧν γ' ἂν ἐξηλεγχόμην· ξυνειδότες γὰρ οὗτοι 960
ἤλεγχον ἄν μου τὴν τέχνην· ἀλλ' οὐκ ἐκομπολάκουν

---

[1] Lenting: οὐδὲν codd.
[2] scripsi: κανόνων εἰσβολὰς codd.

| | |
|---|---|
| AE. | And you, enemy of the gods, what kind of poetry was it that you used to make? |
| EU. | Not poems about horse-cocks or goat-stags, like yours, creatures they draw on Persian hangings. But as soon as I took over the art from you, swollen with bombast and tiresome vocabulary, my first act was to thin her down and take off some of her weight by means of pretty little verses, long walks, and white beets, and I gave her extract of Babble made by boiling out-of-the-way books. Then I nourished her up again with monodies, mixing in some Cephisophon.[1] And then I didn't talk whatever rot came into my head or blunder in and mix the story all up in the telling, but the first character to come out immediately told the lineage of the play. |
| DI. | And a better lineage it was, by Zeus, than your own. |
| EU. | Then from word one on I left no one idle, but women had speaking parts and no less did slaves, and so did masters and maidens and old women. |
| AE. | And after doing this should you not have been put to death for such effrontery? |
| EU. | No, by Apollo. In doing this I was acting more democratically. |
| DI. | Best leave *that* alone, my good man! You don't have the clearest field before you on that point. |
| EU. | And then I taught these, our audience, to prattle— |
| AE. | Yes, you did. Would that before teaching them you had spilled your guts out! |
| EU. | and I taught them to measure out the line of subtle attack, to square the corners of their words, to think, to see, to understand, to be passionate twist-and-turners, to contrive, to suspect mischief, to be highly clever in everything— |
| AE. | I agree. |
| EU. | by introducing into my plays the ordinary things of use and daily life. On the basis of these I was open to refutation. For these spectators, who know these things as well as I, could have put my art to the test. But I didn't engage in empty |

---

[1] The comic poets accused him of writing parts of Euripides' plays and seducing his wife: see T 1.5, 1.26, 58.

ἀπὸ τοῦ φρονεῖν ἀποσπάσας, οὐδ' ἐξέπληττον αὐτούς,
Κύκνους ποῶν καὶ Μέμνονας κωδωνοφαλαροπώλους.
γνώσει δὲ τοὺς τούτου τε κἀμοὺς ἑκατέρου μαθητάς.
τουτουμενὶ Φορμίσιος Μεγαίνετός θ' ὁ Μάγνης,[1]    965
σαλπιγγολογχυπηνάδαι, σαρκασμοπιτυοκάμπται,
οὑμοὶ δὲ Κλειτοφῶν τε καὶ Θηραμένης ὁ κομψός.    967

...............
ΕΥ.   τοιαῦτα μέντοὐγὼ φρονεῖν    971
      τούτοισιν εἰσηγησάμην,
      λογισμὸν ἐνθεὶς τῇ τέχνῃ
      καὶ σκέψιν, ὥστ' ἤδη νοεῖν
      ἅπαντα καὶ διειδέναι    975
      τά τ' ἄλλα καὶ τὰς οἰκίας
      οἰκεῖν ἄμεινον ἢ πρὸ τοῦ
      κἀνασκοπεῖν, "πῶς τοῦτ' ἔχει;
      ποῦ μοι τοδί; τίς τοῦτ' ἔλαβε;"
ΔΙ.   νὴ τοὺς θεούς, νῦν γοῦν Ἀθη-
      ναίων ἅπας τις εἰσιὼν
      κέκραγε πρὸς τοὺς οἰκέτας
      ζητεῖ τε· "ποῦ 'στιν ἡ χύτρα;
      τίς τὴν κεφαλὴν ἀπεδήδοκεν
      τῆς μαινίδος; τὸ τρύβλιον    985
      τὸ περυσινὸν τέθνηκέ μοι;
      ποῦ τὸ σκόροδον τὸ χθιζινόν;
      τίς τῆς ἐλάας παρέτραγεν;"
      τέως δ' ἀβελτερώτατοι
      κεχηνότες μαμμάκυθοι,    990
      μελιτίδαι καθῆντο.
ΧΟ(ΡΟΣ)
      "τάδε μὲν λεύσσεις, φαίδιμ' Ἀχιλλεῦ" [Aesch. fr. 131]·
      σὺ δὲ τί, φέρε, πρὸς ταῦτα λέξεις; μόνον ὅπως
      μή σ' ὁ θυμὸς ἁρπάσας
      ἐκτὸς οἴσει τῶν ἐλαῶν·    995
      δεινὰ γὰρ κατηγόρηκεν.
      ἀλλ' ὅπως, ὦ γεννάδα,
      μὴ πρὸς ὀργὴν ἀντιλέξεις,

---

[1] codex A: Μανῆς plerique codd.

bombast tearing them loose from their good sense nor did I stun them by putting in my plays Cycnuses and Memnons with bells and cheek-pieces on their steeds. You will easily recognize the disciples of each of us, his and mine. His are Phormisio and Megaenetus the Magnesian, lance-trumpet-and-mustachio men and pine-bending-flesh-tearers, while mine are Clitophon and the clever Theramenes.[1]

............

EU. This was the kind of wisdom I instructed the audience here to possess. I put reason in my art and thought so that now they notice and distinguish everything and in particular they manage their households better than before and ask searching questions, 'How is this doing? Where is that? Who took that other thing?'

DI. Yes, by the gods, now every Athenian goes into his house, shouts at his slaves and asks, 'Where is the jar? Who bit the head off of this sprat? Has the cup I had last year been smashed? Where is yesterday's garlic? Who has been nibbling at this olive?' Before this they used to sit around slack-jawed like a bunch of ninnies.

CH. 'Brilliant Achilles, you see what is happening.'[2] But tell me what you will say in reply to this. Just take care that your anger does not carry you beyond the olive trees.[3] The accusations he has made are terrible. But be sure not to reply

---

[1] Clitophon was a young aristocrat, an admirer of the Sophist Thrasymachus. Theramenes, who had participated in the oligarchic revolution of 411, had survived to play an infamous role in the restored democracy, bringing about the condemnation of the generals who were victorious at Arginusae. He acquired the nickname 'Buskin', suggesting that, like the loose tragic shoe, he adapted himself to either foot. See Xenophon, *Hellenica* 2.3.27-31.

[2] The opening line of Aeschylus' *Myrmidons*.

[3] I.e. beyond the boundary of the race-course.

ἀλλὰ συστείλας ἄκροισι
χρώμενος τοῖς ἱστίοις, 1000
εἶτα μᾶλλον μᾶλλον ἄξεις
καὶ φυλάξεις, ἡνίκ' ἂν τὸ
πνεῦμα λεῖον καὶ καθεστηκὸς λάβῃς.
ἀλλ' ὦ πρῶτος τῶν Ἑλλήνων πυργώσας ῥήματα σεμνὰ 1004
καὶ κοσμήσας τραγικὸν λῆρον, θαρρῶν τὸν κρουνὸν ἀφίει.

ΑΙ. θυμοῦμαι μὲν τῇ ξυντυχίᾳ, καί μου τὰ σπλάγχν' ἀγανακτεῖ,
εἰ πρὸς τοῦτον δεῖ μ' ἀντιλέγειν· ἵνα μὴ φάσκῃ δ' ἀπορεῖν με,
ἀπόκριναί μοι, τίνος οὕνεκα χρὴ θαυμάζειν ἄνδρα ποητήν;

ΕΥ. δεξιότητος καὶ νουθεσίας, ὅτι βελτίους τε ποοῦμεν 1009
τοὺς ἀνθρώπους ἐν ταῖς πόλεσιν.

ΑΙ.                ταῦτ' οὖν εἰ μὴ πεπόηκας,
ἀλλ' ἐκ χρηστῶν καὶ γενναίων μοχθηροτάτους ἀπέδειξας,
τί παθεῖν φήσεις ἄξιος εἶναι;

ΔΙ.                τεθνάναι· μὴ τοῦτον ἐρώτα.

ΑΙ. σκέψαι τοίνυν οἵους αὐτοὺς παρ' ἐμοῦ παρεδέξατο πρῶτον,
εἰ γενναίους καὶ τετραπήχεις, καὶ μὴ διαδρασιπολίτας 1014
μηδ' ἀγοραίους μηδὲ κοβάλους, ὥσπερ νῦν, μηδὲ πανούργους,
ἀλλὰ πνέοντας δόρυ καὶ λόγχας καὶ λευκολόφους τρυφαλείας
καὶ πήληκας καὶ κνημῖδας καὶ θυμοὺς ἑπταβοείους.

ΕΥ. καὶ δὴ χωρεῖ τουτὶ τὸ κακόν· κρανοποιῶν αὖ μ' ἐπιτρίψει.

ΔΙ. καὶ τί σὺ δράσας οὕτως αὐτοὺς γενναίους ἐξεδίδαξας; 1019
Αἰσχύλε, λέξον, μηδ' αὐθάδως σεμνυνόμενος χαλέπαινε.

ΑΙ. δρᾶμα ποήσας Ἄρεως μεστόν.

ΔΙ.                ποῖον;

ΑΙ.                τοὺς Ἕπτ' ἐπὶ Θήβας·
ὃ θεασάμενος πᾶς ἄν τις ἀνὴρ ἠράσθη δάιος εἶναι.

ΔΙ. τουτὶ μέν σοι κακὸν εἴργασται· Θηβαίους γὰρ πεπόηκας
ἀνδρειοτέρους εἰς τὸν πόλεμον· καὶ τούτου γ' οὕνεκα τύπτου.

ΑΙ. ἀλλ' ὑμῖν αὔτ' ἐξῆν ἀσκεῖν, ἀλλ' οὐκ ἐπὶ τοῦτ' ἐτράπεσθε.
εἶτα διδάξας Πέρσας μετὰ τοῦτ' ἐπιθυμεῖν ἐξεδίδαξα 1026

angrily, my noble sir, but reef your sails, use only the edge of them, then let them out a little at a time and wait for the moment when the breeze blows smooth and calm. Well, inventor of the towering and impressive phrase, tricker-out of tragic balderdash, take courage now and open your floodgates.

AE. I am annoyed and it vexes my inward parts that I must reply to this man. But so that he will not claim I am at a loss for words—[to Euripides] tell me this, for what quality ought we to admire a poet?

EU. For cleverness and for advice, because we make men better in the cities.

AE. But if you have not done so but have taken good and noble men and produced[1] criminals, what punishment will you say you deserve?

DI. Death. Don't ask him.

AE. Then look at the kind of men he received from me, what noble and stalwart fellows they were, not shirkers of civic duty, not the vulgar humbugs of today or knaves but men whose every breath was spears and lances, white-plumed helmets, breast-plates and greaves, and hearts bound in seven-layered oxhide.[2]

EU. Here's the plague, just as predicted! He'll kill me with his helmet-making!

DI. And what did you do to them to make them so noble? Tell us, Aeschylus, don't be sullen and stubborn.

AE. I wrote a play full of Ares.

DI. What play was that?

AE. *Seven against Thebes*. And every man, when he had seen it, longed to be a valiant soldier.

DI. But that was really a bad deed on your part: you made the Thebans braver in war. For your trouble, take that! [He hits him gently.]

AE. But you could have trained for war, but you didn't turn your efforts in that direction. After that I put on *Persians*,

---

[1] There is deliberate blurring of the distinction between the characters a poet produces in his plays and the quality of the citizens his plays produce.
[2] Like the shield of Ajax at *Iliad* 7.220.

νικᾶν ἀεὶ τοὺς ἀντιπάλους, κοσμήσας ἔργον ἄριστον.
ΔΙ. ἐχάρην γοῦν, ἡνίκ' ἐκώκυσας περὶ Δαρείου τεθνεῶτος,
ὁ χορὸς δ' εὐθὺς τὼ χεῖρ' ὡδὶ συγκρούσας εἶπεν "Ἰαυοῖ".
ΑΙ. ταῦτα γὰρ ἄνδρας χρὴ ποιητὰς ἀσκεῖν. σκέψαι γὰρ ἀπ' ἀρχῆς
ὡς ὠφέλιμοι τῶν ποιητῶν οἱ γενναῖοι γεγένηνται.   1031
Ὀρφεὺς μὲν γὰρ τελετάς θ' ἡμῖν κατέδειξε φόνων τ' ἀπέχεσθαι,
Μουσαῖος δ' ἐξακέσεις τε νόσων καὶ χρησμούς, Ἡσίοδος δὲ
γῆς ἐργασίας, καρπῶν ὥρας, ἀρότους· ὁ δὲ θεῖος Ὅμηρος
ἀπὸ τοῦ τιμὴν καὶ κλέος ἔσχεν πλὴν τοῦδ' ὅτι χρήστ' ἐδίδαξεν,
τάξεις, ἀρετάς, ὁπλίσεις ἀνδρῶν;
ΔΙ.                                         καὶ μὴν οὐ Παντακλέα γε 1036
ἐδίδαξεν ὅμως τὸν σκαιότατον. πρώην γοῦν, ἡνίκ' ἔπεμπεν,
τὸ κράνος πρῶτον περιδησάμενος τὸν λόφον ἤμελλ'
    ἐπιδήσειν.
ΑΙ. ἀλλ' ἄλλους τοι πολλοὺς ἀγαθούς, ὧν ἦν καὶ Λάμαχος ἥρως·
ὅθεν ἡμὴ φρὴν ἀπομαξαμένη πολλὰς ἀρετὰς ἐπόησεν,   1040
Πατρόκλων, Τεύκρων θυμολεόντων, ἵν' ἐπαίροιμ' ἄνδρα
    πολίτην
ἀντεκτείνειν αὐτὸν τούτοις, ὁπόταν σάλπιγγος ἀκούσῃ.
ἀλλ' οὐ μὰ Δί' οὐ Φαίδρας ἐπόουν πόρνας οὐδὲ Σθενεβοίας
οὐδ' οἶδ' οὐδεὶς ἥντιν' ἐρῶσαν πώποτ' ἐπόησα γυναῖκα.
ΕΥ. μὰ Δί', οὐ γὰρ ἐπῆν τῆς Ἀφροδίτης οὐδέν σοι.
ΑΙ.                                          μηδέ γ' ἐπείη· 1045
ἀλλ' ἐπὶ σοί τοι καὶ τοῖς σοῖσιν πολλὴ πολλοῦ 'πικαθῆτο,
ὥστε γε καὐτόν σε κατ' οὖν ἔβαλεν.
ΔΙ.                                       νὴ τὸν Δία τοῦτό γέ τοι δή.
ἃ γὰρ εἰς τὰς ἀλλοτρίας ἐπόεις, αὐτὸς τούτοισιν ἐπλήγης.
ΕΥ. καὶ τί βλάπτουσ', ὦ σχέτλι' ἀνδρῶν, τὴν πόλιν ἁμαὶ Σθενέ-
    βοιαι;
ΑΙ. ὅτι γενναίας καὶ γενναίων ἀνδρῶν ἀλόχους ἀνέπεισας   1050
κώνεια πιεῖν αἰσχυνθείσας διὰ τοὺς σοὺς Βελλεροφόντας.

|     | and by adorning a noble action I made the Athenians long to be always victorious over the foe. |
| --- | --- |
| DI. | I enjoyed it when you made them wail around the ghost of Darius and the Chorus stuck up its hands like this and said 'Lackaday!' |
| AE. | These are the lessons poets must inculcate. See how useful noble poets have been from the very beginning. Orpheus gave us mystery-rites and told us to abstain from murder, Musaeus told us the cure of diseases and gave us oracles, Hesiod told us how to work the soil, the seasons for fruits and how to plow. And the divine Homer—what is the source of his glory and fame but this, that he taught noble accomplishments such as military formations and courage and the proper way to arm? |
| DI. | But he didn't get through to that fool Pantacles. The other day when he was part of the escort, he had put his helmet on and was trying to attach the crest to it without taking it off! |
| AI. | But he taught lots of other brave men, like the hero Lamachus. Homer's spirit has rubbed off on mine, and it is from him I get the examples of courage I put in my poetry, lion-hearted Patrocluses and Teucers, in order to inspire the citizen to measure himself against them whenever he hears the battle-trumpet sound. But, by Zeus, I did not put whores like Phaedra or Stheneboea in my poetry, nor does anyone know of a woman in love I ever put in a play of mine. |
| EU. | No, by Zeus, you had not the slightest charm of Aphrodite about you. |
| AE. | And may I never have it! But the goddess sat heavily upon you and upon your family, and you yourself she has thrown for a complete fall. |
| DI. | By Zeus, that's certainly true. For what you used to do[1] to other men's wives now comes home to strike you.[2] |
| EU. | And what harm to the city, heartless man, did my Stheno-boeas ever do? |
| AE. | You persuaded noble women, wives of noble husbands, to drink hemlock out of shame because of your Bellerophons. |

---

[1] Either in real life (cf. T 2.9) or in portraying heroines in his tragedies.
[2] Apparently an allusion to the alleged adultery of Euripides' wife.

ΕΥ. πότερον δ' οὐκ ὄντα λόγον τοῦτον περὶ τῆς Φαίδρας
ξυνέθηκα;
ΑΙ. μὰ Δί', ἀλλ' ὄντ'· ἀλλ' ἀποκρύπτειν χρὴ τὸ πονηρὸν τόν γε ποηι
καὶ μὴ παράγειν μηδὲ διδάσκειν· τοῖς μὲν γὰρ παιδαρίοισιν
ἔστι διδάσκαλος ὅστις φράζει, τοῖσιν δ' ἡβῶσι ποηταί. 1055
πάνυ δὴ δεῖ χρηστὰ λέγειν ἡμᾶς.
ΕΥ. ἢν οὖν σὺ λέγῃς Λυκαβηττοὺς
καὶ Παρνασσῶν ἡμῖν μεγέθη, τοῦτ' ἔστι τὸ χρηστὰ
διδάσκειν,
ὃν χρῆν φράζειν ἀνθρωπείως;
ΑΙ. ἀλλ', ὦ κακόδαιμον, ἀνάγκη
μεγάλων γνωμῶν καὶ διανοιῶν ἴσα καὶ τὰ ῥήματα τίκτειν.
κἄλλως εἰκὸς τοὺς ἡμιθέους τοῖς ῥήμασι μείζοσι
χρῆσθαι· 1060
καὶ γὰρ τοῖς ἱματίοις ἡμῶν χρῶνται πολὺ σεμνοτέροισιν.
ἁμοῦ χρηστῶς καταδείξαντος διελυμήνω σύ.
ΕΥ. τί δράσας;
ΑΙ. πρῶτον μὲν τοὺς βασιλεύοντας ῥάκι' ἀμπισχών, ἵν' ἐλεινοὶ
τοῖς ἀνθρώποις φαίνοιντ' εἶναι.
ΕΥ. τοῦτ' οὖν ἔβλαψα τί δράσας;
ΑΙ. οὔκουν ἐθέλει γε τριηραρχεῖν πλουτῶν οὐδεὶς διὰ ταῦτα,
ἀλλὰ ῥακίοις περιειλάμενος κλάει καὶ φησὶ πένεσθαι. 1066
ΔΙ. νὴ τὴν Δήμητρα, χιτῶνά γ' ἔχων οὔλων ἐρίων ὑπένερθεν.
κἂν ταῦτα λέγων ἐξαπατήσῃ, περὶ τοὺς ἰχθῦς ἀνέκυψεν.
ΑΙ. εἶτ' αὖ λαλιὰν ἐπιτηδεῦσαι καὶ στωμυλίαν ἐδίδαξας,
ἣ 'ξεκένωσεν τάς τε παλαίστρας καὶ τὰς πυγὰς
ἐνέτριψεν 1070
τῶν μειρακίων στωμυλλομένων, καὶ τοὺς Παράλους ἀνέπεισεν
ἀνταγορεύειν τοῖς ἄρχουσιν. καίτοι τότε γ', ἡνίκ' ἐγὼ 'ζων,
οὐκ ἠπίσταντ' ἀλλ' ἢ μᾶζαν καλέσαι καὶ "ῥυππαπαῖ" εἰπεῖν.

..............
ποίων δὲ κακῶν οὐκ αἴτιός ἐστ'; 1078
οὐ προαγωγοὺς κατέδειξ' οὗτος,
καὶ τικτούσας ἐν τοῖς ἱεροῖς, 1080
καὶ μειγνυμένας τοῖσιν ἀδελφοῖς,

EU. But was it a lie that I told about Phaedra?
AE. No, by Zeus, the truth. But a poet ought to hide what is wicked and not put it on stage or produce it. For while young boys have a teacher who gives them advice, young men have the poets. It is our bounden duty, then, to say what is good.
EU. And so if you speak your mountain-high masses of words, whole Lycabettuses and Parnassuses, is that what you mean by a poet producing what is good, a poet who ought to be speaking humanely?
AE. But when thoughts and ideas are big, you hopeless creature, one must give birth to words that equal them. And furthermore, it is reasonable for the demi-gods to use bigger words. And in fact they wear clothing that is much more august than ours. This good practice, which I initiated, you have outraged.
EU. By doing what?
AE. First, you dressed your kings in rags, so that they might seem pitiable to mortal men.
EU. What harm was there in that?
AE. On account of this no rich man now is willing to equip a trireme[1] but wraps himself in rags and claims poverty.
DI. Yes, by Demeter, and he wears a tunic of fleecy wool underneath. And if he carries off this deception, he pops up near the fish-stalls.[2]
AE. And then you taught people to engage in chatter and babble, which has emptied the wrestling-schools and worn out the buttocks of the young men and convinced the crew of the Paralos to talk back to their officers. But when I was still alive, they only knew how to ask for their grub and say 'Yo-heave-ho.'...What misfortunes is he not responsible for? Did he not introduce panders onto the stage[3] and women giving birth in shrines[4] and women sleeping with their

---

[1] Equipping a trireme was one of the 'liturgies', or public services, rich men were called on to perform at their own expense.
[2] Fish were regarded as an expensive delicacy.
[3] The Nurse in the *Hippolytus*.
[4] An allusion to the *Auge*.

καὶ φασκούσας οὐ ζῆν τὸ ζῆν;
κᾆτ' ἐκ τούτων ἡ πόλις ἡμῶν
ὑπογραμματέων ἀνεμεστώθη
καὶ βωμολόχων δημοπιθήκων 1085
ἐξαπατώντων τὸν δῆμον ἀεί,
λαμπάδα δ' οὐδεὶς οἷός τε φέρειν
ὑπ' ἀγυμνασίας ἔτι νυνί. 1088
..................
ΠΛ(ΟΥΤΩΝ)
   κρίνοις ἄν.
ΔΙ.     αὕτη σφῷν κρίσις γενήσεται. 1467
   αἱρήσομαι γὰρ ὅνπερ ἡ ψυχὴ θέλει.
ΕΥ.  μεμνημένος νυν τῶν θεῶν οὓς ὤμοσας
   ἦ μὴν ἀπάξειν μ' οἴκαδ', αἱροῦ τοὺς φίλους. 1470
ΔΙ.  ἡ γλῶττ' ὀμώμοκ', Αἰσχύλον δ' αἱρήσομαι.
ΕΥ.  τί δέδρακας, ὦ μιαρώτατ' ἀνθρώπων;
ΔΙ.         ἐγώ;
   ἔκρινα νικᾶν Αἰσχύλον. τιὴ γὰρ οὔ;
ΕΥ.  αἴσχιστον ἔργον προσβλέπεις μ' εἰργασμένος;
ΔΙ.  τί δ' αἰσχρόν, ἢν μὴ τοῖς θεωμένοις δοκῇ; 1475
ΕΥ.  ὦ σχέτλιε, περιόψει με δὴ τεθνηκότα;
ΔΙ.  τίς οἶδεν εἰ τὸ ζῆν μέν ἐστι κατθανεῖν,
   τὸ πνεῖν δὲ δειπνεῖν, τὸ δὲ καθεύδειν κῴδιον;
ΠΛ.  χωρεῖτε τοίνυν, ὦ Διόνυσ', εἴσω.
ΔΙ.        τί δαί;
ΠΛ.  ἵνα ξενίσω ⟨'γώ⟩ σφω πρὶν ἀποπλεῖν.
ΔΙ.         εὖ λέγεις 1480
   νὴ τὸν Δί'· οὐ γὰρ ἄχθομαι τῷ πράγματι.
ΧΟ.  μακάριός γ' ἀνὴρ ἔχων
   ξύνεσιν ἠκριβωμένην.
   πάρα δὲ πολλοῖσιν μαθεῖν.
   ὅδε γὰρ εὖ φρονεῖν δοκήσας 1485
   πάλιν ἄπεισιν οἴκαδ' αὖθις,
   ἐπ' ἀγαθῷ μὲν τοῖς πολίταις
   ἐπ' ἀγαθῷ δὲ τοῖς ἑαυτοῦ
   ξυγγενέσι τε καὶ φίλοισι,

brothers[1] and claiming that Life is not Life?[2] And as a result our city is filled to the brim with under-secretaries and scurrilous democrat-apes who constantly make fools of the common people, and from being out of condition no one is able any longer to run the torch-race.

............

PLUTO
    Kindly render your verdict.

DI.    This shall be my verdict for the two of you. I shall choose him whom my heart desires.

EU.    Therefore, remembering the gods in whose name you swore that you would surely bring me back home, choose the one you love.

DI.    My tongue has sworn, but I'll choose Aeschylus.[3]

EU.    What is this you have done, unspeakable man?

DI.    Me? I named Aeschylus the winner. Why not?

EU.    Can you commit such a shameful deed against me and look me in the face?

DI.    What's shameful if the audience think not so?[4]

EU.    Hard-hearted man, will you suffer me then to be dead?

DI.    Who knows if life is really death, breathing is dining, and sleeping is a fleece-blanket?[5]

PL.    Dionysus, you and your friend go inside.

DI.    Why?

PL.    So that I can give you a feast before you sail off.

DI.    By Zeus, a good idea! The suggestion does not vex me. [Exit Pluto, Dionysus, and Aeschylus into the palace, Euripides to the side.]

CHORUS
    Yes, blessed is the man who has accuracy of judgement. One can see this in many ways. This man, having proved himself to be a man of good sense, is going back home again, to the benefit of the citizens and to the benefit of his own kinsmen

---

[1] An allusion to the *Aeolus*.
[2] Cf. fr. 638 (*Polyidus*).
[3] Parody of *Hippolytus* 612.
[4] A quotation from Euripides' *Aeolus* (fr. 19), with substitution of 'the audience' for 'the doers': cf. T 44.
[5] A parody of Eur. fr. 638, from the *Polyidus*.

διὰ τὸ συνετὸς εἶναι. 1490
χαρίεν οὖν μὴ Σωκράτει
παρακαθήμενον λαλεῖν,
ἀποβαλόντα μουσικὴν
τά τε μέγιστα παραλιπόντα
τῆς τραγῳδικῆς τέχνης. 1495
τὸ δ' ἐπὶ σεμνοῖσιν λόγοισι
καὶ σκαριφησμοῖσι λήρων
διατριβὴν ἀργὸν ποεῖσθαι,
παραφρονοῦντος ἀνδρός. 1499

**78** id. fr. 682 K.-A., schol. *Ran.* 775

στρεψίμαλλος τὴν τέχνην Εὐριπίδης

**79** Cratinus fr. 342 K.-A. et Ar. fr. 488 K.-A., Scholia Areth. (B) Plat. *Apol.* p. 19C

Ἀριστοφάνης...ἐκωμῳδεῖτο ἐπὶ τῷ σκώπτειν μὲν Εὐριπίδην, μιμεῖσθαι δ' αὐτόν. Κρατῖνος
 τίς δ' εἶ σύ; ⟨τάχ' ἂν⟩[1] κομψός τις ἔροιτο θεατής.
 ὑπολεπτολόγος, γνωμιδιώκτης, εὐριπιδαριστοφανίζων
καὶ αὐτὸς δ' ἐξομολογεῖτο Σκηνὰς καταλαμβανούσαις·
 χρῶμαι γὰρ αὐτοῦ τοῦ στόματος τῷ στρογγύλῳ,
 τοὺς νοῦς δ' ἀγοραίους ἧττον ἢ 'κεῖνος ποῶ.

**80** Strattis apud Arist. *de Sensu* 443 b 30-1

ἀληθὲς γὰρ ὅπερ Εὐριπίδην σκώπτων εἶπε Στράττις [fr. 47.2 K.-A.],
 ὅταν φακῆν ἕψητε, μὴ 'πιχεῖν μύρον.

**81** Axionicus fr. 3 K.-A. ap. Athen. 4.76, 175B

καὶ Ἀξιόνικος ἐν Φιλευριπίδῃ·

---
[1] Headlam: τίς δὲ σύ; codd.

and friends, because he is wise. And so the elegant thing is not to sit next to Socrates and babble, losing all sense of the Muses and omitting the weightiest points of the tragic art. To waste one's time on high-sounding words and idiotic chicken-scratchings is the mark of a madman.

**78** Aristophanes, fragment quoted in the scholia to the *Frogs*

Euripides, tangled and complex in his art

### (b) Other comic poets

**79** Cratinus, fr. 342 K.-A. and Aristophanes, fr. 488 K.-A. quoted in the scholia to Plato

Aristophanes...was mocked because, while he made fun of Euripides, he still imitated him. Cratinus says

> 'Who are you?' some clever play-goer may ask. 'Weaver of subtle words, chaser of epigrammatic saws, euripidaristophanist.'

And he himself admits the charge in his *Women Seizing the Stage*:

> I make use of the neat rotundity of his style, but the sentiments I put in verse are less vulgar than his.

**80** Strattis quoted in Aristotle, *On Sense*

It is a true point Strattis made in his mockery of Euripides, 'When you cook bean-soup, do not add myrrh.'

**81** Axionicus quoted in Athenaeus

And Axionicus says in his *Lover of Euripides*,

οὕτω γὰρ ἐπὶ τοῖς μέλεσι τοῖς Εὐριπίδου
ἄμφω νοσοῦσιν, ὥστε τἆλλ' αὐτοῖς δοκεῖν
εἶναι μέλη γιγγραντὰ καὶ κακὸν μέγα

**82** Arist.

(a) *Poet.* 1453 a 22-30: ἡ μὲν οὖν κατὰ τὴν τέχνην καλλίστη τραγῳδία ἐκ ταύτης τῆς συστάσεώς ἐστι [τῆς εἰς τὴν δυστυχίαν sc.]. διὸ καὶ οἱ Εὐριπίδῃ ἐγκαλοῦντες τοῦτ' αὐτὸ[1] ἁμαρτάνουσιν ὅτι τοῦτο δρᾷ ἐν ταῖς τραγῳδίαις καὶ πολλαὶ αὐτοῦ εἰς δυστυχίαν τελευτῶσιν. τοῦτο γάρ ἐστιν ὥσπερ εἴρηται ὀρθόν· σημεῖον δὲ μέγιστον· ἐπὶ γὰρ τῶν σκηνῶν καὶ τῶν ἀγώνων τραγικώταται αἱ τοιαῦται φαίνονται, ἂν κατορθωθῶσιν, καὶ ὁ Εὐριπίδης, εἰ καὶ τὰ ἄλλα μὴ εὖ οἰκονομεῖ, ἀλλὰ τραγικώτατός γε τῶν ποιητῶν φαίνεται.

(b) *Poet.* 1454 a 37-1454 b 2: φανερὸν οὖν ὅτι καὶ τὰς λύσεις τῶν μύθων ἐξ αὐτοῦ δεῖ τοῦ μύθου συμβαίνειν, καὶ μὴ ὥσπερ ἐν τῇ Μηδείᾳ ἀπὸ μηχανῆς καὶ ἐν τῇ Ἰλιάδι τὰ περὶ τὸν ἀπόπλουν.

(c) *Poet.* 1456 a 25-30: καὶ τὸν χορὸν δὲ ἕνα δεῖ ὑπολαμβάνειν τῶν ὑποκριτῶν, καὶ μόριον εἶναι τοῦ ὅλου καὶ συναγωνίζεσθαι μὴ ὥσπερ Εὐριπίδῃ ἀλλ' ὥσπερ Σοφοκλεῖ.

(d) *Poet.* 1461 b 19-21: ὀρθὴ δ' ἐπιτίμησις καὶ ἀλογίᾳ καὶ μοχθηρίᾳ, ὅταν μὴ ἀνάγκης οὔσης ⟨εἰς⟩[2] μηθὲν χρήσηται τῷ ἀλόγῳ, ὥσπερ Εὐριπίδης τῷ Αἰγεῖ, ἢ τῇ πονηρίᾳ, ὥσπερ ἐν Ὀρέστῃ ⟨τῇ⟩ τοῦ Μενελάου.

(e) *Rhet.* 1404 b 18-25: διὸ δεῖ λανθάνειν ποιοῦντας, καὶ μὴ δοκεῖν λέγειν πεπλασμένως ἀλλὰ πεφυκότως...κλέπτεται δ' εὖ, ἐάν τις ἐκ τῆς εἰωθυίας διαλέκτου ἐκλέγων συντιθῇ· ὅπερ Εὐριπίδης ποιεῖ καὶ ὑπέδειξε πρῶτος.

---

[1] Thurot: τὸ αὐτὸ codd.
[2] post Gomperz (πρὸς) ego

The pair of them are so mad-keen on the songs of Euripides that everything else seems to them mere penny-whistle stuff, a great bore.

## O. *Other Judgements*[1]

**82** Aristotle, *Poetics* and *Rhetoric*

(a) The tragedy that is artistically the best is of this shape [i.e. moving from good fortune to bad]. Hence those who criticize Euripides on this very point, that he does this in his tragedies and that many of them end in unhappiness, are in error. For, as we have said, this is the correct way to proceed. The best proof is that plays like this on the stage and in the tragic competitions appear, if successfully performed, the most tragic, and Euripides, even if he does not manage his art well in other respects, is clearly the most *tragic*, at least, of the poets.

(b) It is clear therefore that the resolutions of plots must come from the plot itself, not, as in the *Medea*, from the stage-crane or like the episode of the embarkation in the *Iliad*.

(c) One should regard the chorus too as one of the actors and it should be a part of the whole and share in the action, as in Sophocles, not as in Euripides.

(d) It is proper to criticize both irrationality and baseness of character when, in the absence of necessity, the poet uses the irrationality to no purpose, as Euripides does the arrival of Aegeus, or makes unnecessary use of wickedness, as Euripides does of Menelaus's in the *Orestes*.

(e) We must therefore conceal our art and appear to speak not in an artificial but in a natural manner...Someone can conceal his art well if he puts together elements taken from the common language of everyday life. This is what Euripides does and was the first to show the way to his successors.

---

[1] Cf. also Athenaeus 14.67, 652D, Dio of Prusa 66.6.

**83** [Plut.] *Vitae decem oratorum*, 841F

τὸν δέ [νόμον εἰσήνεγκε Λύκουργος sc.], ὡς χαλκᾶς εἰκόνας ἀναθεῖναι τῶν ποιητῶν, Αἰσχύλου Σοφοκλέους Εὐριπίδου, καὶ τὰς τραγῳδίας αὐτῶν ἐν κοινῷ γραψαμένους φυλάττειν καὶ τὸν τῆς πόλεως γραμματέα παραναγινώσκειν τοῖς ὑποκρινουμένοις, οὐδ'[1] ἐξεῖναι παρ' αὐτὰς ὑποκρίνεσθαι.

**84** Crantor ap. D.L. 4.26 [=Mullach, iii 131]

Ἐθαύμαζε δὲ ὁ Κράντωρ πάντων δὴ μᾶλλον Ὅμηρον καὶ Εὐριπίδην, λέγων ἐργῶδες ἐν τῷ κυρίῳ τραγικῶς ἅμα καὶ συμπαθῶς γράψαι.

**85** Plut. *De recta ratione audiendi* 13, 45AB

μέμψαιτο δ' ἄν τις Ἀρχιλόχου μὲν τὴν ὑπόθεσιν, Παρμενίδου δὲ τὴν στιχοποιίαν, Φωκυλίδου δὲ τὴν εὐτέλειαν, Εὐριπίδου δὲ τὴν λαλιάν, Σοφοκλέους δὲ τὴν ἀνωμαλίαν, κτλ.

**86** [Longinus] *De Sublim.*

(a) 15.3-6: ἔστι μὲν οὖν φιλοπονώτατος ὁ Εὐριπίδης δύο ταυτὶ πάθη, μανίας τε καὶ ἔρωτας, ἐκτραγῳδῆσαι, κἀν τούτοις ὡς οὐκ οἶδ' εἴ τισιν ἑτέροις ἐπιτυχέστατος, οὐ μὴν ἀλλὰ καὶ ταῖς ἄλλαις ἐπιτίθεσθαι φαντασίαις οὐκ ἄτολμος. ἥκιστά γέ τοι μεγαλοφυὴς ὢν ὅμως τὴν αὐτὸς αὐτοῦ φύσιν ἐν πολλοῖς γενέσθαι τραγικὴν προσηνάγκασεν....4. τῷ γοῦν Φαέθοντι παραδιδοὺς τὰς ἡνίας ὁ Ἥλιος [fr. 779 N[2]]

>   ἔλα δὲ μήτε Λιβυκὸν αἰθέρ' εἰσβαλών·
>   κρᾶσιν γὰρ ὑγρὰν οὐκ ἔχων ἁψῖδα σὴν
>   κάτω διήσει,

φησίν, εἶθ' ἑξῆς·

>   ἵει δ', ἐφ' ἑπτὰ Πλειάδων ἔχων δρόμον.
>   τοσαῦτ' ἀκούσας παῖς ἔμαρψεν ἡνίας·
>   κρούσας δὲ πλευρὰ πτεροφόρων ὀχημάτων
>   μεθῆκεν, αἱ δ' ἔπταντ' ἐπ' αἰθέρος πτύχας.
>   πατὴρ δ' ὄπισθε νῶτα Σειρίου βεβὼς

---

[1] scripsi: οὐκ codd.'

**83** Pseudo-Plutarch, *Lives of the Ten Orators*

Lycurgus also introduced a law to dedicate bronze statues of the poets Aeschylus, Sophocles, and Euripides, and to copy their tragedies and keep them in a public depository, stipulating that the city's secretary should read them for comparison to the actors who were to perform them, and that it should be unlawful to depart from this text in performance.

**84** Crantor quoted by Diogenes Laertius

Crantor admired Homer and Euripides far above the rest. For he said it was a difficult task to write in a tragic and stirring fashion using the language of everyday life.

**85** Plutarch, *On Listening to Lectures*

One could find fault with Archilochus for his subject-matter, Parmenides for his versification, Phocylides for the triviality of his sentiments, Euripides for his talkativeness, Sophocles for his inconsistency...

**86** 'Longinus', *On the Sublime*

(a) Euripides expends his best efforts in the tragic depiction of these two emotions, madness and love, and in these he is more successful, I think, than in any others, though he does not lack the enterprise to attack the other forms of imagination as well. Although he is not by natural bent sublime, still in many places he compels his own nature to be tragic....In his *Phaethon*, Helios, as he hands over the reins, says,

> 'See that you drive not into the Libyan air: since it has no moisture, it will send the wheels of your chariot downward...'

and what follows:

> '...but turn your course to the seven Pleiades.' When he had heard this, the boy snatched up the reins, and striking the flanks of his winged team, he set them in motion, and they flew off to the heavenly vales. But his father, standing on the back of the Dog-star, rode after, admonishing

ἵππευε παῖδα νουθετῶν· ἐκεῖσ' ἔλα,
τῇδε στρέφ' ἅρμα, τῇδε.

ἆρ' οὐκ ἂν εἴποις, ὅτι ἡ ψυχὴ τοῦ γράφοντος συνεπιβαίνει τοῦ ἅρματος καὶ συγκινδυνεύουσα τοῖς ἵπποις συνεπτέρωται; οὐ γὰρ ἄν, εἰ μὴ τοῖς οὐρανίοις ἐκείνοις ἔργοις ἰσοδρομοῦσα ἐφέρετο, τοιαῦτ' ἄν ποτε ἐφαντάσθη. ὅμοια καὶ τὰ ἐπὶ τῆς Κασσάνδρας αὐτῷ [fr. 935 N²],

ἀλλ', ὦ φίλιπποι Τρῶες.

5. τοῦ δ' Αἰσχύλου φαντασίαις ἐπιτολμῶντος ἡρωικωτάταις, ...ὅμως ἑαυτὸν ὁ Εὐριπίδης κἀκείνοις ὑπὸ φιλοτιμίας τοῖς κινδύνοις προβιβάζει. 6. καὶ παρὰ μὲν Αἰσχύλῳ παραδόξως τὰ τοῦ Λυκούργου βασίλεια κατὰ τὴν ἐπιφάνειαν τοῦ Διονύσου θεοφορεῖται—

ἐνθουσιᾷ δὴ δῶμα, βακχεύει στέγη [Aesch. fr. 58 Radt]·

ὁ δὲ Εὐριπίδης τὸ αὐτὸ τοῦθ' ἑτέρως ἐφηδύνας ἐξεφώνησε [Ba. 726],

πᾶν δὲ συνεβάκχευ' ὄρος.

(b) 40.2-3: ἀλλὰ μὴν ὅτι γε πολλοὶ καὶ συγγραφέων καὶ ποιητῶν οὐκ ὄντες ὑψηλοὶ φύσει, μήποτε δὲ καὶ ἀμεγέθεις, ὅμως κοινοῖς καὶ δημώδεσι τοῖς ὀνόμασι καὶ οὐδὲν ἐπαγομένοις περιττὸν ὡς τὰ πολλὰ συγχρώμενοι, διὰ μόνου τοῦ συνθεῖναι καὶ ἁρμόσαι ταῦτα †δ' ὅμως† ὄγκον καὶ διάστημα καὶ τὸ μὴ ταπεινοὶ δοκεῖν εἶναι περιεβάλοντο, καθάπερ ἄλλοι τε πολλοὶ καὶ Φίλιστος, Ἀριστοφάνης ἔν τισιν, ἐν τοῖς πλείστοις Εὐριπίδης, ἱκανῶς δεδήλωται. μετά γέ τοι τὴν τεκνοκτονίαν Ἡρακλῆς φησι [H.F. 1245]

γέμω κακῶν δὴ κοὐκέτ' ἔσθ' ὅποι τεθῇ.

σφόδρα δημῶδες τὸ λεγόμενον, ἀλλὰ γέγονεν ὑψηλὸν τῇ πλάσει ἀναλογοῦν· εἰ δ' ἄλλως αὐτὸ συναρμόσεις, φανήσεταί σοι διότι τῆς συνθέσεως ποιητὴς ὁ Εὐριπίδης μᾶλλόν ἐστιν ἢ τοῦ νοῦ.

**87** Quintil. 10.1.67-9

sed longe clarius inlustraverunt hoc opus Sophocles atque Euripides, quorum in dispari dicendi via uter sit poeta melior, inter plurimos

him: 'drive that way, now turn your chariot this way, this way'.

Would you not say that the soul of the writer is mounted with the rider on the chariot and that it shares with the horses the danger of this flight? It could never have produced such imaginings unless it had run in close competition with those celestial doings. He does the same in the speech of Cassandra[1] that begins

Nay, Trojans, famed for horses.

While Aeschylus attempts imaginings of a most heroic sort...still, Euripides from ambition to surpass him treads the same perilous path. Where in Aeschylus the palace of Lycurgus is miraculously rapt at the appearance of Dionysus,

the palace feels the god's possession, the very roof leaps in ecstasy,

Euripides expresses this same idea in a different way, making it milder:

the whole mountain joined in a single ecstatic dance.

(b) It has been abundantly shown that many writers both of prose and of poetry who are not by nature sublime, perhaps even pedestrian, while using for the most part words that are common and vulgar and suggestive of nothing out of the ordinary, yet manage, by the way they combine and fit these words together, to clothe themselves in dignity and distinction and to avoid seeming lowly. Among authors of this sort are Philistus, Aristophanes in some of his works, and Euripides to a very high degree. After the murder of his children Heracles says, 'I am stowed full of miseries and have no room for more'. The phrase is exceedingly vulgar but it becomes elevated by being in keeping with the fictional situation. If you put the passage together in some other way, it will become apparent to you that Euripides is a poet of composition rather than one of thought.

## 87 Quintilian, *The Education of an Orator*

But Sophocles and Euripides added far more lustre to this genre. Many people ask which of these poets, so different in style, was the

---

[1] Probably in the *Alexandros*.

quaeritur. idque ego sane, quoniam ad praesentem materiam nihil pertinet, iniudicatum relinquo. illud quidem nemo non fateatur necesse est, his qui se ad agendum comparant utiliorem longe fore Euripiden. namque is et sermone (quod ipsum reprehendunt quibus gravitas et cothurnus et sonus Sophocli videtur esse sublimior) magis accedit oratorio generi et sententiis densus, et illis quae a sapientibus tradita sunt paene ipsis par, et dicendo ac respondendo cuilibet eorum qui fuerunt in foro diserti comparandus, in adfectibus vero cum omnibus mirus, tum in his qui miseratione constant facile praecipuus. hunc et admiratus maxime est, ut saepe testatur, et secutus, quamquam in opere diverso, Menander.

**88** Dio Prus. (a) 35(52).11, (b) 35(52).15

(a) ἥ τε τοῦ Εὐριπίδου σύνεσις καὶ περὶ πάντα ἐπιμέλεια, ὥστε μήτε ἀπίθανόν τι καὶ παρημελημένον ἐᾶσαι μήτε ἁπλῶς τοῖς πράγμασι χρῆσθαι, ἀλλὰ μετὰ πάσης ἐν τῷ εἰπεῖν δυνάμεως, ὥσπερ ἀντίστροφός ἐστι τῇ τοῦ Αἰσχύλου ⟨ἁπλότητι,⟩[1] πολιτικωτάτη καὶ ῥητορικωτάτη οὖσα καὶ τοῖς ἐντυγχάνουσι πλείστην ὠφέλειαν παρασχεῖν δυναμένη.

(b) ὅ τε Σοφοκλῆς μέσος ἔοικεν ἀμφοῖν εἶναι, οὔτε τὸ αὔθαδες καὶ ἁπλοῦν τὸ τοῦ Αἰσχύλου ἔχων οὔτε τὸ ἀκριβὲς καὶ δριμὺ καὶ πολιτικὸν τὸ τοῦ Εὐριπίδου....

**89** Archimedes, *FGE*, p. 24, *AP* 7.50

Τὴν Εὐριπίδεω μήτ' ἔρχεο μήτ' ἐπιβάλλου,
δύσβατον ἀνθρώποις οἶμον, ἀοιδοθέτα·
λείη μὲν γὰρ ἰδεῖν καὶ ἐπίτροχος,[2] ἢν δέ τις αὐτὴν
εἰσβαίνῃ, χαλεποῦ τρηχυτέρη σκόλοπος.
ἢν δὲ τὰ Μηδείης Αἰητίδος ἄκρα χαράξῃς,
ἀμνήμων κείσῃ νέρθεν· ἔα στεφάνους.

---

[1] Reiske
[2] Hollis: ἐπίρροθος codd.

better. I naturally leave this question unanswered since it is irrelevant to the present topic. But certainly everyone must admit that to those preparing themselves for oratory Euripides will be by far the more useful. For he is closer to the genre of oratory in his manner of speaking (a fact for which he is criticized by those who regard Sophocles' tragic solemnity as more elevated); he is full of aphorisms, and as regards what is handed down by the sages, he is nearly the equal of the sages themselves; in speaking and in replying he is to be compared with any of those who were eloquent in the forum; but it is in the emotions that he is remarkable and in those that have to do with pitying he is easily the first and foremost. Menander admired him greatly and, as he often testifies, followed him, though in a different genre.

**88 Dio of Prusa**

(a) The intelligence of Euripides and his care in all matters to leave nothing implausible and carelessly done and not to make use simply of the facts but to treat them with all rhetorical power is as it were the converse of Aeschylus' simplicity; it is most political and rhetorical and can furnish great benefit to those who encounter it.

(b) Sophocles seems to occupy a middle place between the two, without the self-will and simplicity of Aeschylus and without the precise particularity of Euripides or his bitter atmosphere of political discussion...

**89 Archimedes**

Maker of songs, do not walk upon the road of Euripides, think not on that, a path hard for mortals to tread. For while it is smooth and easy in appearance, if someone walks it, it is rougher than the harsh thorn. If you in your scribbling touch the fringes of the story of Medea, Aeetes' daughter, you will lie below without a name. Leave these garlands alone.

**90** Hieron. Rhod. fr. 36 Wehrli, ap. Athen. 13.5, 557E [=Sophocles T 58a Radt]

φιλογύνης δ' ἦν καὶ Εὐριπίδης ὁ ποιητής. Ἱερώνυμος γοῦν ἐν ἱστορικοῖς ὑπομνήμασίν φησιν οὕτως· "εἰπόντος Σοφοκλεῖ τινος ὅτι μισογύνης ἐστὶν Εὐριπίδης, 'ἔν γε ταῖς τραγῳδίαις', ἔφη ὁ Σοφοκλῆς· 'ἐπεὶ ἐν [γε] τῇ κλίνῃ φιλογύνης'."

**91** Athen. 1.4, 3A

ἦν δέ, φησί ['Αθηναῖος sc.], καὶ βιβλίων κτῆσις αὐτῷ [Λαρενσίῳ sc.] ἀρχαίων Ἑλληνικῶν τοσαύτη ὡς ὑπερβάλλειν πάντας τοὺς ἐπὶ συναγωγῇ τεθαυμασμένους, Πολυκράτην τε τὸν Σάμιον... Εὐριπίδην τε τὸν ποιητὴν κτλ.

**92** Plut. *Vita Niciae* 29.2-3, 542CD

ἔνιοι δὲ καὶ δι' Εὐριπίδην ἐσώθησαν. μάλιστα γὰρ ὡς ἔοικε τῶν ἐκτὸς Ἑλλήνων ἐπόθησαν αὐτοῦ τὴν μοῦσαν οἱ περὶ Σικελίαν, καὶ μικρὰ τῶν ἀφικνουμένων ἑκάστοτε δείγματα καὶ γεύματα κομιζόντων ἐκμανθάνοντες ἀγαπητῶς μετεδίδοσαν ἀλλήλοις. τότε γοῦν φασι τῶν σωθέντων οἴκαδε συχνοὺς ἀσπάζεσθαί τε τὸν Εὐριπίδην φιλοφρόνως, καὶ διηγεῖσθαι τοὺς μὲν ὅτι δουλεύοντες ἀφείθησαν, ἐκδιδάξαντες ὅσα τῶν ἐκείνου ποιημάτων ἐμέμνηντο, τοὺς δ' ὅτι πλανώμενοι μετὰ τὴν μάχην τροφῆς καὶ ὕδατος μετελάμβανον τῶν μελῶν ᾄσαντες. οὐ δεῖ δὴ θαυμάζειν ὅτι τοὺς Καυνίους φασὶ πλοίου προσφερομένου τοῖς λιμέσιν ὑπὸ λῃστρίδων διωκομένου μὴ δέχεσθαι τὸ πρῶτον, ἀλλ' ἀπείργειν, εἶτα μέντοι διαπυνθανομένους εἰ γιγνώσκουσιν ᾄσματα τῶν Εὐρι-

P. *Miscellanea*

a. Hatred of Women[1]

**90** Hieronymus of Rhodes quoted by Athenaeus

Euripides the poet was a lover of women. At any rate Hieronymus in his *Historical Notes* says, 'When someone said to Sophocles that Euripides was a woman-hater, he replied, "In his tragedies; though in bed he is a lover of women."'

b. His library[2]

**91** Athenaeus

He [Athenaeus] says that he [Larensius] possessed so many ancient Greek books that he surpassed all those who were admired for their collections, Polycrates of Samos...and Euripides the poet...

c. Admiration of non-Athenians

**92** Plutarch, *Life of Nicias*

Some also arrived home safely because of Euripides. For, as it appears, the Sicilians, more than any of the other Greeks outside of Greece, had a longing for his poetry, and when arrivals brought samples and tastes of it, they learned them off by heart and were glad to share them with each other. On this occasion, at any rate, they say that of those who got home safely a large number greeted Euripides kindly and some related that they were released from slavery for teaching their owners all they remembered of his poems, and others that when they were wandering after the battle they received food and drink for singing his lyrics. So one should not be surprised at the report that the Caunians, when a vessel came into their harbors pursued by pirates, did not at first receive it but shut their gates, but later when they had enquired whether they knew any

---

[1] See also T 1.23-5, 1.29-30, 2.6, 4.13-15, and 5.6, Diphilus fr. 74 K.-A., and Athenaeus 13.81, 603E [=Hieronymus Rhodius, fr. 35 Wehrli].

[2] See also T 58 and 77.943.

πίδου, φησάντων δ' ἐκείνων, οὕτω παρεῖναι καὶ συγκαταγαγεῖν τὸ πλοῖον.

**93** Luc. 59.1

Ἀβδηρίταις φασὶ Λυσιμάχου ἤδη βασιλεύοντος ἐμπεσεῖν τι νόσημα, ὦ καλὲ Φίλων, τοιοῦτο· πυρέττειν μὲν γὰρ τὰ πρῶτα πανδημεὶ ἅπαντας ἀπὸ τῆς πρώτης εὐθὺς ἐρρωμένῳ[1] καὶ λιπαρεῖ τῷ πυρετῷ, περὶ δὲ τὴν ἑβδόμην τοῖς μὲν αἷμα πολὺ ἐκ ῥινῶν ῥυέν, τοῖς δ' ἰδρὼς ἐπιγενόμενος, πολὺς καὶ οὗτος, ἔλυσεν τὸν πυρετόν. ἐς γελοῖον δέ τι πάθος περιίστη τὰς γνώμας αὐτῶν· ἅπαντες γὰρ ἐς τραγῳδίαν παρεκίνουν καὶ ἰαμβεῖα ἐφθέγγοντο καὶ μέγα ἐβόων· μάλιστα δὲ τὴν Εὐριπίδου Ἀνδρομέδαν ἐμονῴδουν καὶ τὴν τοῦ Περσέως ῥῆσιν ἐν μέλει διεξῄεσαν, καὶ μεστὴ ἦν ἡ πόλις ὠχρῶν ἁπάντων καὶ λεπτῶν τῶν ἑβδομαίων ἐκείνων τραγῳδῶν,

σὺ δ' ὦ θεῶν τύραννε κἀνθρώπων Ἔρως [fr. 136.1 N[2]],

καὶ τὰ ἄλλα μεγάλῃ τῇ φωνῇ ἀναβοώντων καὶ τοῦτο ἐπὶ πολύ, ἄχρι δὴ χειμὼν καὶ κρύος δὲ μέγα γενόμενον ἔπαυσε ληροῦντας αὐτούς. αἰτίαν δέ μοι δοκεῖ τοῦ τοιούτου παρασχεῖν Ἀρχέλαος ὁ τραγῳδός, εὐδοκιμῶν τότε, μεσοῦντος θέρους ἐν πολλῷ τῷ φλογμῷ τραγῳδήσας αὐτοῖς τὴν Ἀνδρομέδαν, ὡς πυρέξαι τε ἀπὸ τοῦ θεάτρου τοὺς πολλοὺς καὶ ἀναστάντας ὕστερον ἐς τὴν τραγῳδίαν παρολισθαίνειν, ἐπὶ πολὺ ἐμφιλοχωρούσης τῆς Ἀνδρομέδας τῇ μνήμῃ αὐτῶν καὶ τοῦ Περσέως ἔτι σὺν τῇ Μεδούσῃ τὴν ἑκάστου γνώμην περιπετομένου.

**94** Arist. *Rhet.* 2.6.20, 1384 b 13-17 et scholia ad loc.

διὸ καὶ τοὺς πρῶτον δεηθέντας τι αἰσχύνονται ὡς οὐδέν πω ἠδοξηκότες ἐν αὐτοῖς· τοιοῦτοι δ' οἱ ἄρτι βουλόμενοι φίλοι εἶναι (τὰ γὰρ βέλτιστα τεθέανται, διὸ εὖ ἔχει ἡ τοῦ Εὐριπίδου[2] ἀπό-

---

[1] scripsi: -ως codd.
[2] Εὐριππίδου Wilamowitz: Ὑπερίδου Ruhnken

songs of Euripides and the men on board said they did, they allowed the boat to come to land.[1]

**93** Lucian, *How to Write History* 1

They say, my handsome Philo, that during the reign of Lysimachus [305-281] a disease with these symptoms fell upon the inhabitants of Abdera. All the population together caught a fever, one that was strong and persistent from the very first day. Around the seventh day a plentiful discharge of blood from the nostrils in some cases, or a profuse sweat in others, broke up the fever. But it brought their minds around into a laughable condition. For they were all out of their minds for tragedy and they uttered iambic verse and shouted it aloud. For the most part they sang individually the *Andromeda* of Euripides and they performed in song the speech of Perseus, and the city was full of these sallow and emaciated seventh-day tragic actors, reciting 'Eros, of gods and men alike the lord' and all the rest at the top of their voices. And this lasted for a long time until winter—and it was a cold one—came and stopped their raving. The cause of this, as I think, was provided by Archelaus, the tragic actor. He enjoyed high reputation at that time and at the height of summer, in a fierce heat, he acted the *Andromeda* for them. The result was that the majority caught fever immediately after the theater, and when they recovered later they slipped back into tragedy, since the *Andromeda* haunted their memories and Perseus with the Medusa was still flitting about each man's mind.

d. Embassy to Syracuse[2]

**94** Aristotle, *Rhetoric* and scholia

People are ashamed to refuse those making a first request of them since they have not yet been seen in a bad light by them. Such also are those who have recently decided to be friends (for they have seen one's best qualities, and so Euripides' reply to the Syracusans

---

[1] Cf. T 4.21.
[2] It is likely that the subject of this story was a different Euripides or someone with a similar name, such as Heurippides.

κρισις πρὸς τοὺς Συρακοσίους), καὶ τῶν πάλαι γνωρίμων οἱ μηδὲν συνειδότες.

schol: Εὐριπίδης πρὸς τοὺς Συρακοσίους πρέσβυς ἀποσταλεὶς καὶ περὶ εἰρήνης καὶ φιλίας δεόμενος, ὡς ἐκεῖνοι ἀνένευον, εἶπεν· ἔδει, ἄνδρες Συρακόσιοι, εἰ καὶ διὰ μηδὲν ἄλλο, ἀλλά γε διὰ τὸ ἄρτι ὑμῶν δέεσθαι, αἰσχύνεσθαι ἡμᾶς ὡς θαυμάζοντας.

**95** Plut. *Vita Lycurgi* 31.5, 59BC

λέγεται δὲ καὶ τῶν λειψάνων αὐτοῦ [Λυκούργου sc.] κομισθέντων οἴκαδε κεραυνὸν εἰς τὸν τάφον κατασκῆψαι· τοῦτο δὲ οὐ ῥᾳδίως ἑτέρῳ τινὶ τῶν ἐπιφανῶν πλὴν Εὐριπίδῃ συμπεσεῖν ὕστερον, τελευτήσαντι καὶ ταφέντι τῆς Μακεδονίας περὶ Ἀρέθουσαν. ὥστε ἀπολόγημα καὶ μαρτύριον μέγα εἶναι τοῖς ἀγαπῶσι τὸν Εὐριπίδην τὸ μόνῳ συμπεσεῖν αὐτῷ μετὰ τελευτὴν ἃ τῷ θεοφιλεστάτῳ καὶ ὁσιωτάτῳ πρότερον συνέπεσε.

**96** [Ion], *FGE*, pp. 157-8, *EG* 468-71, *AP* 7.43

Χαῖρε μελαμπετάλοις, Εὐριπίδη, ἐν γυάλοισι
Πιερίας τὸν ἀεὶ νυκτὸς ἔχων θάλαμον,
ἴσθι δ' ὑπὸ χθονὸς ὢν ὅτι σοι κλέος ἄφθιτον ἔσται,
ἶσον Ὁμηρείαις ἀενάοις χάρισιν.

**97** anonymus, *AP* 7.46

Οὐ σὸν μνῆμα τόδ' ἔστ', Εὐριπίδη, ἀλλὰ σὺ τοῦδε·
τῇ σῇ γὰρ δόξῃ μνῆμα τόδ' ἀμπέχεται.

was a good one) and those of one's old acquaintances who know nothing bad of one.

Scholia: Euripides was sent as an ambassador to the Syracusans to request peace and friendship, and when they said no, he replied, 'Gentlemen of Syracuse, if for no other reason than that we are but lately asking something of you, you ought to be ashamed to refuse us on the ground that we admire you'.

### e. His tomb struck by lightning[1]

**95** Plutarch, *Life of Lycurgus*

It is said that when his [Lycurgus'] remains were brought home lightning fell on the tomb. This scarcely happened to any other famous person except at a later date Euripides, who died and was buried near Arethusa in Macedonia. And this seems a great witness in defense of the poet for those who love him, the fact that to him alone there befell that which happened previously to the most god-beloved and pious of men.

### Q. *Epigrams*[2]

**96** Epigram falsely ascribed to Ion of Chios

Hail, Euripides, dwelling in a chamber of eternal night in the dark-blossomed vales of Pieria! Though you are under earth, yet know that your fame shall be eternal, equal to the everlasting charm of Homer.

**97** Anonymous epigram

This is not your memorial, Euripides, but rather you are the memorial of this, for by your glory this monument is surrounded.

---

[1] See also T 1.19 and 99.
[2] See also T 1.18, 63, 64, 66, and 89.

**98** anonymus, *AP* 7.47

Ἅπασ' Ἀχαιὶς μνῆμα σόν ⟨γ'⟩, Εὐριπίδη·
οὔκουν ἄφωνος, ἀλλὰ καὶ †λαλητέος[1].

**99** Bianor Bithynius, *GP* 1645-8, *AP* 7.49

Ἁ Μακέτις σε κέκευθε τάφου κόνις, ἀλλὰ πυρωθεὶς
Ζανὶ κεραυνείῳ γαῖαν ἀπηχθίσαο·
τρὶς γὰρ ἐπαστράψας, Εὐριπίδη, ἐκ Διὸς αἰθὴρ
ἥγνισ' ἐς ἀθανάταν σῆμα τόδ'[2] ἱστορίαν.

**100** [Euripides], *Epistulae*

1. Εὐριπίδης Ἀρχελάῳ

(1) τὸ μὲν ἀργύριον ἀνεπέμψαμέν σοι πάλιν, ὅπερ ἡμῖν Ἀμφίας ἐκόμιζεν, οὐ δόξαν κενὴν θηρώμενοι, ἐπεί[3] γε καί ⟨σ'⟩ ἀχθεσθήσεσθαι μᾶλλον ἢ ἀποδέξεσθαι ἡμᾶς δι' αὐτὸ ἐνομίζομεν, τοὺς δ' ἄλλους αὐτὸ δὴ τοῦτο καὶ μάλιστα πάντων συκοφαντεῖν ἐπιχειρήσειν ὡς ἐπίδειξιν οὖσαν τὸ πρᾶγμα καὶ πρόσχημα μᾶλλον εἰς τοὺς πολλούς, οὐ μεγαλοφροσύνην οὐδεμίαν. ὥστε τούτοιν μὲν ἀμφοῖν ἕνεκα κἂν ἐδεξάμεθα (καὶ Κλείτων δὲ ἐπέστειλεν ἡμῖν, ὅπως λάβοιμεν, ἀπειλήσας ὀργιεῖσθαι μὴ λαβοῦσιν)· ἀλλ' ⟨          ⟩[4] ὡς τὸ μὲν αὔταρκες ἡμῖν τε καὶ τοῖς φίλοις παρόν, τὸ δ' ὑπὸ σοῦ πεμφθὲν πλεῖον ἢ ὅσου ἥ τε κτῆσις ἥρμοζε καὶ ἦν ἡμῖν ἡ φυλακὴ ῥᾳδία.

(2) περὶ δὲ τῶν Πελλαίων νεανίσκων καὶ πρότερον ἤδη ἐπεστείλαμέν σοι δεόμενοι, καὶ νῦν δεόμεθα σῶσαί τε αὐτοὺς καὶ ἀνεῖναι τῶν δεσμῶν· οὐδὲν γὰρ ἀδικεῖν ἐοίκασιν ἢ οὐδὲν βλάψειν ἀφεθέντες ἔτι. μέτριον δὲ καὶ τὸ χαρίσασθαι δεομένοις ἡμῖν καὶ τὸ ἐλεῆσαι δὲ τὸν πατέρα αὐτῶν, γέροντα (ὡς ἔστι πυνθάνεσθαι) τῶν εὐγενεστάτων ἐν Πέλλῃ καὶ κατὰ τἆλλα δόκιμον,[5] ὃς αὐτὸς ἐλθὼν Ἀθήναζε ἐφ' ἡμᾶς κατέφυγεν, ἐλπίσας δύνασθαί τι

---

[1] λαλίστατος dubitanter Lloyd-Jones
[2] Gow-Page, e.g.: -σε τὰν θνητὰν σήματος codd.
[3] Herscher: εἰ μή codd.
[4] nonnulla hic intercidisse suspicatus est Herscher
[5] scripsi: δοκίμων codd.

**98** Anonymous epigram

All Greece is your monument, Euripides, and therefore you are not dumb but vocal.

**99** Bianor of Bithynia

The Macedonian dust of your grave covers you, yet fire-struck by Zeus the Thunderer you freed yourself of the burden of earth. For the upper air lightened thrice by the will of Zeus, Euripides, and sanctifed your monument to everlasting renown.

R. *Fictitious Letters*

**100** pseudo-Euripides, *Letters*[1]

1. Euripides to Archelaus

(1) The money which Amphias attempted to deliver I have sent back to you. This was not a quest for idle glory since I thought you might even be annoyed with me rather than approve of me for this deed, while the others would attempt to slander me for this very thing on the ground that it was ostentation and pretense before the crowd and no true greatness of spirit. Therefore for these two reasons I might even have accepted it (and Cleiton also wrote to me, telling me to take it and threatening to get angry if I turned it down). But <I decided against acceptance> since my friends and I had a sufficiency, while your gift is worth more than my property may properly be worth and more than I can easily guard.

(2) About the young men of Pella I wrote to you before and pleaded, and now too I plead that you spare them and release them from prison. For they seem not to be guilty of wrong-doing, or at any rate it seems they will do no more harm if they are let go. It is an act of reason to grant me this favor when I ask you and also to show mercy to their father, one of the most nobly born old men (as one can hear) in Pella and also distinguished in other respects. He himself came to Athens and sought refuge with me, thinking that I

---

[1] Most recently edited, with a German translation, by Hanns-Ulrich Gößwein (Meisenheim am Glan, 1975).

παρὰ σοί, καὶ ἐδεήθη ταῦτα ἐπιστεῖλαί σοι. ἀλλὰ μὴ φαυλότερος γένῃ περὶ ἡμᾶς ἢ ἐκεῖνος ὑπέλαβεν.

2. Εὐριπίδης Σοφοκλεῖ

(1) ἐκομίσθη Ἀθήναζε, ὦ Σοφόκλεις, ἡ περὶ τὸν εἰς Χίον πλοῦν γενομένη σοι συμφορά· καὶ ἴσθι οὕτω διατεθεῖσαν τὴν πόλιν ἅπασαν, ὡς μηδὲ τοὺς ἐχθροὺς ἧσσον ἀχθεσθῆναι τῶν φίλων. τὸ δὲ τοσούτου κακοῦ ἥκοντος περισῴζεσθαί σε καὶ τὸ τῶν συνόντων σοι φίλων μηδὲ θεραπόντων ἀποβαλεῖν μηδένα οὐκ ἄλλο τι ἔγωγε ἢ θεοῦ πρόνοιαν γενέσθαι πείθομαι. ἡ μέντοι περὶ τὰ δράματα συμφορά (ἣν τίς οὐχὶ κοινὴν ἁπάσης τῆς Ἑλλάδος νομίσειεν ἄν;) δεινὴ μέν, ἀλλὰ περιόντος γε σοῦ ῥᾳδίως ἐπανορθωθήσεται.

(2) σκόπει δ', ὅπως ἀσφαλεστέραν ἢ ταχυτέραν ποιήσαιο τὴν ἐπάνοδον· καὶ εἴ τι ἄρα ἡ θάλασσα ἢ τὸ κρύος παραχρῆμα νηχόμενόν γε ἢ ὕστερον κακῶσαι δοκεῖ, ῥαίσας τὸ σῶμα πρότερον ἡσυχῇ ἐπάνιθι. καὶ τὰ οἴκοι ἴσθι κατὰ νοῦν καὶ ὅσα ἐπέστειλας ἐπιτελῆ ὄντα. ἄσπασαι Χιωνίδην τε καὶ Λαπρέπην, καὶ εἰδέτωσαν ἡμᾶς οὐχ ἥκιστα καὶ ἐπ' αὐτοῖς χαίροντας ὅτι σῴζονται. Ἀντιγένην τὸν ἰατρόν, εἴπερ ἔτι ἐν Χίῳ καταλαμβάνεις καὶ μὴ ἀπῆρκέ πω εἰς Ῥόδον, ἄσπασαι (καὶ ἴσθι ἀνδρῶν βέλτιστον ὄντα) καὶ τοὺς Κρατίνου υἱεῖς.

3. ⟨Εὐριπίδης⟩ Ἀρχελάῳ [βασιλεῖ]

(1) ἀφίκετο Ἀθήναζε πρὸς ἡμᾶς ὁ Πελλαῖος γέρων ἅμα τοῖς ἑαυτοῦ νεανίσκοις, καὶ ἐγένετο ἡ ὄψις, ὦ βέλτιστε βασιλεῦ, ἡδεῖα μὲν ἐμοὶ τῷ θεωμένῳ τε καὶ δι' ὃν ταῦτα ἐγένετο, καλὴ δὲ καὶ σοὶ ἀπόντι καὶ φέρουσα δόξαν πολλὴν καὶ ζῆλον παρὰ τοῖς τε ἐπιτηδείοις τοῖς ἐμοῖς καὶ Ἀθηναίων ὁπόσοι εἶδον· εἶδον δὲ πολλοί, καὶ οὐδεὶς ὅστις οὐκ ἠγάσθη τέ σου τῆς φιλανθρωπίας καὶ συνεύξατό σοι τὰ ἀγαθά. περιῄει γὰρ ⟨ὁ⟩ γέρων οὐ πολλαῖς πάνυ ἡμέραις πρότερον ἐνθάδε ῥυπῶν τε καὶ ⟨κεκαρμένην τὴν⟩[1] κόμην ἔχων ἐν οὕτω πάνυ λιτῇ τινι ἐλπίδι τεθειμένος τὴν σωτηρίαν τῶν παίδων, λαμπρὸς ⟨δ'⟩ ἐξαίφνης καὶ μετὰ δυοῖν παίδοιν νεανίαιν, θύων τε τοῖς θεοῖς ἐμέ τε ὑμνῶν καὶ περιέπων, ὅτι σώ-

---

[1] post Barnes (κόμην ⟨κεκαρμένην⟩)scripsi

had some power with you, and he begged me to write this to you. So do not act less nobly towards me than he supposed you would.

2. Euripides to Sophocles

(1) Word has reached Athens, Sophocles, of the misfortune that befell your voyage to Chios. You must be quite clear that the whole city is of such a mind that not even your enemies feel less pain than your friends. But the fact that, when such a calamity had occurred, you escaped death and lost not a single one of the friends and slaves who were with you—this I regard as nothing other than divine providence. The misfortune regarding your plays—and who would not regard it as the common misfortune of Hellas?—is terrible, to be sure, but since you are still alive it can easily be put to rights.

(2) Take care, however, that you make your return journey with more safety than speed. And if it seems that the sea or the cold did you any harm, either at once when you were swimming in it or subsequently, let your body recover first and return home without haste. Know that affairs at home are as you would like them to be, and all the instructions you wrote have been carried out. Give my greetings to Chionides and Lapretes, and let them know that not the least cause of my joy is their survival. My greetings to Antigenes the doctor, if you find him still in Chios and he has not yet gone to Rhodes (know that he is a splendid fellow) and also to the sons of Cratinus.

3. Euripides to Archelaus

(1) The old man from Pella arrived at Athens at my house together with his sons, and the sight, my good king, was pleasant to me, who beheld it and was the cause of it, but also glorious for you in your absence and brought much fame and admiration from all my friends and from all the Athenians who saw it. There were many who saw it, and every single one of them admired your humane spirit and prayed for blessings on you. For the old man not many days before was walking around here in Athens unkempt and with his head shaven in mourning, so slender were the hopes he had of his boys' survival, but suddenly now beaming with joy and with his two young lads, sacrificing to the gods and singing my praises

σαιμι αὐτῷ τοὺς υἱέας, καὶ τὴν πόλιν τὴν τῶν Ἀθηναίων, ὅτι τοιούτους πολίτας τρέφει.

(2) ἐγὼ δὲ πολλὰ μὲν καὶ ἕτερα εἰπεῖν ἔχω, οὐ βούλομαι δέ, ἐπιδεικνὺς ὅσῳ πλείονα ἐκ τούτου σεαυτὸν ὤνησας ἢ ἄλλον τινὰ ἀνθρώπων, δοκεῖν διὰ τοῦτο ἐλάττω σοι χάριν ἔχειν. ὁμολογῶ δὲ αὐτός τε εὖ τὰ μέγιστα πεπονθέναι καὶ πειράσεσθαι τοῦ καλοῦ τούτου ἔργου πολλὰ πάνυ καὶ μεγάλα παρασχεῖν σοι χαριστήρια, ὅτι οὔτε τὸν δείλαιον γέροντα ἐκεῖνον, ὅτε ἠτύχει, τῆς ἐφ' ἡμῖν οὔτε ἡμᾶς τῆς ἐπὶ σοὶ γενομένης ἐψεύσω ἐλπίδος.

4. ⟨Εὐριπίδης Ἀρχελάῳ⟩
(1) καὶ τὰ περὶ τοὺς Πελλαίους, ὦ βέλτιστε Ἀρχέλαε, καὶ πολλὰ ἄλλα πεπολίτευταί σοι καλῶς καὶ πρὸς ἐμὲ καὶ πρὸς ἑτέρους ἐπιεικεῖς τε καὶ σπουδῆς ἀξίους πολλούς, καὶ οὐχ ἧσσον αὐτά, εὖ ἴσθι, ὅσα πρὸς ἄλλους τινάς, ἢ ὅσα πρὸς ἡμᾶς ἰδίᾳ πέπρακταί σοι καλῶς, ἐπιμελές μοι εἰδέναι, οὐ φιλοπράγμονι ὄντι, ἀλλὰ χαίροντι ἐφ' οἷς εὐδοκιμοῦντα πυνθάνομαί σε, καὶ χάριν σοι οὐκ ἐλάττω ὑπὲρ αὐτῶν ἔχω· οὐ γὰρ ἀφ' ὧν αὐτὸς ἔπαθόν τι ἰδίᾳ δεῖν[1] μᾶλλον ἡσθῆναι ἢ ὅτι σε τοιοῦτον ὄντα ἔγνων ἔγωγε νομίζω. ταὐτὸ δὴ τοῦτό μοι περίεστιν ἀπὸ παντὸς ἔργου, ὅ τι ἂν εἰς ὁντινοῦν τῶν ἐπιεικῶν πυνθάνωμαί σε καλῶς πεπολιτευμένον.

(2) καὶ μέμνησο τούτων, ὦ βέλτιστε Ἀρχέλαε, ὅτι τὰ μὲν ἄλλα οὐδὲν πλέον ἢ πολλοὺς πόνους καὶ πολλὰς φροντίδας ἔδωκέ σοι ὁ θεός, ἓν δὲ ἔδωκεν ἀγαθόν, δύνασθαι εὖ ποιεῖν οὓς ἂν ἐθέλῃς, θέλειν δὲ δεῖ τοὺς ἀξίους. καὶ τὰ μὲν ἄλλα ἐπ' αὐτῷ βουλομένῳ ἐστὶν ἀφελέσθαι, ἓν δὲ οὐδὲ βουληθείς ποτε ἀφαιρήσεται, τὸ πολλοὺς εὖ πεποιηκέναι. ὥστε εὖ ἴσθι, ὅτι οὐδεμία μείζων ἀνδρὶ γενομένῳ ποτὲ ἐν δυνάμει μεταμέλεια καὶ πολυωδυνία γίγνεται ἢ εἰ διδόντος τοῦ θεοῦ μηδένα ἔδρασεν ἀγαθὸν μηδὲ ἕν, βουλομένῳ δὲ δρᾶν πέπαυται διδοὺς ὁ θεός. ἀλλ' οὐ σύ γε ἂν τοῦτο πώποτε πάθοις, οὐδὲ ἀνιάσῃ ὅτι οἴχεται ὁ καιρὸς εἰς ἀνθρώπων εὐεργεσίας ἀνεθεὶς φροῦδος ἤδη καὶ πέπαυται παρὼν ὁ θεός, ἀλλὰ καὶ παρέσται μὲν ἀεὶ καὶ στήσεται κατόπιν ἀξίῳ γε ὄντι καὶ χρωμένῳ

---

[1] Aldina: οὐδὲν codd.

and honoring me for saving his sons' lives and the city of Athens for producing such citizens.

(2) I could tell you many other things, but I do not wish, in demonstrating how much more benefit you did to yourself by this deed than to any other mortal, to seem to be less thankful to you on that account. I admit that I myself have received the greatest benefaction and will try to give you many great evidences of gratitude because you did not disappoint the poor old man, in his hour of misfortune, of the hope he placed in me nor me of the hope I placed in you.

4. Euripides to Archelaus

(1) Both in the matter of the Pellaeans, most excellent king, and in many others you have acted well both in regard to me and in regard to many other good men worthy of your efforts, and I am not less concerned to learn, you may be sure, about the actions performed with regard to others than about those good deeds you have done to me as an individual. This concerns me not because I am a busybody but because I take pleasure in the renown I perceive you enjoying and I am no less grateful to you for these deeds. For it is not from the treatment I have received as an individual that I think I am the more pleased but because I have made the acquaintance of a man of your character. This same thing befalls me whenever I hear of any deed well done to anysoever of the good.

(2) Remember this, my good Archelaus, that in other respects God has given you nothing but a multitude of toils and worries, but one thing good he has given, the power to benefit whomever you wish, and you ought to wish to do this to those who are worthy. It lies in God's power, when he will, to take away your other possessions, but not even if he wishes to will he take *this* away: the fact of having done good to many. Therefore be aware that there is no greater regret and cause for pain for a man who has enjoyed power than that while God gave him the power, he failed to do even one good deed to anyone, while when he wished to do so God ceased to give him the power. This will never be the case with you, nor will you be vexed because the occasion for doing good to men has gone clean away and God has withdrawn his presence, but he will always

ταῖς αὐτοῦ χάρισι δεξιῶς.

(3) ἀλλὰ δῆτα, κἂν ἐπίσχῃ πνέων, πάντως ἤδη καὶ πόλεις καὶ ἔθνη καὶ ἰδιῶται πολλοὶ καὶ ᾔσθοντο τῆς σῆς δυνάμεως οὐ σὺν κακῷ καὶ ἔχουσιν ἀπόμοιραν τῆς σῆς εὐπραξίας. καὶ οἱ μὲν πόνοι παύσαιντ' ἂν ἐκστάντος σοῦ καὶ τὸ κινδυνεύειν καὶ αἱ φροντίδες, τὸ δὲ συνειδὸς ὧν τε ἔπαθον τοῖς παθοῦσι καὶ σοὶ τῷ πεποιηκότι αἰεὶ μενεῖ οὐ μικρὸν οὔτε κτῆμα οὔτε ἀπόλαυσμα, ἀλλὰ ἀρκοῦν τοῦτο καὶ ἐν δυσπραξίαις ἡδονὰς παρέχειν. ταῦτά τε δὴ παρακελεύομαι πράσσειν τε ἀεὶ καὶ μὴ ἀποκάμνειν, ὥσπερ οὐδ' ἀποκάμοις ἄν (οὐδ' ἔστι τις τούτου κόρος), τὰ δ' ἄλλα πράως ὁμοίως καὶ δεξιῶς χρῆσθαι τῇ παρούσῃ δυνάμει· καὶ γὰρ τοῦτο αὐτὸ οὐκ ἄλλον τινὰ ἀνθρώπων, οὐδ' ὅστις τεθνήξεσθαι παραχρῆμα μέλλων σοῦ κελεύσαντος ἀφεθῇ, ἐκεῖνον μᾶλλον ἢ σεαυτὸν εὐφρανεῖ τὸ τοιοῦτον εἶναι τὸν τρόπον.

(4) ἔτι γε μὴν καὶ τὸ τοὺς ἁπανταχόθι τιμῆς καὶ λόγου τινὸς τῶν Ἑλλήνων ἀξίους καὶ μάλιστα τοὺς κατὰ τὰς τέχνας σπουδαζομένους καὶ πάλιν αὖ μάλιστα τούτων ἁπάντων τοὺς ποιεῖν ἢ λέγειν τι κατὰ παιδείαν δυναμένους μετακαλεῖσθαί σε πανταχόθεν καὶ χορηγίαις τῶν ἐπτηδείων ἀφθόνοις καὶ ταῖς ἄλλαις φιλοφροσύναις τημελεῖν, ὅπως ἀπαλλαγέντες τῶν ἄλλων φροντίδων ἐπιδιδῶσιν αἰεὶ διὰ σὲ καὶ προΐωσιν ἐν ταῖς ἑαυτῶν ἕκαστοι τέχναις, καὶ τὸ τούτων ἀναπιμπλάναι τὸν οἶκον, ἀλλὰ μὴ κολάκων καὶ βωμολόχων ἀνθρώπων, καὶ τούτους θεραπεύειν αὐτόν, οὐχ ὑπ' ἐκείνων θεραπεύεσθαι μᾶλλον ἐθέλειν, ὁμολογοῦντα (ὥσπερ ἔστι πυνθάνεσθαι πολλάκις) ὅτι ἐπ' ἐκείνοις μᾶλλόν ἐστι τὸ σὲ εἶναι ὁποῖος εἶ καὶ τὸ τοιοῦτον ὄντα παρὰ τοῖς ἔπειτα ἀνθρώποις λόγου τυχεῖν ἢ ἐπὶ σοὶ τὸ ἐκείνους εὐτυχεῖν· ἐκείνοις μέν γε, κἂν ὑπολίπωσιν αἱ παρὰ σοῦ δωρεαί, καὶ πλοῦτον αὐτάρκη καὶ δόξαν εἶναι καὶ ἡδονὴν τὰς τέχνας—τίς ⟨σ'⟩ οὐκ ἂν ἀγάσαιτο καὶ μακαρίσειε τούτων ἁπάντων, καὶ μάλιστα ὅτι ὁμολογοῦσιν ἤδη καὶ ἴσασι πάντες εἰς τοῦτό σε ἥκοντα τῆς πρὸς τοὺς συνόντας σοι φιλανθρωπίας, ὥστε τὴν μὲν ἰσχὺν καὶ πάνυ σοι συμβάλλεσθαι, τὸ δὲ ὄνομα μηδὲν ἀντιπράσσειν τὸ τοῦ βασιλέως εἰς τὸ στέργεσθαι ὑπὸ τῶν φίλων;

be present and will stand behind you since you are worthy and since you make correct use of his gifts.

(3) But in truth, even if you cease to breathe, cities and peoples and private citizens have at any rate felt your power, not to their hurt, and have a share in your benefaction. The toils will cease when you are gone away and the danger and the worry, but the consciousness of the treatment they have received will remain forever with those who have received it and with you who gave it, no small possession and no small enjoyment but a sufficient source, even in adversity, of pleasure. I urge you to act always thus and not to grow weary, as indeed you will not do (for of this action there is no satiety), and to use your present power with equal mildness and propriety in other ways. And this very fact will give no more joy to the man about to die but released at your command than it does to yourself, the fact that you are that kind of man in your character.

(4) Further, the fact that you send for those among the Greeks who in any place have won honor or regard and especially those who are highly regarded in the arts, and what is more, those men most of all who can write or speak literarily; and that you care for them with bountiful supply of their necessities and with other kindnesses so that being freed from all other worries they may make continual progress through you and go forward in their respective arts; and that you fill up your house with them rather than with flatterers and buffoons and that you yourself serve them rather than being willing to be served by them, since you admit (as one can often hear reported) that it is more in their power that you are the kind of man you are and that you win from after ages the name for being so than it is in your power that they be fortunate, since they, if gifts from you should fail, have in their arts independent wealth and glory and pleasure—for all these accomplishments who would not marvel at you and felicitate you, most especially because they all admit and know full well that you have attained to such a degree of humanity that while your kingly power makes a great contribution to you in this goal, the name of king is in no way a hindrance to your being loved by your friends?

5. ⟨Εὐριπίδης⟩ Κηφισοφῶντι

(1) καὶ ἀφικόμεθα εἰς Μακεδονίαν, ὦ βέλτιστε Κηφισοφῶν, τό τε σῶμα οὐ μοχθηρῶς διατεθέντες καὶ ὡς οἷόν τε μάλιστα ἦν ἐπιεικῶς κομιζόμενοι συντόμως, καὶ ἀπεδέξατο ἡμᾶς Ἀρχέλαος, ὡς εἰκός τε ἦν καὶ προσεδοκῶμεν ἡμεῖς, οὐ δωρεαῖς μόνον, ὧν οὐδὲν ἐχρῄζομεν ἡμεῖς, ἀλλὰ καὶ φιλοφροσύναις, ὧν οὐδ' ἂν εὔξαιτό τις μείζους παρὰ βασιλέων. καὶ κατελάβομεν Κλείτωνα ἐρρωμένον, καὶ ἔστιν ἡμῖν σὺν ἐκείνῳ τὰ πολλὰ καί, ὅταν τύχῃ, σὺν Ἀρχελάῳ ἄμεμπτος ἡ διαγωγή, πρός τε τοῖς ἔργοις οὐδὲν κωλυόμεθα τοῖς τούτων γίγνεσθαι. ἀλλὰ καὶ πολὺς μὲν ἔγκειται ὁ Κλείτων, πολὺς δὲ ὁ Ἀρχέλαος, ἑκάστοτε φροντίζειν ἀεί τι καὶ ποιεῖν τῶν εἰωθότων ἀναγκάζοντες, ὥστ' ἔμοιγε μισθὸν οὐκ ἀηδῆ μὲν οὖν, ⟨ἀλλ'⟩[1] οὐδὲ ἄπονον δοκεῖ Ἀρχέλαος ἀναπράσσεσθαι τῶν τε δωρεῶν, ὧν ἔδωκέ μοι εὐθέως ἀφικομένῳ, καὶ ὅτι εἱστίᾳ με λαμπρότερον ἢ ἐμοὶ φίλον ἑκάστης ἡμέρας.

(2) περὶ δὲ ὧν ἐπέστειλας ἡμῖν σὺ μὲν εὖ ποιεῖς ἐπιστέλλων ἃ δοκεῖς ἡμῖν εἰδέναι διαφέρειν· ἴσθι μέντοι μηδὲν μᾶλλον ἡμῖν ὧν νῦν Ἀγάθων ἢ Μέσατος λέγει μέλον ἢ τῶν Ἀριστοφάνους φληναφημάτων οἶσθά ποτε μέλον. καὶ τούτοις γε ἂν ἀδικήσαις ἡμᾶς εἰς τὰ μάλιστα ἀποκρινάμενός ποτε, κἂν ὅλως μὴ παυομένους τῆς ἀναγωγίας αὐτοὺς ὁρᾷς. ἢν μέντοι τις τῶν ἀξίων περὶ Εὐριπίδου λέγειν τι ἢ ἀκούειν αἰτιᾶται ἡμᾶς τῆς πρὸς Ἀρχέλαον ὁδοῦ, ἃ μὲν τὸ πρόσθεν εἴπομεν περὶ τοῦ μὴ δεῖν εἰς Μακεδονίαν ἡμᾶς ἀποδημεῖν ἐπιστάμενος, ἃ δὲ μετὰ ταῦτα ἡμᾶς ἀπηνάγκασε βαδίσαι ἀγνοῶν, τοῦτον δὲ ἄξιον νόμιζε δηλοῦν αὐτῷ ἅπερ οἶσθα, ὦ Κηφισοφῶν· καὶ οὕτως πεπαύσεται ἀγνοῶν τὰς αἰτίας καὶ ἅμα, ὅπερ εἰκός ἐστι τὸν ἀγνοοῦντα πάσχειν, καταγιγνώσκων ἡμῶν ὡς φιλοχρημάτων γενομένων.

(3) οὐ γάρ που δὴ πορφύραν καὶ σκῆπτρον φορεῖν ἢ φρούρια λαβόντας ἐν Τριβαλλοῖς ἡγεῖσθαι ὑπάρχους καλουμένους ὀρεχθῆναί τις ἂν φήσειεν ἡμᾶς καὶ διὰ τοῦτο δὴ στείλασθαι τὴν πρὸς Ἀρχέλαον ὁδόν, ἀλλὰ δηλονότι πλούτου ἕνεκα. εἶτα πῶς ὄν, ὅτε νέοι τε καὶ ὅτε μέσοι τὴν ἡλικίαν ἦμεν, καὶ ὃν ἔτι ζώσης ἡμῖν τῆς μητρός (ἧς ἕνεκα ἂν μόνης ἐβουλόμεθα πλουτεῖν, εἴπερ ἄλλως ἐβουλόμεθα) οὐχ ὅπως ἐδιώξαμεν, ἀλλὰ καὶ ἀπεωσάμεθα ἐγκείμενον, τὸν αὐτὸν τοῦτον πλοῦτον ἤδη τηλικοῖσδε οὖσιν ἡμῖν

---

[1] Herscher

## 5. Euripides to Cephisophon

(1) I have arrived in Macedon, my good Cephisophon, in no bad state physically and after as short a journey as possible. Archelaus has received me—properly and as expected—not only with gifts, which I do not need, but also with kindnesses than which one could not pray for greater from kings. I found Cleiton in good health, and with him for the most part, and with Archelaus as occasion allows, I pass my time most agreeably, and there is no objection to my taking part in their work. But Cleiton is very pressing, and so is Archelaus, and they compel me always to think and to write in my customary genre. And so I think that Archelaus is exacting from me a payment—not unpleasant, but not without toil—for the gifts he gave me on my arrival and for the fact that he feasts me every day more splendidly than I like.

(2) As regards your letters to me, you do well to write what you think it interests me to know. But you should be clear that I have no more concern for what Agathon or Mesatus says than I had once, as you are aware, for the fooleries of Aristophanes. And you will do me a grave injustice if you reply to these men, even if you see that they let up not at all from their vulgarity. But if anyone worthy to speak or hear a word about Euripides should find fault with my journey to Archelaus, knowing what I said earlier about there being no necessity for me to go to Macedon but not knowing the subsequent circumstances that forced me to go, regard him as someone worthy to hear all you know, Cephisophon. And in this way he will cease to be ignorant of the causes and at the same time to condemn me—as is natural for one in ignorance to do—as greedy for gain.

(3) For of course no one would assert that I desired to wear purple or carry a sceptre or be a commander with a garrison among the Triballi and be called Viceroy and that it was for this reason that I made the journey to Archelaus, but rather, naturally, that I did so for the sake of wealth. But how can anyone reasonably suppose that that wealth which in my middle years and while my mother was still alive (the only reason I ever had to desire wealth, if I ever desired it) I was so far from pursuing that I even thrust it away when it was laid upon me—this same wealth is now desirable to me at my present advanced age, unless they supposed that my reason for winning

ἱμερτὸν εἶναι εἰκότως ἄν τις νομίσειεν, εἰ μὴ διὰ τοῦτο ἄρα πολλὰ λαβεῖν σὺν ἀδοξίᾳ τέ τινι ἡμετέρᾳ καὶ οὐδὲ ἀπολαύσει ἔτι οὐδεμιᾷ ἐπεθυμήσαμεν, ἵνα ἐν βαρβάρῳ γῇ ἀποθάνωμεν καὶ ἵνα πλείονα Ἀρχελάῳ καταλίπωμεν χρήματα;

(4) ἔτι δὲ δὴ κἂν[1] προσθείης ὅτι, ἐπειδὴ τάχιστα ἀφικόμεθα εἰς Μακεδονίαν, ὀλίγαις ὕστερον ἡμέραις τεσσαράκοντα τάλαντα ἀργυρίου διδόντος Ἀρχελάου καὶ ἀγανακτοῦντος, ὅτι οὐ λαμβάνοιμεν, ἀντέσχομεν μὴ λαβεῖν· τῶν τε ἄλλων δωρεῶν, ὁπόσα⟨ς⟩ ἢ Κλείτων ἔδωκεν ἡμῖν ἢ Ἀρχέλαος ἔπεισε λαβεῖν, οὐκ ἔσθ' ὅ τι ἐνθάδε ὑπολελείμμεθα, ἀλλ' οἴχονται αὐτὰ φέροντες, οἵπερ καὶ ταύτην τὴν ἐπιστολὴν φέρουσιν, ὑμῖν τοῖς αὐτόθι ἑταίροις καὶ ἐπιτηδείοις νεμήσοντες ἅπαντα. τίς ⟨οὖν⟩ ἂν οὕτω εὑρεθείη ἔτι σκαιὸς καὶ βάσκανος τὸν τρόπον, ὅστις ἂν φιλοχρηματίᾳ με θελχθέντα ταύτην ἀποδημῆσαι ὑπολάβοι τὴν ἀποδημίαν; ἀλλὰ δήπου ἀλαζονείαν τινὰ ἢ τοῦ δύνασθαί τι μέγα ἐπιθυμίαν ἐροῦσιν.

(5) ἀλλ' ἡ μὲν δύναμις ἡμῖν καὶ μένουσιν Ἀθήνησιν ἡ παρὰ Ἀρχελάου καὶ πάλαι ἦν (ἄλλως τε καὶ Κλείτων τοσοῦτον ἐδύνατο μέγα) τοῦ μηδέ⟨ν'⟩ ἄλλον ἢ ὃν προηρούμην ἐξ ἀρχῆς τρόπον βιοῦν ἐμέ, μηδ' ὅπου μὴ ἐθέλοιμι ἀποθανεῖν, τελευταῖον δὲ μὴ παρέχειν λόγους εἰσαεὶ τοῖς κακῶς βουλομένοις ἡμᾶς λέγειν. εἰ δὲ δὴ καὶ δυνάμεώς τινος ὠρέχθημεν, τί ἄλλο ταύτῃ τῇ δυνάμει ἢ πρῶτον μὲν εἰς τὰ τῆς πόλεως, ἔπειτα εἰς τὰ τῶν φίλων χρήσασθαι ἐμέλλομεν; ἀλαζονείας τε ἕνεκα πολὺ ἂν μᾶλλον ἐν ὄψει τῶν τε φίλων καὶ οὐχ ἥκιστα τῶν ἐχθρῶν δύνασθαί τι ἐβουλόμεθα. καὶ μὴν εὐμετάβολόν γέ με οὔτε εἰς τὰ ἐπιτηδεύματα οὔτε εἰς ὑμᾶς τοὺς φίλους καὶ οὐχ ἧσσον εἰς τοὺς ἐχθροὺς σκοπῶν εἴποι τις ἄν, οἷς ἅπασιν ἐκ νέου μέχρι τοῦ νῦν τοῖς αὐτοῖς κέχρημαι πλὴν ἑνὸς ἀνδρός, Σοφοκλέους· πρὸς γὰρ δὴ τοῦτον μόνον ἴσασί με τάχα οὐχ ὁμοίως ἀεὶ τὴν γνώμην ἔχοντα.

(6) ὃν ἐγὼ ἐμίσησα μὲν οὐδέποτε, ἐθαύμασα δὲ ἀεί, ἔστερξα δὲ οὐχ ὁμοίως ἀεί, ἀλλὰ φιλοτιμότερον μέν τινα εἶναί ποτε δόξας ὑπεῖδον, βουληθέντα δὲ ἐκλύσασθαι τὰ νείκη προθυμότατα ὑπεδεξάμην. καὶ ἀλλήλους μέν, ἐξ ὅτου συνέβη, στέργομέν τε καὶ στέρξομεν· τοὺς δ' ἐμβάλλοντας ἡμῖν πολλάκις τὰς ὑπονοίας, ἵνα ἐκ τοῦ ἡμᾶς ἀπεχθάνεσθαι, τὸν ἕτερον θεραπεύοντες, αὐτοὶ πλεῖον ἔχωσι, †διαβεβλήμεθα[2]. καὶ νῦν, ὦ βέλτιστε Κηφι-

---

[1] Herscher: καὶ codd.
[2] fort. ἀποβεβλήμεθα

great wealth along with a measure of personal disgrace and without the least enjoyment was so that I might die in barbary and leave more money to Archelaus?

(4) You might add further that a few days after I arrived in Macedon, when Archelaus offered me forty talents of silver and was annoyed at my declining it, I refused to take it. And of the other gifts which either Cleiton gave me or Archelaus persuaded me to take, not a single one have I kept here, but rather the bearers of this letter have taken them all to distribute to all of you there who are my companions and friends. Who could be found so uncouth and malignant in nature that he would suppose that I made this journey under the spell of greed? But of course they will allege vanity or a desire for great power.

(5) But even if I remained at Athens I had power from Archelaus for a long time (especially since Cleiton had such great influence), the power of living no other life than the one I chose, of not dying where I did not wish to die, and last of not giving a handle for all time to come to those who wish to slander me. If I had in fact desired a certain degree of power, to what other end would I have used it than first for my city's good and then for that of my friends? And as regards vanity, I would much rather have enjoyed influence under the eyes of my friends and especially my enemies. The truth is that no one who examined me could say that I was changeable either as regards my way of life or as regards you my friends and, to no less an extent, my enemies. From my youth up to the present day I have had the same men as friends and the same for enemies with the exception of one man, Sophocles. People know that in regard to him alone my attitude has been different.

(6) I never hated him, to be sure, and I always admired him, but I did not always love him as I do now. I thought he was a man rather given to ambition and so I looked askance at him, but when he proposed to make up our hostility I eagerly accepted him. And since the time of our reconciliation we have loved one another and will continue to do so. As for those who seek to sow suspicion between us so that, as a result of our falling out, they might serve one or the other of us and gain thereby, we have cast them off. And now, my good Cephisophon, I am sure that these are the men who

σοφῶν, οἶδ' ὅτι οὗτοί εἰσιν οἱ τοὺς περὶ ἡμῶν λόγους ἐμβάλλοντες εἰς τοὺς ὄχλους· ἀλλ' ὥσπερ ἀεὶ ἄπρακτοι αὐτῶν αἱ κακαὶ γλῶσσαι ἐγένοντο καὶ γέλωτα ἐξ αὐτῶν καὶ μῖσος, οὐδὲν πλέον ὠφλίσκανον, καὶ νῦν ἴσθι ὅτι οὐκ ἄπρακτοι μόνον ἀλλὰ καὶ ἐπὶ κακῷ σφίσιν ἔσονται. σὺ μέντοι εὖ ποιεῖς περὶ τούτων ἡμῖν γράφων, ἐπειδήπερ οἴει ἡμῖν διαφέρειν· ἀλλ' ὥσπερ εὖ ποιεῖς γράφων, οὕτως ἀδικεῖν σε φήσαιμ' ἂν ἡμᾶς ἀντιλέγοντα ὑπὲρ αὐτῶν τοῖς οὐκ ἀξίοις.

are sowing these reports of me among the multitude. But just as their calumniations have always proved useless and they have incurred only laughter and hatred from them, so be sure that now too they will not only be useless but even harmful to their authors. You do well to write to me about these things when you think they are of importance to me. But just as you do well to write, so I shall say that you do me wrong if you reply on these matters to those who are not worthy.

# PART TWO

# TEXTUAL DISCUSSIONS

# TEXTUAL DISCUSSIONS

## CYCLOPS

**52-4.** L gives στασιωρὸν, an accusative that doesn't construe. We have the choice of inserting πρὸς before μηλοβότα with Wecklein or changing the accusative to a vocative with Wilamowitz. The first means that the στασιωρός would have to be Silenus. But this is a rather vague periphrasis for him—as is apparent from the fact that other identifications have been proposed—and further it gives him a prominence in the operation that he does not clearly deserve: we expect 'Back to the cave with you', not 'Back to Silenus'. Wecklein writes, 'Stallwächter des Kyklopen ist Silen nach 29'. 'Stallputzer' would be more accurate.

There are objections to Wilamowitz' solution, but they are not fatal. Diggle, *CQ* 65 (1971), 42-4, raises two. The epithet στασιωρός applied to the sheep would mean that he was Homer's famous ram, but Homer's ram, according to *Od.* 9.447-52, never tarries on his way home. Diggle also questions the appropriateness of the epithet since 'we are talking about a sheep, not a sheepdog'. Neither objection is fatal. On Wilamowitz' hypothesis, the animal is the head of the flock in this play, and nothing forces us to attribute to him all the characteristics of Homer's ram. And while a sheep-dog would be a guardian of the flock, a ram, with fully developed horns and an instinct for charging, could also be so called without extravagance.

Diggle's text is also less satisfactory metrically than Wilamowitz's. There is period-end at 51 in L's text (hiatus) and again at 53 (catalexis followed by anacrusis).[1] The addition of ⟨πρὸς⟩ in 53 means that we have period-end at the end of 52, making four lines in a row. Elsewhere in this play two consecutive lines is the limit, and not even all of these are beyond the range of attack. (Lines 65-6, for example, should probably be printed in that order and dovetailed to give ^gl¨ / gl¨. See also on 661-2 below.) Period-end at 53

---

[1] For catalexis at the end of one line followed by anacrusis at the beginning of the next as a marker of period-end, see T. C. W. Stinton's important paper, 'Pause and Period in the Lyrics of Greek Tragedy', *CQ* 27 (1977), 27-66, rpt. in *Collected Papers on Greek Tragedy* (Oxford, 1990), pp. 310-39.

is justified by the pause accompanying apposition, and I have punctuated it with a comma. This text, with Wilamowitz' vocative, is defensible, but we could eliminate period-end here by a different colometry, dod$^d$ / dod¨: μηλοβότα στασιωρέ, Κυ-/κλωπος ἀγροβάτα. For dod$^d$ (=ibycean) see Aesch. *Cho.* 315, *Alc.* 244 (~248) and Seaford on *Cycl.* 73-4. For clausular dod¨ see 81 and also (with my colometry) *Alc.* 990 (~1001).

**60-2.** Transmitted εἴσω is implausible. Neither the grassy meadows nor the cave are plausibly described as *within* the crags of Aetna. Furthermore, neither L's ἀμφιβαίνεις (which doesn't scan) nor Triclinius' ἀμφιβαλεῖς is suitable, and, as Seaford point out, this prepositional prefix, attached to any verb, would imply some kind of encompassment, which doesn't fit well here. The prefix would look better on an adjective. Read Seidler's εἴσει and the first problem is solved.[1] Meadows and cave are no longer within Aetna. We also have a main verb, and one that, flanked by two genitives, could easily have been corrupted to a look-alike preposition. As for the ἀμφι- adjective we now require, Seaford's ἀμφίθυρον, though possible, is a touch irrelevant, for the number of entrances can make no difference to the sheep. To describe the cave as 'vast' or 'roomy', however, would be to the point, and Hartung's ἀμφιλαφῆ, though the corruption is not easy to account for, gives good sense. It remains to attach the genitive Αἰτναίων σκοπέλων to either αὐλάν or νομούς. In 130 Aetna is somewhere other than Polyphemus' cave. We must, accordingly take the genitive with νομούς, giving 'the grassy haunts of Aetna'. For the word-order, in which the main verb is embedded in a phrase belonging with the participle, see *Ion* 1069-72 and *Ba.* 530-2.

**73-5.** L's ὦ φίλος ὦ φίλε is without parallel, ὦ φίλος is an expression used seven times in Euripides (*Andr.* 510, 530, 1204, *Sup.* 278, *Tro.* 267, 1081, *IT* 830), and it is clearly genuine. It is also not hard to see how it could have generated its otiose companion by a supralinear gloss. Attempts to heal these lines that involve deleting ὦ φίλος are unlikely to be right.

---

[1] Willink arrived independently at the same conjecture.

Seaford points out that Βακχεῖος is nowhere else a noun, and this is confirmed from the TLG disk. We must either emend to Βάκχιε or find a noun for it. Since we are going to have to alter the unparalleled ὦ φίλος ὦ φίλε in any case, it seems better to leave Βακχεῖε unaltered and to try to find a noun, possibly one obliterated mistakenly when the gloss ὦ φίλε was thought to be a substitute for the word just to the right of φίλος. The phrase Βακχεῖος ἄναξ, which occurs twice in the Orphic hymns and once (parodically) in Ar. *Ran.* 1259, seems most apposite. Let us suppose that in the phrase ὦ φίλος ὦναξ[1] Βακχεῖε, the third word was obliterated by a gloss on the first two. If we then adopt Nauck's οἰοπολῶν, the rest may be left untouched and the whole gives sense and meter. For overlapping anapestic dimeters, cf. *Or.* 1434-5 and perhaps *Hip.* 1374-5. On the sense of ὦ φίλος, which I render 'Ah me', see M. L. West, *Glotta* 44 (1966), 139-44.

**149-56.** In 153-54 as transmitted in L, Odysseus' surprised 'What? Have you seen it?' can just possibly be defended in either of two ways. (1) Odysseus uses ὁρᾶν as a verb of general sense perception ('What? Have you perceived it?') and Silenus misunderstands him and supplies a more specific verb ('No, by Zeus, but I smell it'). There are parallels for this use of the verb in Alexis, fr. 222.3-4, ἅπαντες ὀρχοῦντ' εὐθὺς ἂν οἴνου μόνον ὀσμὴν ἴδωσιν, cited by Kassel, *Maia* 25 (1973), 101-2.[2] Still, the resultant joke is rather lame and seems like an unsuccessful attempt at creating in Silenus the linguistic naiveté of a Dogberry. (2) Odysseus' question relates to Silenus' καλήν, which he pretends to understand as 'visually beautiful'. This makes Odysseus into a βωμολόχος, whereas elsewhere he is played quite 'straight'. His joke is rather lame too.

Tastes in these matters, notoriously, are different, but I persuade myself that a slightly more amusing few lines result if we assume that ὀσμήν is the work of some overly literal-minded scribe 'correcting' 153 from 154 and that the passage originally ran as follows:

---

[1] This is Willink's improvement of an earlier suggestion of mine, ὦ φίλος ὦ Βακχεῖ' ἄναξ, giving ¨gl, alien to the meter of the passage.

[2] See also I. Waern, 'Zur Synästhesie in griechischer Dichtung', *Eranos* 50 (1952), 14-22.

Οδ. ἰδού. Σι. παπαιάξ, ὡς καλὴν χροιὰν ἔχει.
Οδ. εἶδες γὰρ αὐτήν; Σι. οὐ μὰ Δί', ἀλλ' ὀσφραίνομαι.

Od. 'There'. (Spoken as he pours the wine into a cup, perhaps at eye level so that Silenus might well not see into it.) Si. 'My oh my, what a lovely color it has!' Od. 'What? Have you seen it?' Si. 'No, but I smell it'. The joke is a little bit in the spirit of Old Comedy, perhaps, but not, I think, fatally so. Silenus is now the βωμολόχος and the spirit of his remarks is not unlike the extravagance in 553, where he says the wine kissed him because of his good looks. Such is his affinity for wine that his nose does the duty of his other senses. Alternatively, Willink has suggested to me φυὴν for ὀσμὴν.

**164-6.** Since μαίνομαι does not construe with an infinitive anywhere else in Euripides or, to judge from LSJ, anywhere else at all, Kirchhoff was acting intelligibly when he altered ἐκπιεῖν and ῥῖψαι to participles, and this is the text Diggle adopts: 'if I drank down a single cup of this wine and hurled myself from the Leucadian cliff into the brine, I would be mad', i.e. delirious with joy. But since 'I would be mad' does not immediately suggest joy, and since the two verbs seem rather to describe actions Silenus wants to perform, something along the lines of F. W. Schmidt's μαιοίμην or the Aldine edition's βουλοίμην (keeping the infinitives) gives better sense. (Though it is not found elsewhere in Euripides, μαίομαι is a tragic verb.) Paley's κἂν gives the right nuance, 'even a *single cup*' (cf. 473), and perhaps κἂν κύλικα βουλοίμην is the closest we can get. But if we had a choice, we might dispense with the polite optative: a simple 'I long' would be better. The ἄν seems to guarantee the optative, but careful readers of Greek will have noticed that in the development of the Greek language κἄν begins to take on the function of simple καί and is used where there is no optative verb for the ἄν to modify: see Smyth 1766b, who cites Soph. *El.* 1482: ἀλλά μοι πάρες κἂν σμικρὸν εἰπεῖν. (See also the examples in K.-G. i.244-5.) This tempts one to speculate that Euripides might have written ὡς ἐκπιεῖν κἂν κύλικα μαίομαι μίαν. If a verb attested in Euripides is preferred, we might write κύλικ' ἐφίεμαι.

**169-72.** The attempt to replace παρεσκευασμένου with a compound of σκεπάζω (παρεσκεπασμένου Hermann, περιεσκεπασμένου Jacobs) fails the test of sense. It may be true that maenads, as Seaford says, 'tend to *resist* satyric advances', but in a passage such as this such resistance can form no part of what Silenus wants. (In a more leisurely treatment Silenus might have said that coy resistance adds to one's pleasure, but there is no room for such sentiments in the basic and earthy description here.) That being so, we must reconsider what can be done with παρασκευάζω. Blaydes made the participle neuter, no doubt *subaudito ἐστίν*. This is at least possible, and I have printed it. At a drinking party such as Silenus imagines, you may grasp the woman's breasts at once. To touch her nether regions with your hand (i.e. with your hand directly on them) lies still in the future.

**198-200.** At *CQ* 33 (1984), 334-8 I drew attention to one of the commonest of Greek 'figures of thought' in which someone says 'It would be terrible if I did A on the one hand and B on the other', where only B is something terrible and A is put in merely as a foil to B. Here we have the same figure of thought, but the elements are reversed: the terrible thing, running from one man, is put first and the foil to it, standing bravely against a numberless throng, is put second.

**286-91.** Elsewhere in tragedy when two verbs, as in 287, are joined with τε καί and the first of them has an object preceding it, the object invariably goes with the second of them as well: see *Hcld.* 138, *Andr.* 672 (non-Euripidean), *Tr.* 468, *IA* 969; Soph. *El.* 1471, *Ph.* 671.[1] Here λέγομεν cannot take σ' as its object. Furthermore, καὶ λέγομεν ἐλευθέρως trails off rather lamely: what does 'speaking freely' have to do with 'supplicating'? Style and sense together are improved by writing ψέγομεν: 'We both supplicate you and give you our frank censure'. Rhetorically it is a good move, when you are about to criticize someone's behavior, to prepare the way with some such gambit as 'I fear I must speak bluntly'. And censuring is precisely what he goes on to do, describing the course

---

[1] This same principle seems to apply to other coordinated verbs as well: see *GRBS* 29 (1988), 116-17.

Polyphemus proposes to take in direct and damning terms. Odysseus calls himself and his men φίλοι of Polyphemus in view of the services they have rendered to his father Poseidon, rescuing his Greek temples from pillaging by the Trojans. Polyphemus, he says, proposes 'to kill them and make an unholy meal' for his jaws (289) and to spit and cook them and fill his belly and jaws (302-3), an action that qualifies as 'the gluttony of your jaw' and 'impiousness' (310-11). Even though these actions are only planned and still lie in the future, to describe them in those terms is surely ψόγος of Polyphemus, and Odysseus is rhetorically correct to call it so before engaging in it.

The corruption is a fairly common one: see *Andr.* 419, *Su.* 565, Soph. *OT* 338 (λέγοις Γ), *El.* 551 (λέγε R); Hartung's conjecture at E. *Su.* 565, and Dawe's at Soph. *El.* 1467; reverse error (apparently) at *Cho.* 989.

**320-8** (1) The asyndeton at the beginning of 322 is hard to explain. It would be slightly easier if τὸ λοιπόν were the subject of μέλει, but it seems clear from what follows (the understood subject of ἐκχέῃ) and from Euripides' use elsewhere (see Seaford *ad loc.*) that τὸ λοιπόν is adverbial and that with οὔ μοι μέλει we must understand Διός. That means the two sentences in 321 and 322a are about the same subject, Zeus, but the statements they make about this subject do not fall under any of the usual categories for which asyndeton is the proper expression, as can be seen if we attempt to punctuate at the end of 321 with a colon. Also Polyphemus' 'for the future' implies that he has talked about caring for Zeus in the past.[1] I have marked a lacuna before 322, e.g.

Ζηνὸς δ' ἐγὼ κεραυνὸν οὐ φρίσσω, ξένε,
οὐδ' οἶδ' ὅ τι Ζεύς ἐστ' ἐμοῦ κρείσσων θεός.
⟨ἀλλ' εἴ τι τοῦδε καὶ πάροιθ' ἐφρόντισα,⟩
οὔ μοι μέλει τὸ λοιπόν· ὡς δ' οὔ μοι μέλει,
ἄκουσον.

---

[1] These two points, asyndeton and the difficulty of τὸ λοιπόν, were made by Wecklein, SB München, phil.-hist. Kl. 1921, 5, p. 91. He conjectures οὔ μοι μέλει τὸ μηδέν, attractive in some ways but destroying the deliberate and rhetorically effective repetition of οὔ μοι μέλει at either end of 322.

(2) L in 326 has ἐν στέγοντι, for which editors print Reiske's εὖ τέγγων τε. This is fairly close to the reading of L but it gives clumsy style, doubtful sense, and questionable word-order. The style is too heavy in participles and—more important—their tenses and relationship are somewhat incoherent: '*taking* my water-tight shelter in this cave, *feasting* on roasted calf or some wild beast and well *moistening* my upturned belly, *having in addition drunk up* a storage-jar of milk, I strike, etc'.. It is not clear why ἐπεκπιών is aorist when the others are present. Furthermore, either ἐπεκπιών is an aorist participle explicating a present, τέγγων, which is awkward and hard to parallel. Or we must suppose that Polyphemus 'moistens' his belly by spilling things on it. But the liquid part of the meal has not been mentioned yet—this is dinner in the usual Greek style, with food first and drink after—and 'moistening' is out of place. It is all a bit of a muddle.

There is worse. Reiske can be forgiven for not reading Denniston on postponed τε (*GP* 516-18), but we cannot. Apart from cases where prepositions or articles are in the first position, τε in third or later place is extremely rare. Denniston cites eleven examples from tragedy. Of these Aesch. *Eu.* 559 is doubtful and Eur. *Alc.* 819 spurious. The remaining examples cannot be explained away, nor can πηκτοῦ γάλακτός τ' in *Cyclops* 190, but they provide no grounds for confidently introducing such word-order by conjecture. Reiske's contribution must be rejected.

Before we replace it, let us make an easy correction. In 327 ἐπεκπιών is remarkable in itself, apart from the difficulty of its relation to τέγγων. The verb is not found elsewhere in Greek literature ('drink dry on top of' is not that plausible anyway) and there is good reason to look with a kindly eye on Musgrave's εἶτ' ἐκπιών, which presupposes the easy and common uncial error ΕΠ for ΕΙΤ.

As for the rest, reason says that εὖ τέγγων τε is unlikely to impossible, intuition that the replacement for ἐν στέγοντι should be or contain a main verb. 'When Zeus sends his rain from above, taking my water-tight shelter in this cave and feasting on roasted calf or some wild beast I <e.g. fill to bursting> my upturned belly, then having drunk dry a whole storage-vat of milk, I strike, etc'. Since the syllable before γαστέρ' must be short, only a μι-verb like ἐμπίπλημι could fill the entire space. But if we supposed that the last syllable of transmitted ἐν στέγοντι was genuine, another approach suggests itself. We may take τι as internal accusative and find some verb that could govern both an internal and an external object. Good sense is given by expressions such as 'do a good turn to' (εὖ ποιῶ τι), 'bring some cheer to' (εὐφραίνω τι), or 'cause to swell a bit' (ἐξογκῶ τι). My choice, however, would be 'give some hospitality to' (ἑστιῶ τι). This is close to the reading of L (ΕϹΤΕΙΩΤΙ[1] read as ἑϲτεγο͂ντι) and gives suitably Cyclopean sense: the only guest Polyphemus sees at his meal is the protuberance of his own upturned belly.

(3) Line 328, together with the last word of 327, has been the occasion for some fantastical exercises of ingenuity. Seaford says that πέπλον κρούω, 'I strike my peplos', refers to masturbation, and he cites Catullus 32.10-11, 'Nam pransus iaceo et satur supinus/ pertundo tunicamque palliumque'. Catullus neither says nor implies anything about masturbation, and if we took this parallel at face value, Polyphemus would be saying 'After a big dinner I lie in a state of unrelieved sexual excitement'. Far from boasting of his ability to ignore Zeus and satisfy his own needs, he would be confessing his helplessness to satisfy those needs, for Catullus' 'pertundo tunicam etc.', far from being a boast of independence, is an urgent appeal to Ipsicilla[2] for immediate and much-needed relief.

Seaford, however, does not press the parallel in this way. Even though what Catullus does to his clothing he does, as it were, from the inside and without the aid of his hands, Seaford has his Cyclops say 'I strike my peplos', presumably with his hand and from the outside. The parallel, of course, now does Seaford no good. What is more, the expression is astonishingly oblique and coy. Two further questions: First, does a person wishing to relieve his sexual tension normally do so *through* his clothing, and if not, why is the Cyclops made to suppose so here? Second, how much noise does the procedure make, and would anyone even in the most extravagant and hyperbolic of moods compare it to the thundering of Zeus (Euripides) or even to the ritual breast-beating of mourners (Seaford)? This

---

[1] Ancient papyri sometimes exhibit EI for I even where iota is short.
[2] For the spelling of the lady's name, see A. S. Gratwick, *CQ* 41 (1991), 547-51.

editorial fantasy cannot be maintained.¹ Likewise to be dismissed as impossibly oblique is πέπλον κρούω (sc. ventris efflatu), 'I break wind'.

There are good reasons for thinking that πέπλον is corrupt. In Euripides the plural of this word is used to mean 'clothing' in general: *Hec.* 734 etc. The singular, however, usually denotes a woman's garment, an affair of many gathers worn over the upper body: *Ba.* 938, *Hec.* 468, 578, *Med.* 786, 949, 982. In the few cases where the word is used of a man's garment, all but the present passage show it being held in front of the face: *HF* 1205, *IT* 1218, *IA* 1550. It is not, therefore, the ordinary Euripidean word for a full-length man's garment, and although Deianeira uses it (*Trach.* 602) of the long robe she is sending Heracles, we may look on it here with some suspicion. Suspicion darkens several shades when we consider the kind of enjambment transmitted πέπλον gives: a comma or stronger pause before the final iamb followed by enjambment with the next line is very rare, a fact noted by Wilamowitz *ad HF* 280.² In brief, not only does πέπλον κρούω give absurd sense but πέπλον / κρούω is dubious Euripidean style and πέπλος is not the word we would expect anyway.

Musgrave's πέδον and Hartung's πίθον give better and still better sense respectively, but both exhibit the same unusual enjambment. Best in sense and style (and closest to the *ductus*) is W. Gilbert's πλέων: 'Then when I have drunk dry a full storage jar of milk, I beat on it, making a din to rival Zeus's thunder'. The speech thus lists the pleasures of food and drink and lastly (Q.E.D.) of defiance of Zeus à la Salmoneus, who also imitated Zeus's thunder by natural means. Sex does not belong in this discussion. Polyphemus' situation in this respect cannot be counted among the advantages he enjoys,

---

[1] For further examples of Seaford's peculiar fancies, see the review by D. Bain, *TLS* 84 (1985), 209. Seaford is not dismayed and adds more of the same in *LCM* 12 (1987), 142-3.

[2] If we leave out cases where the comma is one of two surrounding a vocative or other parenthetic expression earlier in the line (e.g. *Pho.* 431 and 576) and cases of 'Sophoclean' enjambment of ἐπεί or ὅπως (*Pho.* 1318, *Or.* 1161), seven prima facie candidates remain: *El.* 779, *HF* 975, *IT* 1435, *Pho.* 22, *HF* 593, *And.* 50, and *Or.* 521. The first three occur in excited questions and in the fourth, though the reading of the mss. is almost certainly wrong, we do not know what word was replaced by βρέφος and hence whether it belongs in sense to what precedes or what follows. The three that remain show that πέπλον is not impossible but are not grounds for great confidence.

and most Greeks would feel pity or derision for a man reduced to solitary self-communion. Only an extreme eccentric like Diogenes the Cynic could boast about the independence he thereby enjoyed. Here, finally, is how I print the passage:

ὅταν ἄνωθεν ὄμβρον ἐκχέῃ,
ἐν τῇδε πέτρᾳ στέγν' ἔχων σκηνώματα,
ἢ μόσχον ὀπτὸν ἤ τι θήρειον δάκος
δαινύμενος ἐστιῶ τι γαστέρ' ὑπτίαν,
εἶτ' ἐκπιὼν γάλακτος ἀμφορέα πλέων
κρούω, Διὸς βρονταῖσιν εἰς ἔριν κτυπῶν.

**340-4** Jackson's χαλκόν for λέβητα (getting rid of a split anapest and an unconvincing γε) is accepted by both Seaford and Diggle, but there are indications that Jackson picked the wrong word to attack. The vessel in question, called by whatever name, is not on stage and it has not been mentioned in the immediate vicinity. This means that τόνδε is almost certainly wrong. Furthermore why should this common kitchen pot, mentioned in passing in 246, be suddenly dignified with the adjective πατρῷον, as if Polyphemus, whose father, after all, is Poseidon, were reduced to displaying ordinary kitchen vessels amongst his *Erbstücke*? If these remarks are to the point, the upshot is that where τόνδε stands now there once stood a noun, naming an object suitable to be given to Odysseus as a mock guest-gift and deserving the epithet 'belonging to my father', and that for λέβητά γ' we should read λέβητά θ'.

Nauck, who had the same idea, suggested λίβα λέβητά θ'. But while 'my father's water' gives good sense, λίψ does not occur in Euripides. I suggest ἄλα λέβητά θ'.[1] ἄλς is 'salt' when masculine, 'sea' when feminine.[2] Though πατρῷος could be an adjective of two terminations and feminine, it is probably masculine here. The resultant ironies are heavy-handed and Cyclopean. Odysseus shall receive guest-gifts, fire to warm him (cf. *Or.* 47, πυρὶ δέχεσθαι), the salt that is the emblem of shared hospitality (cf. Archil. fr. 173

---

[1] In the forest of slanting lines represented by ΟΝΑΛΑΛΕ, ΑΛΑ was lost. A subsequent scribe filled in two syllables in accordance with his understanding of meter and adjusted θ', now rendered nonsense, to γ'.

[2] ἄλς, salt, does not occur in any tragic author. But that is because the *thing* is not named, not because this word is avoided. Salt is called Poseidon's gift and connected with hospitality in Lycophron 134-5.

W.), and a cauldron. The fire will cook him, the salt flavor him, and the cauldron wrap his limbs around, thereby answering his plea (301) for guest-presents and clothing.

In 344 Diggle, like many other editors, prints Scaliger's διαφόρητον. I do not find this adjective particularly appealing: neither 'wrap about your flesh *when it is torn in pieces*' nor 'wrap about your flesh *so as to make it torn in pieces*' seems inevitably and perfectly convincing, and I would especially point out that the violent rending of διαφορεῖν is hard to see in the act of cutting up with a knife and missing entirely from the process of boiling until tender. Seaford's δυσφόρητος is an improvement, though when the disadvantages of Polyphemus' guest-gifts are being conveyed elsewhere through irony, an unironically dyslogistic word is not particularly welcome. Since the last of these presents is an ironic reply to 300, where Odysseus had asked for the gift of clothing, it may not be amiss to look for the meaning 'ill-clad' here and write δυσφάρωτον. The word is ἅπαξ εἰρημένον, like all the other conjectures ever made here, but it is has analogies in Sophocles' ἀφύλλωτος and Euripides' λογχωτός, as well as in Callimachus' ἀπεδίλωτος. According to the variorum edition of Euripides published by A. and J. M. Duncan at Glasgow in 1821, this proposal was previously made by Barnes.

**370-1.** In view of 356-7, which call out for the analysis sp lk | 3 ia, we should try to produce a similar rhythm in 370-1. (Sp lk followed by unsyncopated iambo-trochaics occurs at Aesch. *Ag.* 160 ff., as Willink points out to me, along with the same rare 5 da we have in 358/373. Deliberate reminiscence is a possibility.) Wecklein's deletion of ὦ before τλᾶμον improves sense as well as meter, for, as Seaford shows *ad loc.*, ὦ τλᾶμον means 'O suffering one', while τλᾶμον is used to indicate disapproval: cf. *Ba.* 1184. Further in the line I have written ὅστε for ὅστις: ὅστε maintains a somewhat precarious existence in the lyrics of tragedy, and Porson thought of banishing it altogether. I have not found any instance of its being corrupted to ὅστις, but the latter is an obvious gloss on the former.

**434-40** Line 440 gives no metre at all and 439 give metre only if we are prepared to shorten the first syllable of σίφων, elsewhere long. Diggle addresses the problem of 439 by stylish and adroit rearrangement of words, τὸν φίλον χηρεύομεν (uel -ομαι) / σίφωνα τόνδε, but confesses bafflement at the rest.

Diggle's approach here is based on the sense 'I have been widowed (i.e. deprived) for a long time with respect to this siphon here (=penis)', and this is rendered plausible by the use of χήρα to denote sexual deprivation in Aeschylus, *Dictyulci* 824 ff. 'This siphon', accompanied by a gesture, would be instantly intelligible even if the word had never previously been used with this reference (and we have no other instance). Still, while the Chorus have alluded once in passing to their sexual deprivation (68-72), and while there is a passing reference by Odysseus to 'dwelling in Dionysus' halls along with the Naiads' in 429-30, it seems a bit strange that in answer to a peroration whose main features are (1) get far away from the Cyclops and (2) get back your old friend Dionysus, the Chorus imply that they are delighted to get away from the Cyclops principally because of their sexual deprivation. Perhaps the Chorus replied to Odysseus along these lines:

καὶ τὸν ἀρχαῖον φίλον
Διόνυσον ἀνάλαβ', οὐ Κύκλωπι προσφερῆ.
Χο. ὦ φίλτατ', εἰ γὰρ τήνδ' ἴδοιμεν ἡμέραν
Κύκλωπος ἐκφυγόντες ἀνόσιον κάρα.
ὡς διὰ μακροῦ γε τὸν φίλον θηρεύομεν
σίφωνα τόνδε κἀκφυγεῖν οὐκ εἴχομεν.

In answer to Odysseus' suggestion that they escape from the Cyclops and recover Dionysus, they reply that they have been on the track of 'that dear wine-siphon' for some time, a circumstance only hinted at in 112 but now spelled out in full, but have been unable to escape. (According to Prinz-Wecklein, θηρεύομεν was first suggested by Scaliger.) The phrase τὸν φίλον σίφωνα τόνδε refers with affectionate disparagement to the bibulous Dionysus, who is the most immediate topic of conversation. We now have a use of σίφων that is attested, for Hesychius gives as one of its meanings ῥυπαρὸς ἄνθρωπος ἢ λίχνος. It was evidently a term of abuse. 'Wine-siphon' is an apt metaphor for a person who is in one sense or another 'greedy', and while ῥυπαρός seems a bit strange, Dionysus in many representations of him deserves the epithet λίχνος.

**661-2.** The reading of L, τόρνευ' ἕλκε, μή σ' ἐξοδυνηθεὶς / δράσῃ τι μάταιον, gives unconvincing rhythm, analyzed by Seaford as dochmius and anonymous colarion? / reizianum.[1] In addition to the doubt raised by 'anonymous colarion', there is the further problem that pendent close followed by anacrusis means period-end,[2] and that is not welcome here. The Parisian apograph omits σ', and even though this ms. has no independent authority as a witness to the tradition, this omission gives adequate (arguably improved) sense and vastly improves the meter: gl¨ / ph. Both cola occur in the play: gl¨ at 41, 43, 45-7, etc. and ph at 658. For the sequence gl¨ / ph, see *Sup.* 1007-8, *El.* 188-9, *HF* 683-4, *Ion* 1229-30, 1242-3, *Hel.* 521-2, 526-7, 1336-7, 1454-5, *Pho.* 229-30, *Ba.* 880-1.

**689-93** In 690 Odysseus gives his true name, and Polyphemus in 691 reacts with surprise at it. 'The very same name my father gave me, Odysseus', says Odysseus as his words are transmitted in L. The repetition of the name seems surprisingly weak. (Contrast *I.T.* 779 where Iphigeneia draws attention to her repetition and gives it a motive.) Could it be a subsequent addition to the text?

The evocation of the occasion when Odysseus received his name suggests that Odysseus may wish to draw attention to its significance. The etymology given by Homer at *Od.* 19.407 ff. derives the name from ὀδύσσασθαι, a verb meaning 'to hate or be angry with' or (just possibly in Homer's etymology) 'to be hated'.[3] Sophocles, fr. 965 Radt alludes to this etymology and derives Odysseus' name from the hatred his enemies feel towards him. I suggest that Euripides did something similar but not identical here and that he wrote, e.g. ὅπερ μ' ὁ φύσας ὠνόμαζ' ὀργῆς χάριν. This derives Odysseus' name from the anger of Odysseus himself. Euripides has been concerned all throughout the play to recast his story and his hero in ways required by the Attic stage, where there can be no question of a great stone blocking the entrance and where the blinding of Polyphemus has to be remotivated. This he has done by giving him the character of a warrior touchy about his reputation and con-

---

[1] Dale dovetails and analyzes as doch + chor / pher.
[2] See T. C. W. Stinton, 'Pause and Period' (above, p. 145, n. 1).
[3] See W. B. Stanford *ad loc.* and in *CP* 47 (1952), 209-13.

cerned to make good any slight to it (198-200) and by reference to 'requital' (τιμωρία, 441), as well as by the suggestion (353-5) that Zeus is at work punishing Polyphemus by the hand of Odysseus. The vengeance once exacted, he has Odysseus give the etymology of his name, hatred or wrath, implying that this is one of Odysseus' leading characteristics. Odysseus then goes on to say, 'And it was fated (ἔμελλες) that you should pay the penalty for your unholy feast'. Names, in other words, are bestowed presciently and foretell what must come to pass.

To explain the text of L we can suppose a note above ὀργῆς χάριν read Ὀδυσσέα ἐκ τοῦ ὀδύσσασθαι ἤτοι ὀργίζεσθαι.

## ALCESTIS

**64.** F. W. Schmidt's πείσῃ for παύσῃ has some attractions, but on balance it is not likely to be right. What Apollo predicts is not Death being 'persuaded' or 'won over' or 'obeying' but being overcome by force: see 69. The line may be correctly transmitted: with παύσῃ, understand ἐχθροὺς τοὺς τρόπους ἔχων from 61-2. Or, if this is too difficult, with 63 intervening, one might consider ἦ μὴν σὺ παύσῃ, καίπερ ὠμὸς ὤν, ἄγρας: 'though you are ruthless, you will cease from your hunt [of Alcestis]'.

**98-104.** Diggle's ὅ for ἅ and Blaydes's πρέπει for πιτνεῖ restore sense up to the connective. Thereafter we must ask what we expect the sense to be. What kind of female hand is it that resounds in grief in a bereaved house? What shall replace οὐδὲ νεολαία, which does not scan and in which the second word is nowhere else an adjective and would not give proper sense if it were? We expect something like 'nor do the hands of her kinswomen resound'. We might hazard the guess οὐδὲ συναίμων / δουπεῖ χεὶρ γυναικῶν, or, since 'kindred hand of women' is good Greek hypallage for 'hand of kindred women', οὐδὲ σύναιμος.

**121-6.** In a passage which talks about what Asclepius could do for Alcestis if he were alive, we do not want 'only' to apply to Alcestis: 'Only Alcestis would have come back from the dead if Asclepius were alive' makes no sense. What we want is 'Only Asclepius, if he were alive, could remedy the situation'. Diggle writes μόνα, but this must be rejected. If transmitted μόνος is correct,[1] it goes with the apodosis and means that Asclepius must be the subject of both protasis and apodosis. We should note that two mss. read προλιπών.

The sense we require is 'Only Asclepius, if he were alive, could bring her back from the dead'. There is more than one way of saying this within the metrical constraints imposed, but προλιπεῖν ἦνεν, joint property of Willink and myself, does the needful with-

---

[1] Adverbs have been proposed: Hermann suggested μόνον and Wakefield μούνως. The second need not detain us: a check of the TLG reveals that neither μόνως nor μούνως occurs in poetry, the sole exception being *AP* 12.254.6. As for the first, Euripides does not use the adverb μόνον before 'if.' And if he did, one would expect it to go with the protasis, not cohering with ἄν and the apodosis.

out unduly extravagant change. For a closely related verb with an infinitive, see Soph. *OT* 720: κἀνταῦθ' Ἀπόλλων οὔτ' ἐκεῖνον ἤνυσεν / φονέα γενέσθαι πατρὸς κτλ. The corruption posited is in two stages: for προλιπεῖν to προλιπών, cf. *Hcld.* 228, 828, and, for the reverse error, *Alc.* 18, *El.* 804 (?), *Or.* 749. Once this had happened, 'correction' of the masculine participle to a feminine would be all but inevitable.

**204-5.** Diggle attempts to avoid the lacuna posited by Elmsley, but so many qualifiers tumbling over one another surely are grounds for suspicion: 'slackened, a wretched burden in his arms, but yet, though only a little, still breathing, she wants, etc.' Furthermore, καίπερ without any participle expressed is extremely rare in Euripides: only fr. 655.[1] So too is ὅμως marking opposition between two participles.[2] Better to take ὅμως with βούλεται and καίπερ with ἐμπνέουσ'. Just what stood in the lacuna this implies is impossible to know. The supplement I print, ⟨κεῖται, τὸ σῶμα δ' οὐκέτ' ὀρθῶσαι σθένει⟩ is one possibility. Greater prominence is given to δέ, however, if we suppose that the sense is 'But slack in limb, a wretched burden in his arms, <she is scarcely able to reply to her husband's exhortation>', for which the Greek might be <μόλις πρὸς ἀνδρὸς νουθέτημ' ἀμείβεται.⟩

**290-2.** One cannot prove with mathematical certainty that 291 has not been correctly transmitted, but it is possible to come just short of this. Note first that there are three parallel infinitives depending on the accusative absolute, κατθανεῖν, σῶσαι, and εὐκλεῶς θανεῖν. Most will find the repetition of the first by the third either puzzling, irritating, or suspicious. The first infinitive can be construed loosely as a consecutive infinitive: 'they were far along in life *so as to die*'. It is when we continue that the real trouble emerges.

---

[1] Even this is not certain. The single line of this fragment might have been followed by another containing a participle, e.g. οὐκ ἂν προδοίην καίπερ ἄψυχον φίλον / ⟨εἶναι δοκοῦντα τοῖς πολλοῖς ἐμὸν πόσιν⟩.

[2] At *Hip.* 358-9, οἱ σώφρονες γὰρ οὐχ ἑκόντες ἀλλ' ὅμως κακῶν ἐρῶσι, the opposition is not between two participles, one of them to be understood, but between οὐχ ἑκόντες (ἐρῶσι) and ἀλλ' ὅμως ἐρῶσι. Passages such as *HF* 100 or *El.* 26-8 likewise furnish no parallel.

The anaphora καλῶς μέν...καλῶς δὲ means that we must supply the same idea for the infinitives in 292 as we have in 291, but this means understanding καλῶς ἧκον αὐτοῖς βίου with both σῶσαι παῖδα and εὐκλεῶς θανεῖν. This is barely—but only barely—possible. For while one can say, 'They were far along in life so as to die', it strains language and thought more than a little to say 'They were far along in life so as to save their son and die a glorious death'. Length of years is not the natural predisposing cause for saving one's son and dying gloriously as it is the predisposing cause of simply dying.

The conclusion to be drawn from this would be considerably less clear if it were not for another fact: there is no good reason on the usual view of how the line is construed to use ἥκω as an impersonal verb with a dative. Dale says ἧκον αὐτοῖς = καίπερ ἡκόντων αὐτῶν, but she cites no parallel. Elsewhere in phrase such as τοῦ βίου εὖ ἥκοντι (Hdt. 1.30.4) the verb has a personal subject. We must conclude that ἧκον is impersonal because ἥκει=καθήκει, a usage illustrated by Soph. *OC* 738. The genitive βίου has nothing to do with the εὖ ἥκω τινός construction but must be given another function.

Dale admits the passage is puzzling and puts in a good word for Hayley's καλῶς μὲν αὐτοῖς ἧκον ἐκστῆναι βίου. This corresponds in every respect to the intuitions above: καλῶς αὐτοῖς ἧκον means 'though it well befitted them', βίου is genitive of separation with ἐκστῆναι, and when καλῶς αὐτοῖς ἧκον is supplied in the next line, the line makes good sense. 'Yet your father and your mother abandoned you, though it well befitted them to retire from life, well befitted them to save their son and die a glorious death'. The repetition is κατθανεῖν / θανεῖν is avoided.

The only flaw in this is the probabilities of transmission. Hayley's conjecture assumes that a suprascript gloss κατθανεῖν came to be written in place of ἐκστῆναι and the meter repaired by a simple transposition. But κατ(α)θανεῖν is not a glossator's word but purely poetic, and the likelihood is that anyone glossing ἐκστῆναι βίου would have written ἀποθανεῖν. Even if he had not, someone correcting the meter would have been more likely to change κατθανεῖν to ἀποθανεῖν rather than to rearrange words.

It is sometimes necessary to assume an obliterating gloss, a kind of corruption in which *ex hypothesi* the look of the transmitted letters gives one no help in recovering the original. But if other expedients are available, they may carry more conviction. I thought of κόρον ἔχειν ἧκον, good sense, but rather far from transmitted κατθανεῖν ἧκον; and also καταμελεῖν ἧκον, easily corrupted into the text we have but rhetorically perhaps not precisely what we want. Willink suggests καταφρονεῖν, easier still as corruption, but to my taste a trifle too Pauline. Others may be able to do better.

**313-14.** Is it natural—is it even possible—to say of a motherless girl whose father has remarried that she 'has gotten a wife for her father'? It does not seem so. The only one who 'gets' a mate in this situation is the widowed father. In view of this, it is tempting to write τοίας (Reiske) τυχόντος συζύγου τοῦ σοῦ πατρός, but this will strike most as too costly since it involves changing every word in the line but συζύγου. We should perhaps regard the transmitted dative as genuine, construe it with τυγχάνω in the sense 'befall', as at Aesch. *PV* 346, and write τοίας τυχούσης συζύγου τῷ σῷ πατρί, 'if a wife of this kind should fall to your father's lot'.

**527.** 'The one who is doomed to die is dead already', says Admetus. He intends that Heracles should understand this as 'one who has promised to die is as good as dead', while to himself it means 'she who has promised to die has in fact died'. This is the only point the line should make, and when the two halves of our tradition, each in its separate way, go on to say 'and one who is dead is no more', they weaken the substantive point Admetus is making by adding a mere tautology. Jackson saw this clearly, and his solution was to write κἀνθάδ' ὢν οὐκ ἔστ' ἔτι for L's χὠ θανὼν οὐκ ἔστ' ἔτι. But this is not perfectly convincing: Jackson's parallel for this use of ἐνθάδε = 'among the living' is a corrupt line (*Hel.* 1225) and no others are available. And it would not be utterly fastidious to complain that the antithesis 'although he is here he is non-existent' lacks crispness. For goods of this quality, I suggest, one should not be willing to pay the high price Jackson's changes exact in paleographical implausibility.

The slightest possible change also gives the simplest sense, as Schwartz saw long ago. Read καὶ for χὠ: 'The one doomed to die is dead and having died is no more'. This merely elaborates the point in the first half of the line. Such plenitude of expression is not unheard of in tragic stichomythia, where the length of each speech is invariable but the idea to be expressed may need no more than a word or half a line.

**673-5.** At 674 Diggle's apparatus reads 'ὦ παῖ suspectum'. *Et pour cause*. First, 675 begins with the same words. If ὦ παῖ in 674 were genuine, the repetition of those words by Pheres would have to be an echo of the chorus-leader's words. But the echo would have no point, and, what is more significant, the two- or four-line choral 'buffers' that stand between the *rheseis* of so many tragic *agones* are never in Euripides alluded or adverted to by the next speaker. Even strong suggestions, like *Andr.* 423-4, are ignored.

The same conclusion is made inevitable by a further fact. In the whole of tragedy, one speaker addresses another who not a slave with the vocative παῖ or τέκνον (without a defining genitive or equivalent) only if (a) he or she is the parent or grandparent or other older relative of the addressee (e.g. *Ba.* 329); (b) he or she is a household servant addressing a young family member (e.g. *Hip.* 211); or (c) he or she is noticeably an old person and the addressee noticeably a young person (e.g. *Hcld.* 380).[1] None of these is the case here. For the chorus-leader, who is not portrayed as an old man, to address Admetus, who is in his prime and is furthermore his sovereign, as 'my son' would be inconceivably patronizing. The source of these offending words is all too plain, the eye of a scribe wandering to the line below. The case against these words would hardly be stronger if a papyrus turned up with a variant that made sense.

---

[1] The few exceptions are sufficiently different from the present case that they do not undermine the point being made. At E. *El.* 197, *Hel.* 1355, and S. *El.* 251 the Chorus are not old, but Electra and Helen are young. Both, in any case, are female, and one might expect that where addressing a male and a king in his prime as 'my son' would be bad form, the same tendency that allows one to refer to a full-grown woman as a κόρη might be operative here as well. In Sophocles' *Electra*, the heroine addresses her younger brother, dead as she imagines, in this way, as well as the young man, Orestes in fact, who bears his urn. The context of E. fr. *889a.1 in which a speaker addresses someone as ὦ παῖ and then admits he is an old man, is unknown. The same rules apply to the vocative (ὦ) τέκνον.

Under normal circumstances, when a word or words are obliterated by an accident like this, it is impossible to discover with any certainty what the author originally wrote. In this case, however, we can restore the beginning of 674 with near certainty, for the paradoxical reason that there is corruption in the previous line. It is a virtual certainty that παύσασθ', the transmitted first word of 673, is wrong. Consider the situation. Pheres makes his entrance bearing adornments for the corpse of Alcestis and comments on the nobility of her sacrifice. To this Admetus replies in these terms: you were not invited to this funeral; you are no φίλος of mine; you are not my father, and I must have been a suppositious child; you should have died since you had little time left in any case and have had all the goods that life has to offer; I was a dutiful son and this is the way you treat me; better hurry up and beget another son for I shall not care for you in your old age. When two speeches have been delivered, one polite and perfectly in order, the other in extremely bad form, shall the chorus-leader say 'Stop, both of you'? It may be urged that the chorus-leader is trying to be tactful and to distribute blame evenly so that both parties will find it easier to step down. It may be urged that 'Stop!' addressed to Pheres means 'halt before you get started'. But it seems odd to address the same command to two people with such different meanings as 'cease from what you are doing' and 'don't begin'. Furthermore, there are no other examples in Euripides where παῦσαι, παύσασθε, or the like means 'don't begin'. Usual procedure for chorus-leaders in similar situations may be judged by *Andr.* 642-3 and 691-2, where after the first intemperate speech the chorus addresses its moderating words to the first speaker, and after the second to them both, and by *Alc.* 706-7, where after the second angry speech the chorus-leader alludes to both of the speeches but addresses its admonition to the second speaker.

What Euripides wrote at the beginning of 673 must remain uncertain, but the beginning of 674 is, unless I deceive myself, recoverable with a high degree of certainty. We begin with an intuition, shared by Paley in print and by Diggle in a conversation with me, that the first word of 674 must cohere with what precedes, not with what follows, and therefore ἅλις γὰρ ἡ παροῦσα συμφορά is to be taken διὰ μέσου, parenthetic between the first word of 673 and that of 674.[1] We may take it as certain that if any command to stop was issued, it was in the singular. Since there is only one place for such a command to go, given the soundness of most of the words in 673-4, we arrive at a text where only the first word of all remains in any doubt and whence the genesis of the readings of our mss. can be easily explained. I give the text as it must have looked at an intermediate stage.

νεικῶν ἅλις γὰρ ἡ παροῦσα συμφορά
παῦσαι
ὦ παῖ, πατρὸς δὲ μὴ παροξύνῃς φρένας.

Some corrector, realizing that ὦ παῖ in 674 had been miscopied from the following line, consulted the original and copied the correct word above the line. But he may have written it too high in the space, and as a result a later scribe took it for the replacement for the word above it, νεικῶν in my conjectural restoration. Once it had been copied there, the hiatus would have been 'corrected' by making it plural. For a similar thought, likewise expressed by a similar construction interrupted by a parenthesis, see *And.* 691-2: παύσασθον ἤδη—λῷστα γὰρ μακρῷ τάδε—λόγων ματαίων, μὴ δύο σφαλῆθ' ἅμα.

**811.** Dale justifies her conjecture ὀθνεῖος on several grounds, not all of them capable of withstanding scrutiny. (1) The Servant's οἰκεῖος gives the show away too soon. Here one may counter by saying that while telling Heracles that the woman was οἰκεῖος *tout court* would have given the game away, the two adverbs of degree, κάρτα and λίαν, introduce an element of uncertainty. Heracles is told that the woman is 'very much, all too well' connected to the house, and he may well think that some other sort of propinquity obtains than the straightforward and objective tie of marriage, which admits of no degrees. (2) The combination ἦ...μέντοι 'is emphatic affirmative, not the equivalent of μὲν οὖν'. But our passage in the only instance of this rare combination cited by Denniston, and it is hard to exclude the possibility that there is some adversative force in the μέντοι here. (3) 'The corruption of θυραῖος to the lit-

---

[1] Paley *ad loc.* prints the text of the mss. and punctuates so that ὦ παῖ goes with παύσασθ', unlikely to impossible as grammar, impeccable as intuition.

eral-minded οἰκεῖος is likely; not so the reverse.' Hence, the arguments goes, οἰκεῖος must be secondary, and though θυραῖος could be right, we might expect ὀθνεῖος after 810. But in fact corruption could have happened in either direction, either as an unconscious 'polar error' or by a misunderstanding of the point: if a scribe thought the Servant was keeping up the deceit of Heracles, he might feel, as Dale did, that οἰκεῖος gives the show away too soon. It is slightly, but only slightly, easier to imagine the corruption as Dale does, but when we take into account the sense of the whole, the merits of οἰκεῖος are superior: 'she was very closely, all too closely, tied to this house' is better than 'she was very much, all too much, a stranger', not only because such irony is foreign to the tragic servant but because it doesn't work very well as irony.

**829-34.** See *GRBS* 29 (1988), 115-16.

**1037-40.** See *GRBS* 29 (1988), 116-17.

## MEDEA

**6-15.** See *CQ* 41 (1991), 30-5.

**234.** Diggle prints Brunck's τοῦτ' ἔτ', but I simply do not see what sense the result has: if forced to translate, I would have to render it 'this bane is still more painful than a bane', and few will believe that this is what Euripides meant Medea to say. I have daggered the passage, since attempts by me and others at emendation involve implausible corruption.[1]

And yet unless I deceive myself the elements of a very attractive solution are already there in Diggle's apparatus. Diggle defends his own text with the words 'cf. S. OT 1365-6', lines which I transcribe here for the reader's convenience: εἰ δέ τι πρεσβύτερον ἔτι κακοῦ κακόν, / τοῦτ' ἔλαχ' Οἰδίπους. These lines impugn rather than defend Diggle's text, for in a construction like that illustrated by Horace's *est ut viro vir latius imperet*, it is fatal to have one of the words modified by a demonstrative and the other unmodified.[2] Yet the Sophocles parallel is suggestive: Medea might be comparing bane with bane and maintaining that the loss of money together with the acquiring of a master is a calamity beyond the common run. The demonstrative that stands in the way of our achieving this meaning is transmitted in some mss. in the nominative (τοῦτο) and in others as a genitive (τοῦδε). Let us give it another case and then spell out why trouble differs from trouble:

κακοῦ γὰρ τῷδ' ἔτ' (or τῷδέ γ') ἄλγιον κακόν,
⟨ἐὰν παραιρῇ χρήμαθ' ὑβρίσῃ θ' ἅμα.⟩

It is simple to account for the reading of LP, κακοῦ γὰρ τοῦδε, on this theory: one of the commonest of scribal errors is the adjustment of endings to agree mistakenly with neighboring words.

One puzzle remains unsolved: how did τῷδ' ἔτ' or τοῦδ' ἔτ' give rise to τοῦτ' or τοῦτό γ' in the rest of the tradition. I cannot say,

---

[1] We might suppose that Medea means 'What calamity could be more painful than this?' and that Euripides wrote τί γὰρ τοῦδ' ἐστὶν ἄλγιον κακόν; But to explain such a corruption would be difficult indeed.

[2] For proof of this intuitive certainty, see B. Gygli-Wyss, *Das nominale Polyptoton im älteren Griechisch* Göttingen, 1966), pp. 54-64.

but I note that the reverse transformation, presupposed by Diggle, is equally hard to explain.

**240.** In 235-7 Medea's point is that a woman has a lot riding on the decision, normally made for her, whom she is to marry: she can't easily or creditably get rid of a husband once she has married him, and simply sitting out of the game, refusing marriage, is not an option.[1] But in 238-40 she has moved on to a different point, that when she has left her father's house and entered her husband's she will need to be a prophet. What she will need to divine is not what kind of husband she is going to have (Diggle, reading Musgrave's οἵῳ), for she will find that out soon enough, and at this point, since she is already married, divining it in advance will do her no good. Rather, as the reference to her changed circumstances suggest, she needs to know how to get along with her new husband, how to treat him. Meineke's ὅπως for transmitted ὅτῳ is inevitable. But none of the senses of μάλιστα is perfectly persuasive here. If we replace it by ἄριστα (Page), we supply the missing deliberative idea: cf. S. *OT* 407.

**294-306.** 304 has long been bracketed by editors. It was accidentally omitted from A but supplied, presumably from the exemplar, by the rubricator. Its omission therefore tells far less heavily against its genuineness than does its close resemblance to 808 together with its lack of any positive contribution to the sense.[2] But 305 is likewise an interruption to the business at hand. Medea is and claims to be wise (303), and it is her contention that the wise are suspect. She can gain little or nothing by saying εἰμὶ δ' οὐκ ἄγαν σοφή, taking back the whole supposition on which her argument is based. These words too are close to a half line elsewhere: cf. 583, ἔστι δ' οὐκ ἄγαν σοφός.

Without these two lines there is a stronger connection between the generalities Medea starts with and her application of those generalities to herself. In 296-301 she mentions two sorts of φθόνος the

---

[1] ἀνήνασθαι πόσιν could mean either 'reject marriage' or 'reject the husband provided for her'.

[2] Note that homoearkton (τοῖς δ', τοῖς δ') could have caused a copyist who had 304 in his exemplar to omit it. The chances that A in omitting 304 is handing on old tradition seem slim.

wise man receives: ordinary fools think him useless, while those with a reputation for some kind of pre-eminence find a wise man λυπρός. This applies to Medea:

σοφὴ γὰρ οὖσα τοῖς μέν εἰμ' ἐπίφθονος,
σὺ δ' αὖ φοβῇ με.

Here again the many are contrasted with the few. In the eyes of some, Medea incurs ill-will, but Creon, who is pre-eminent, is afraid of her. The language is a bit vague and inexact because Medea's rhetorical purpose requires her to suggest, without saying explicitly, that Creon's fear of Medea is nothing more than the expert's fear and resentment of challenge to his superiority.

**357-61.** See *TAPA* 117 (1987), 267-8.

**364-7.** There is a direct and blatant contradiction between 364 and 365 as is evident in a translation: 'Things are badly off in every way: who will deny it? But these things are not at all this way, do not imagine it.' 'This way' in the context can only mean κακῶς, and therefore 364 asserts, and 365 denies, that the situation is terrible. There would be no contradiction, however, if the first sentence referred to the present and the second to the future, as the sequel suggests. We cannot supply ἔσται in 365. Read therefore:

κακῶς πέπρακται πανταχῇ· τίς ἀντερεῖ;
ἀλλ' οὔτι ταύτῃ ταῦτα, μὴ δοκεῖτέ πω,
⟨μέλλει τελευτᾶν εἴ τι τῇ τέχνῃ σθένω⟩.
ἔτ' εἴσ' ἀγῶνες τοῖς νεωστὶ νυμφίοις κτλ.

The next word is ἔτι, and the subject is the future. Note the asyndeton of 366, marking the strong causal or logical relation with what precedes. Since 366-7 refer to the future, so should 365.

**496-7.** Both Page and Diggle, like Murray before them, put a comma at the end of this line, but this means either construing γονάτων with φεῦ, hard with the intervening nominative χείρ, or speaking of 'attraction' into the construction of ἧς...ἐλαμβάνου. Neither is necessary. The comma should go, and editors should take note of a rare but attested construction of a single verb having two objects or two subjects connected by 'and', one of them a relative pronoun, the other a noun, a construction I hereby christen the 'whom and his bride' construction after *Med.* 163-4, ὄν ποτ' ἐγὼ νύμφαν τ' ἐσίδοιμ' αὐτοῖς μελάθροις διακναιομένους. Three other examples are *Med.* 503, οὓς σοὶ προδοῦσα καὶ πάτραν ἀφικόμην, *El.* 86, ὅς μου κατέκτα πατέρα χἠ πανώλεθρος μήτηρ, and *Hel.* 1648-9, Διόσκοροι...οὓς Λήδα ποτὲ ἔτικτεν Ἑλένην θ'. In Latin dress it may be seen at Ovid, *Tr.* 3.4.40, 'nostra tuas vidi lacrimas super ora cadentes, / tempore quas uno fidaque verba bibi'.

**514.** The only scholar who seems to have felt the inconcinnity between the ironic καλόν and the dyslogistic ὄνειδος ('a fine reproach for a new bridegroom') is Vitelli, who conjectured κακόν. But irony seems in place here, as both the sentiment 515 and the γ' of 514 seem to indicate. What we need is 'a fine feather in a new bridegroom's cap', which in Greek might be καλός γ' ἔπαινος or καλόν γ' ἄγαλμα. Indeed we might wish to punctuate with a comma at the end of 513, making the phrase an 'accusative in apposition to the sentence', in which case we would have to write καλόν γ' ἔπαινον. Whether this is an instance of 'polar error' or of a pedestrian scribe's failure to appreciate the ironic use of words is unclear.

**752.** If we didn't have the notices by Triclinius and the B-scholiast giving ἡλίου θ' ἁγνὸν σέβας as a variant reading at 746, and the ms. Nv, which gives ἡλίου θ' ἁγνὸν σέλας, we never would have guessed that so much was amiss in the transmission of 752. The variant clearly does not belong at 746, because the next verse fits only onto πατέρα θ' Ἥλιον πατρός, not onto the variant. But this phrase, with its choice poetic vocabulary, comes from somewhere, and Porson saw that it fits as a variant for the last half of 752. Once we treat it as such, it beats the competition by a country mile. Its vocabulary, as noted above, is choice, too good, in fact, to be secondary. Furthermore, what concerns Aegeus here is not the sun's bright light but the holiness of its light as an object of reverence. There is nothing *wrong* with the vocabulary of the attested variants, but nothing in them has the same ring of truth, even when grammar and scansion are restored by Page's rearrangement of λαμπρὸν ἡλίου τε φῶς and λαμπρόν θ' ἡλίου φάος to φῶς τε λαμπρὸν ἡλίου. Furthermore, we can explain the corruption of Nv's reading to the readings we have in 752: σέλας was glossed as λαμπρὸν φῶς, both σέλας and ἁγνὸν were obliterated and replaced, and subsequent scribes did what they could with the unmetrical ἡλίου τε λαμπρὸν φῶς.

**846-50.** The hyperbaton of the first ἤ, placed two words later than expected, is startling but can be paralleled. With that established, we face a second problem, the fact that φίλων πόμπιμος χώρα doesn't contribute much to this context. It is easy to see why a city of holy rivers will not accept a child-murderess: holiness abhors the shedding of kindred blood. But there is nothing particularly pointed about asking why 'a city that escorts its friends' will not do so: escorting friends is neither here nor there when it comes to receiving child-murderers, and if it figures at all, it ought to figure in favor of the reception since Medea is Aegeus' friend. What is needed is something from the sphere of religion, and πόμπιμος, 'conducting, leading in procession', needs the genitive θεῶν for φίλων: 'how shall a city of holy rivers or a region that walks by the side of its gods receive you, the child-slayer, the impure, in the company of its citizens?' (Read μετ' ἀστῶν, Jacobs.)

**910.** Every solution to this crux known to me keeps παρεμπολῶντος, either in the genitive as transmitted or altered to another case, usually dative. Yet that is the one word in the line that cannot be correct: we do not want a verb meaning 'traffic underhandedly in, smuggle', for there is nothing at all secret about Jason's dealings with his new bride and father-in-law, there is no reason at all for him to suggest that there was anything underhanded about it, and we do not expect him to engage in gratuitous self-vilification. Indeed, he can avoid claiming any active role in the matter at all except that of picking up what was thrown in his path: cf. 553, where he calls marriage into the royal family a εὕρημα. What we expect him to say is 'It is natural for a woman to be angry when a marriage of a new sort has fallen to her husband's lot'. As it happens V has both γάμου and ἀλλοίου. All that is needed is a participle in the genitive. I suggest παρεμπεσόντος. The word means 'occur, happen', often with the overtones of 'intrude upon', just the sort of nuance that would suit Jason's case.

**945.** Several mss. give this line to Jason, but reason and two mss. plus two scholiasts give it to Medea. It is for Medea to flatter Jason by saying that all women find him irresistible: 'Yes, if she is a woman like the rest'. But in that case we must read γυναικῶν ⟨γ'⟩ with Herwerden.

**1008-10.** See *GRBS* 29 (1988), 117-18.

**1049-55.** See *GRBS* 29 (1988), 118-20.

**1056-80.** See *CQ* 36 (1986), 343-52.

**1076-7.** See *GRBS* 29 (1988), 120-1.

**1314-16.** See *GRBS* 29 (1988), 121-2.

**1415-19.** See *TAPA* 117 (1987), 268-9.

# BIBLIOGRAPHY

## LIST OF EDITIONS USED

Adaeus, epigram, in *GP*.
Aelian, *Varia Historia* , ed. M. R. Dilts (Leipzig, 1974).
Anonymous, Περὶ τραγῳδίας, ed. R. Browning, in ΓΕΡΑΣ: *Studies presented to George Thomson*, Acta Universitatis Carolinae, 1963, Philosophica et Historica I, Graecolatina Pragensia II (Prague, 1963), pp. 69-71.
*AP*: *Anthologia Palatina*, in *Anthologia Graeca*, ed. H. Beckby (Munich, 1965).
Apollodorus Atheniensis, fragments, in *FGrH* #244.
Apostolius, in E. L. von Leutsch and F. G. Schneidewin, edd., *Corpus paroemiographorum Graecorum* (Göttingen, 1851), vol. 2.
Archimedes, epigram, in *FGE*.
Aristophanes, *Acharnenses, Nubes, Pax, Thesmophoriazusae, Ranae*, ed. V. Coulon (Paris, 1952-4).
_____, *Equites*, ed. R. A. Neil (Cambridge, 1909).
_____, *Vespae*, ed. D. M. MacDowell (Oxford, 1971).
_____, *Lysistrata*, ed. J. Henderson (Oxford, 1987).
_____, fragments, in K.-A., vol. 3.2
Aristotle, *Poetica*, ed. R. Kassel (Oxford, 1965).
_____, *Politica*, ed. W. D. Ross (Oxford, 1957).
_____, *Rhetorica*, ed. W. D. Ross (Oxford, 1959).
_____, fragments, ed. V. Rose (Leipzig, 1886).
Athenaeus, *Deipnosophistae*, ed. G. Kaibel (Leipzig, 1887-90).
Aulus Gellius, ed. P. K. Marshall (Oxford, 1968).
Axionicus, fragments, in K.-A.
Babbit, F. C., et al., edd., *Plutarch's Moralia* (Cambridge, Mass., 1927-65).
Cicero, *Tusculanae Disputationes*, ed. M. Giusta (Torino, 1984).
Clemens Alexandrinus, *Stromateis*, ed. O. Stählin, 3rd ed. revised by L. Früchtel (Berlin, 1960).
Cratinus, fragments, in K.-A.
Diggle, J., ed., *Euripidis Fabulae*, vols. 1 and 2 (Oxford 1984, 1981).
Dio Prusaensis, *Orationes*, ed. G. de Budé (Leipzig, 1916-19).
Diogenes Laertius, *Vitae Philosophorum*, ed. H. S. Long (Oxford, 1964).
Dübner, F., ed., *Scholia Graeca in Aristophanem* (Paris, 1877).
*EG*: D. Page, ed., *Epigrammata Graeca* (Oxford, 1975).
Euripides, epinician for Alcibiades, fr. 1 [=*PMG* 755], in C. M. Bowra, *Historia* 9 (1960) 74, rpt. in *On Greek Margins* (Oxford, 1970), p. 141.
_____, epinician for Alcibiades, fr. 2, in *PMG*.
[Euripides], *Epistulae*, ed. Hanns-Ulrich Gößwein (Meisenheim am Glan, 1975).
*FGE*: D. L. Page, ed., *Further Greek Epigrams* (Cambridge, 1981).
*FGrH*: Jakoby, F., *Die Fragmente der griechischen Historiker* (Leiden, 1923-58).
Γένος Εὐριπίδου καὶ βίος, in L. Méridier, ed., *Euripide I* (Paris, 1961), pp. 1-5.
*Gnomologium Vaticanum e codice Vaticano Graeco 743*, ed. L. Sternbach (Berlin, 1963).

GP: A. S. F. Gow and D. Page, edd., *The Greek Anthology: the Garland of Philip and some contemporary epigrams* (Cambridge, 1968).
Harpocration, *Lexicon in decem oratores Atticos*, ed. W. Dindorf (Oxford, 1853; rpt. Groningen, 1969).
Hermesianax, in Powell.
Hermippus, fragments, in Wehrli.
Hieronymus Rhodius, fragments, in Wehrli.
Hypotheses to Euripides' plays, in Diggle, except for *Pho.*, quoted as in *TrGF*, vol. I.
[Ion], epigrams, in *FGE*.
K.-A.: *Poetae Comici Graeci*, edd. R. Kassel et C. Austin (Berlin, 1983-   ).
Koster, W. J. W., et al., *Scholia in Aristophanem* (Groningen, 1960-   ).
[Longinus], *De sublimitate*, ed. D. A. Russell, (Oxford, 1964).
Lucian, *Opera*, ed. M. D. Macleod (Oxford, 1972-87).
Marmor Parium, fragments, in *FGrH* #239.
Nachstädt, W., et al., edd. *Plutarchi Moralia* (Leipzig, 1935-   ).
Nicolaus Damascenus, fragments, in *FGrH* #90.
Oenomaus Gadarensis, fragments, in J. Hammerstaedt, *Die Orakelkritik des Kynikers Oenomaus* (Frankfurt am Main, 1988).
Perrin, B, et al., edd., *Plutarch's Lives* (Cambridge, Mass., 1914-26).
Philochorus, fragments, in *FGrH* #328.
Plutarch, *Amatorius*, in Nachstädt, vol. 4.
_____, *An seni res publica gerenda sit*, in Babbitt, vol. 10.
_____, *De amore prolis*, in Nachstädt, vol. 3.
_____, *Quaestiones Convivales*, in Nachstädt, vol. 4.
_____, *Quomodo adolescens poetas audire debeat*, in Babbit, vol. 1.
_____, *Regum et imperatorum apothegmata*, in Nachstädt, vol. 2.
_____, *Vita Alcibiadis*, in Ziegler, vol. 1.
_____, *Vita Demosthenis*, in Ziegler, vol. 1.
_____, *Vita Lycurgi*, in Perrin, vol. 1.
_____, *Vita Niciae*, in Ziegler, vol. 1.
_____, *Vitae decem oratorum*, in Nachstädt, vol. 5.
[Plutarch], *Placita philosophorum*, in Nachstädt, vol. 5.
*PMG*: Page, D., *Poetae Melici Graeci* (Oxford, 1962).
Pollux, *Onomasticon*, ed. E. Bethe (Leipzig, 1900-31).
Powell, J. U., ed., *Collectanea Alexandrina* (Oxford, 1925).
Quintilian, *Institutio Oratoria*, ed. L. Radermacher (Leipzig, 1971).
Satyrus, *Vita Euripidis* (P. Oxy. 9.1176), ed. G. Arrighetti, *Satiro. Vita di Euripide* (Pisa, 1964).
Scholia to Aristophanes' *Acharn., Vesp.*: in Koster.
Scholia to Aristophanes' *Thesmo., Ran.*: in Dübner.
Scholia to Aristotle's *Rhetorica*, in H. Rabe, *Commentaria in Aristotelem Graeca* 21.2 (Berlin, 1896).
Schwartz, E., ed., *Scholia in Euripidem* (Berlin, 1887-91).
Seneca, *Epistulae Morales*, ed. L. D. Reynolds (Oxford, 1965).
*Suda*, ed. A. Adler (Leipzig, 1928-71).
Theophrastus, *Fragmenta*, ed. F. Wimmer (Paris, 1866; rpt. Frankfurt am Main, 1964).
Thomas Magister, in W. Dindorf, ed., *Scholia Graeca in Euripidis Tragoedias* (Oxford, 1863).
Timaeus Locrius, fragments, in *FGrH* #566.

*TrGF:* B. Snell et al.,*Tragicorum Graecorum Fragmenta* (Göttingen, 1971-  ).
Varro, fragment, in G. Funaioli, ed., *Grammaticae Romanae Fragmenta* (Leipzig, 1907).
Vitruvius, *De architectura*, ed. F. Granger (Cambridge, Mass., 1931-4).
Wehrli, F., ed. *Die Schule des Aristoteles*, (Basel, 1944-74).
Ziegler, K., et al., edd., *Plutarchi vitae parallelae* (Leipzig, 1969-  ).

## OTHER WORKS CITED

Editions of Euripides

J. Diggle, ed., *Euripidis Fabulae* (Oxford, 1981-  ).
Εὐριπίδου Ἅπαντα, Euripidis Opera Omnia, cura et typis Andreae et Joannis M. Duncan (Glasgow, 1821).
F. A. Paley, ed., *Euripides with an English Commentary* (London, 1872-80$^2$).
R. Prinz and N. Wecklein, edd., *Euripidis Fabulae* (Leipzig, 1878-1902).

A. M. Dale, *Alcestis* (Oxford, 1954).
H. W. Hayley, *Alcestis* (Boston, 1898).
D. L. Page, *Medea* (Oxford, 1938).
R. Seaford, *Cyclops* (Oxford, 1984).
U. von Wilamowitz-Moellendorff, *Heracles* (Berlin, 1895$^2$, rpt. Darmstadt, 1969).

Books and Articles

A. M. Dale, *Metrical Analyses of Tragic Choruses* (London, 1971-83).
A. Dieterich, 'Euripides', *RE* VI (1907), 1242-81.
K. J. Dover, 'Aristophanes, *Knights* 11-20', in *Greek and the Greeks* (Oxford, 1987), i 307-10 [=*CR* 9 (1959), 196-9].
B. Gygli-Wyss, *Das nominale Polyptoton im älteren Griechisch* (Göttingen, 1966).
J. Jackson, *Marginalia Scaenica* (Oxford, 1955).
D. Kovacs, 'De Cephisophonte verna, ut perhibent, Euripidis', *ZPE* 84 (1990), 15-18.
——, 'Euripides, *Troades* 95-7: Is Sacking Cities Really Foolish?' *CQ* 33 (1983), 334-8.
M. Lefkowitz, 'The Euripides *Vita*', *GRBS* 20 (1979), 187-210.
——, 'Satyrus the Historian', *Atti del XVII Congresso Internazionale di Papirologia* (Naples, 1984), pp. 339-43.
T. C. W. Stinton, *Collected Papers on Greek Tragedy* (Oxford, 1990).
U. von Wilamowitz-Moellendorff, *Griechische Verskunst* (Berlin, 1921).

# INDICES TO THE TESTIMONIA

(Reference numbers are to the Testimonia and section or line)

## INDEX OF NAMES

Acestor: 4.17
Achaeus of Eretria: 24
Aegae: 64
Aeschylus: 6, 72, 77.757-1499, 86(a)
Agathon: 42, 55-6, 76.88, 77.83-5, 100.5.2
Amphias: 100.1.1
Anaxagoras: 1.4, 2.4-5, 3.4, 4.3-4, 5.4, 5.8, 8, 14
Antisthenes: 44
Archagora, son of Theodotus: 15
Archelaus of Macedon: 1.11, 3.12-13, 4.20, 5.9, 55, 61-2, 66, 100.4, 100.5
Archelaus, tragic actor: 93
Arethusa: 66
Aristophanes compared with Euripides: 79, 86(b)
Arrhibaeus of Macedon: 2.9, 64
Cephisophon: 1.5, 1.29, 3.12, 4.14-15, 58, 100.5
Cleanthes: 44
Cleon: 4.13
Cleito: 1.1, 1.32, 2.1-2, 3.1, 5.1, 9, 70.478, 77.840, 100.5.3-5
Cleiton: 100.1.1, 100.5.1
Crateras: 1.9
Crateuas of Thessaly: 1.9
Decamnichus: 61
Dionysius of Syracuse: 1.27, 69
Dorilaus: 4.17
Euphorion: 28
'Euripidaristophanist': 79
Euripides (see also Table of Contents), age at time of death: 1.18, 2.10; and women: 1.25, 1.29, 1.30, 4.13-14, 5.6, 64, 75, 76; atheistic views: 23, 76.443-52, 77.889-94; cave on the island of Salamis: 1.22, 4.12, 5.5; chorus in: 48, 82(c); cithara: 42; date of birth: 1.2, 1.8, 2.3, 3.2, 6, 7, 8, 25, 67; date of death: 2.12, 67-9; date of first production: 1.36; death and burial in Macedon: 1.18, 1.21, 3.13-14, 4.22-3, 5.9-10, 63-68; deme: 11, 12; embassy to Syracuse: 94; epitaph by Thucydides or Timotheus on his cenotaph in Athens: 1.18, 3.14; first production: 1.9, 3.8, 5.5; first victory: 25; in Egypt with Plato: 20; innovations in tragedy: 1.4, 3.5, 4.11, 42, 77.845-50, 77.937-91, 77.1063-73; lawsuit with Hygiainon about an *antidosis*: 59; library of: 91; literary collaborators: 1.5, 1.26, 1.29; Macedonia: 1.11, 1.18, 1.21, 1.35, 4.19-23, 5.9-10; madness, love, and other passions: 86(a); Magnesia 1.10; *mechane* in: 82(b); moral tendencies of work: 72, 77.1043-88; musical modes: 42; oracles to his father: 1.3, 3.3, 5.2, 13; painter in his youth: 1.6, 2.4 ; parents of: 1.1, 1.32, 2.1, 3.1, 10, 51 (see also Cleito, Mnesarchides); plays, number of: 1.16, 1.38, 2.11-12, 3.6; political opinions: 4.8-9; service to Apollo Zosterios: 1.7; to Apollo Delios: 12; sons of: 1.14, 2.7, 3.10; style: 1.37, 4.1, 4.2, 74.534, 77.96-102, 77.775, 77.841-2, 82(e), 88, 89; sullenness: 1.23, 1.34, 2.6, 3.11, 5.8; teachers of: 1.4, 1.33, 2.4, 3.4, 5.4; tombs struck by lightning: 1.19, 95, 99; tragic contests: 24-48; trained and competed as athlete: 1.3, 3.3, 5.3; use of 'irrational': 82(d); victories, number of: 1.38, 2.12, 3.7, 41; wives of: 1.13, 1.24, 2.7-8, 3.10, 5.6
Euripides, the poet's son: 1.14, 2.7, 3.10, 40
Hegelochus: 38, 39
Heraclitus: 21
Homer: 77.1034, 84, 96

Hygiainon: 59
Ion of Chios: 29
Iophon: 29, 77.73
Lyceum: 15
Lycurgus of Athens: 83
Lycurgus of Sparta: 95
Lysimachus, slave of Archelaus: 2.9
Megaclides: 15
Melanthius: 4.17
Menander: 87
Mesatus: 100.5.2
Mnesarchides, the poet's father: 1.1, 1.32, 2.1, 10; the poet's son: 1.14, 2.7, 3.10
Mnesilochus, the poet's son: 2.7, 3.10; a kinsman (?): 1.5
Morsimus: 4.17
Nicodicus of Arethusa: 2.9
Nicomachus: 43
Pella: 2.10, 63, 100.1.2, 100.3.1

Philistus: 86(b)
Pieria: 63, 96
Piraeus: 18
Plato: 20
Prodicus: 1.4, 5.4,
Promerus, hounds of: 65
Protagoras: 1.4, 3.4, 15-16
Pythangelus: 77.87
Salamis: 1.2
Sicilian Expedition, Athenian survivors saved by reciting Euripides: 4.21, 92
Socrates: 1.4, 2.4, 4.6, 4.7, 5.4, 17-19, 21, 34, 77.1491
Sophocles: 1.20, 1.34, 3.15, 26, 27, 28, 42, 48, 52-4, 68, 74, 77.76-82, 77.787, 85, 87, 90, 100.2, 100.5.5-6
Theognis: 43
Timocrates of Argos: 1.5
Timotheus: 4.24, 57
Xenocles: 31, 77.86

## INDEX OF SOURCES

Adaeus, *AP* 7.51, *GP* 11-16: 66
Aelian, *Varia Historia*, 2.8: 31; 2.13: 18; 2.21: 56
Aëtius, *Plac.* 1.7.1: 23
Alexander Aetolus, fr. 7 Powell: 1.23, 1.28, 3.11, and 5.8
Ammianus Marcellinus 27.4.8: 2.10n.
Anaxagoras, A 1.10, 20a, 20b, 33 D.-K.: p. 33, n. 6
anonymous, Περὶ τραγῳδίας: 42
*Anthologia Palatina* 7.43: 96; 7.44: 63; 7.45: 1.18 and 3.14; 7.46: 97; 7.47: 98; 7.49: 99; 7.50: 89; 7.51: 66
Apollodorus of Athens, *FGrH* 244 F 35: 68
Apostolius, 14.83: 65
Archelaus, A 2 D.-K.: p. 33, n. 5
Archimedes, *AP* 7.50, *FGE*, p. 24: 89
Aristophanes,
 *Acharnians.* 393-489: 70
 *Clouds* 1364-78: 72
 *Frogs* 52-1499 with omissions: 77; 944: 58; 1407-9: 58; 1246: 1.12n.; 1451-3: 58
 *Knights* 11-20: 71
 *Lysistrata* 283-4 and 368-9: 75

 *Peace* 146-8 and 528-34: 74
 *Thesmo.* 3-456 with omissions: 76; 335-7 and 374-5: 4.14; 453-6: 5.6
 *Wasps* 54-61 and 1412-14: 73
 fr. 128 K.-A.: p. 67, n. 4; fr. 392: 17; fr. 488: 79; fr. 565: 4.2; fr. 595: 4.18; fr. 596: 1.29; fr. 682: 78; fr. 694: 4.12
Aristotle,
 *de Sensu* 443 b 30-1: 80
 *Poet.* 1453 a 22-30: 82(a); 1454 a 37-1454 b 2: 82(b); 1456 a 25-30: 82(c); 1460 b 32-5: 52; 1461 b 19-21: 82(d)
 *Pol.* 1311 b 30-4: 61
 *Rhet.* 1384 b 13-17 and scholia: 94; 1404 b 18-25: 82(e); 1416 a 28-35: 59
 fr. 627 Rose: 40
Athenaeus 3A: 91; 61B: p. 55, n. 1; 175B: 81; 424EF: 12; 557E: 90; 561A: p. 37, n. 1; 597B: 64; 603E: p. 123, n. 1; 604D: 54; 652D: p. 115, n. 1
Athenagoras, *Apology* 5.1: p. 39, n. 1

# INDICES

Aulus Gellius 15.20: 5; 17.4.3: 41
Axionicus, fr. 3 K.-A.: 81
Bianor of Bithynia, *AP* 7.49, *GP* 1645-8: 99
Callias, fr. 15 K.-A.: 17
Cicero, *Tusc. Disp.* 4.63: 19
Clement of Alexandria, *Stromat.* 5.70.1: 22
*Comicorum Graecorum Fragmenta in Papyris Reperta*, ed. Austin, fr. adesp. 294(b), 4.9
Crantor, ap. D. L. 4.26, iii 131 Mullach: 84
Cratinus, fr. 342 K.-A.: 79
Critias, *TrGF* 43 F 19: 23
Diagoras of Melos, T 47: 23
Dio of Prusa 35(52) 11 and 15: 88; 66.6: p. 115, n. 1
Diodorus Siculus 1.7.7: p. 33, n. 6; 13.103.4: 68
Diogenes Laertius 2.18: 17; 2.22: 21; 2.44: 33; 2.45: 8; 3.6: 20; 4.26: 84; 9.54: 15; 9.55: 16
Diomedes, p. 488 Keil: 1.11n.
Diphilus, fr. 74 K.-A.: p. 123, n. 1
Eratosthenes, *FGrH* 241 F 12: 1.17
Euripides, works of, cited,
    *Aeolus*: 72.1371f. and 77.863
    *Alexandros*, fr. 42: 77.100
    *Andromeda*: 34, 35, 77.53, 93; fr. 136.1: 93
    *Antiope*: 35
    *Archelaus*: 1.11
    *Auge*: 77.1080
    *Bacchae* 726: 86(e)
    *Bellerophon*: 70.426 and 74.146-8
    *Chrysippus*: 56
    *Danae*: 4.6; 46; 48
    *Daughters of Pelias*: 1.15
    *Electra* 923-4: 1.24
    *Heracles*: 60; line 1245: 86
    *Hippolytus* (the earlier, lost play): 1.24; 77.1043
    *Hippolytus*: 77.1079; line 345: 71.16; 612: 59, 76.276, 77.101, and 77.1471
    *Ino*: 73.1413f.
    *Iphigenia among the Taurians* 1193: 20
    *Ixion*: 16; 45
    *Medea*: 82(a) and (d); 89
    *Melanippe the Wise*, fr. 480 and 481: 47; fr. 484: 76.13-18; fr. 487: 76.272 and 77.100; fr. 499: 1.30
    *Meleager*: 77.864
    *Oeneus*: 70.418-20
    *Orestes*: 82(d); lines 1-3: 19; 279: 38 and 39
    *Palamedes*, fr. 588: 32(e) and 33
    *Peleus*: 77.863
    *Phaethon*, fr. 779: 86(e)
    *Philoctetes*: 70.424
    *Phoenissae*: 35; 36
    *Phoenix*: 70.421; fr. 804.3: 76.413
    *Polyidus*, fr. 638: 77.1082 and 1477
    *Sthenoboea*: 77.1043; fr. 664: 76.404
    *Telephus*: 70.429ff. and 77.855 and 864
    *Tennes*, *Rhadamanthys*, and *Pirithous*: 1.17
    *Trojan Women*: 32(b); line 886: 4.4
    fr. 19: 44 and 77.1475; fr. 42: 77.100; fr. 136.1: 93; fr. 324: 46; fr. 369: 30; fr. 403: 4.19; fr. 480: 27; fr. 481: 47; fr. 487: 77.100; fr. 911: 4.19-20; fr. 912: 4.4; fr. 913: 4.5; fr. 935: 86(a); fr. 1007c: 4.7; fr. 1007d: 4.10
epinician for Alcibiades: 49 and 50
epitaph for the Athenian dead: 51
[Euripides,] *Epistulae*: 100; epigrams, *EG* 462-5: 54; *EG* 478-81: p. 55, n. 1
Eusebius, *Praep. Evang.* 227C: 13
Γένος Εὐριπίδου καὶ βίος: 1
Gnomologium Vaticanum 517: 53
Harpocration, s.v. Φλυέα: 11
Hermesianax, fr. 7.61-8 Powell: 64
Hermippus, fr. 94 Wehrli: 1.27
Hieronymus Rhodius, fr. 35 Wehrli: 54 and p. 123, n. 1; fr. 36: 90
Hypothesis to *Alcestis*: 27; to *Medea*: 28; to *Hippolytus*: 29; to *Phoenissae*: 36
[Ion of Chios], *AP* 7.43, *EG* 468-71: 96; *AP* 7.44, *EG* 472-7: 63

[Longinus], *De sublim.* 15.3-6 and 40.2-3: 86
Lucian 59.1: 93
Marmor Parium, *FGrH* 239 A 50: 6; A 60: 25; A 63: 67
Nicolaus of Damascus, *FGrH* 90 F 103(v): 10
Nicostratus, fr. 28 K.: p. 67, n. 4
Oenomaus, fr. 1 Hammerstaedt: 13
*Oxyrhunchus Papyri* 9.1176: 4; 24.2400: 60
Pausanias 1.2.2: 1.18n.
Philemon, fr. 118 K.-A.: 1.31 and 3.16; fr. 153: 4.11
Philochorus, *FGrH* 328 F 217: 16; F 218: 2.2; F219: 5.4; F 220: 1.17; F 221: 33
Pliny the Elder, NH 31.28: 2.10n.
Plutarch, *Amatorius* 756BC: 47; 770C: 55n.; *An seni res pub. ger.* 795D: 57; *De amore prolis* 496F: 26; *De recta ratione aud.* 45AB: 85; *De vitioso pudore* 531DE: 62n.; *Quaest. Conv.* 717C: 7 and 69; *Quomodo adol. poet. aud. deb.* 19E: 45; 33C: 44; *Regum et imper. apothegm.* 177A: 55 and 62; *Vita Alcib.* 196B: 49; *Vita Demosth.* 846AB: 50; *Vita Lycurg.* 59BC: 95; *Vita Nic.* 528E-529A: 30; 534D: 51; 542CD: 92
[Plutarch], *de plac. phil.* 880DE: 23; *Vitae decem orat.* 841F: 83
Pollux 4.111: 48
Quintilian 10.1.67-9: 87

Sannyrion, fr. 8 K.-A.: 39
Satyrus, *Vita Euripidis*, P. Oxy. 1176: 4
scholia to Aristophanes, *Acharnians* 457: 9; *Birds* 824: 32; *Frogs* 53: 35; 67: 40; 302-4: 38; 775: 78; 944 and 1407-9: 58*Thesmo.* 1012 and 1060: 34
scholia to Aristotle, *Rhetoric* 1384 b 13-17: 94
scholia to Euripides, *Orestes* 279: 39; 371: 37
scholia to Plato, *Apol.* 19C: 79
Seneca, *Ep.* 115.15: 46
Stobaeus, vol. 4, p. 59: 10
Strattis, fr. 1 K.-A.: 39; fr. 47.2: 80; fr. 63: 39
*Suda* s.v. Ἀχαιός, A 4683: 24; s.v. Εὐριπίδης, E 3695: 2; s.v. Νικόμαχος, N 397: 43
Teleclides, fr. 41 K.-A.: 1.5 and 17; fr. 42: 17
Theophrastus, fr. 119 Wimmer: 12
Theopompus, the comic poet, fr. 35 K.-A.: p. 67, n. 4
Theopompus, the historian, *FGrH* 115 F 397: 5.1
Θωμᾶ τοῦ Μαγίστρου σύνοψις τοῦ βίου τοῦ Εὐριπίδου: 3
Timaeus, *FGrH* 566 F 105: 69
Valerius Maximus 3.7 ext. 1: p. 53, n. 1
Varro, fr. 298 Funaioli: 41
Vitruvius, 8 pr. 1: 14; 8.3.16: 2.10n.

## INDICES TO THE TEXTUAL DISCUSSIONS
(Numbers refer to pages)

### INDEX OF SUBJECTS

chorus-leader's two-line interpositions ignored: 163
colometry: 145-6
construction illustrated by *est ut viro vir latius imperet*:: 167
enjambment: 153
gloss extrudes original: 158, 171
homoearkton: 168, n. 2
interlinear correction copied as text: 165
lacunae detected 150, 160, 167, 169
meter
  lyric: 145-6, 147, 155, 157
parenthetical (διὰ μέσου) expressions: 164-5
polar errors: 166, 170

'whom and his bride' construction: 169-70

word-order: 146

## INDEX OF GREEK WORDS

ἄριστα with future indicative in place of deliberative subjunctive: 168
ἥκει as equivalent of καθήκει: 161
κἄν as equivalent of καί: 148
ὅστε: 155
σίφων: 156
τε postponed to third or later place: 151
τλᾶμον: 155
χήρα: 156
ψέγειν corrupted to λέγειν: 150
ὦ παῖ, to whom addressed and by whom in tragedy: 163
ὦ φίλε: 146-7

## INDEX OF PASSAGES CITED

Aeschylus
  *Ag.* 160ff.: 155
  *Cho.* 315: 146; 989: 150
  *Dictyulci* 824ff.: 156
  *Eu.* 559: 151
  *PV* 346: 162
Alexis, fr. 222.3-4
*AP* 12.254.6: 159
Archilochus, fr. 173: 154-5
Aristophanes, *Frogs* 1259: 147
Catullus 32.10-11: 152
Euripides
  *Alc.* 18: 160; 244: 146; 706-7: 164; 819: 151; 990: 146
  *Andr.* 50: 153; 419: 150; 423-4: 163; 510: 146; 530: 146; 642-3: 164; 672: 149; 691-2: 164 and 165; 1204: 146
  *Ba.* 329: 163; 530-2: 146; 880-1: 157; 938: 153; 1184: 155
  *Cy.* 41: 157; 43: 157; 45-7: 157; 190: 151; 198-200: 158; 353-5: 158; 658: 157
  *El.* 26-8: 160; 86: 170; 188-9: 157; 197: 163; 779: 153; 804: 160
  *Hcld.* 138: 149; 228: 160; 380: 163; 828: 160
  *Hec.* 468: 153; 578: 153; 734: 153
  *Hel.* 521-2: 157; 526-7: 157; 1225: 162; 1336-7: 157; 1355: 163; 1454-5: 157; 1648-9: 170
  *HF* 100: 160; 280: 153; 593: 153; 683-4: 157; 975: 153; 1205: 153
  *Hip.* 211: 163; 358-9: 160; 1374-5: 147
  *IA* 969: 149; 1550: 153
  *Ion* 1069-72: 146; 1229-30: 157; 1242-3: 157
  *IT* 779: 157; 830: 146; 1218: 153; 1435: 153
  *Med.* 163-4: 170; 503: 170; 583: 168; 786: 153; 808: 168; 949: 153; 982: 153
  *Or.* 47: 154; 521: 153; 749: 160; 1161: 153; 1434-5: 147
  *Pho.* 22: 153; 229-30: 1571318: 153
  *Sup.* 278: 146; 565: 150; 1007-8: 157
  *Tro.* 267: 146; 468: 149; 1081: 146
  fr. 655: 160; *889a.1: 163
Herodotus 1.30.4: 161
Hesychius: 156
Homer, *Od.* 9.447-52: 145
Orphic Hymns: 147
Ovid, *Tristia* 3.4.40: 170
Sophocles
  *El.* 251: 163; 551: 150; 1467: 150; 1471: 149; 1482: 148
  *OC* 738: 161
  *OT* 338: 150; 407: 168; 720: 160; 1365-6: 167
  *Phil.* 671: 149

# SUPPLEMENTS TO MNEMOSYNE

## EDITED BY J. M. BREMER, L. F. JANSSEN, H. PINKSTER, H. W. PLEKET, C. J. RUIJGH AND P. H. SCHRIJVERS

4. LEEMAN, A.D. *A Systematical Bibliography of Sallust (1879-1964)*. Revised and augmented edition. 1965. ISBN 90 04 01467 5
5. LENZ, F.W. (ed.). *The Aristeides 'Prolegomena'*. 1959. ISBN 90 04 01468 3
7. McKAY, K.J. *Erysichthon. A Callimachean Comedy*. 1962. ISBN 90 04 01470 5
11. RUTILIUS LUPUS. *De Figuris Sententiarum et Elocutionis*. Edited with Prolegomena and Commentary by E. BROOKS. 1970. ISBN 90 04 01474 8
12. SMYTH, W.R. (ed.). *Thesaurus criticus ad Sexti Propertii textum*. 1970. ISBN 90 04 01475 6
13. LEVIN, D.N. *Apollonius' 'Argonautica' re-examined*. 1. The Neglected First and Second Books. 1971. ISBN 90 04 02575 8
14. REINMUTH, O.W. *The Ephebic Inscriptions of the Fourth Century B.C*. 1971. ISBN 90 04 01476 4
16. ROSE, K.F.C. *The Date and Author of the 'Satyricon'*. With an Introduction by J.P.SULLIVAN. 1971. ISBN 90 04 02578 2
18. WILLIS, J. *De Martiano Capella emendando*. 1971. ISBN 90 04 02580 4
19. HERINGTON, C.J. (ed.). *The Older Scholia on the Prometheus Bound*. 1972. ISBN 90 04 03455 2
20. THIEL, H. VAN. *Petron. Überlieferung und Rekonstruktion*. 1971. ISBN 90 04 02581 2
21. LOSADA, L.A. *The Fifth Column in the Peloponnesian War*. 1972. ISBN 90 04 03421 8
23. BROWN, V. *The Textual Transmission of Caesar's 'Civil War'*. 1972. ISBN 90 04 03457 9
24. LOOMIS, J.W. *Studies in Catullan Verse*. An Analysis of Word Types and Patterns in the Polymetra. 1972. ISBN 90 04 03429 3
27. GEORGE, E.V. *Aeneid VIII and the Aitia of Callimachus*. 1974. ISBN 90 04 03859 0
29. BERS, V. *Enallage and Greek Style*. 1974. ISBN 90 04 03786 1
37. SMITH, O.L. *Studies in the Scholia on Aeschylus*. 1. The Recensions of Demetrius Triclinius. 1975. ISBN 90 04 04220 2
39. SCHMELING, G.L. & J.H. STUCKEY. *A Bibliography of Petronius*. 1977 ISBN 90 04 04753 0
44. THOMPSON, W.E. *De Hagniae Hereditate. An Athenian Inheritance Case*. 1976. ISBN 90 04 04757 3
45. McGUSHIN, P. *Sallustius Crispus, 'Bellum Catilinae'. A Commentary*. 1977. ISBN 90 04 04835 9
46. THORNTON, A. *The Living Universe. Gods and Men in Virgil's Aeneid*. 1976. ISBN 90 04 04579 1
48. BRENK, F.E. *In Mist apparelled. Religious Themes in Plutarch's 'Moralia' and 'Lives'*. 1977. ISBN 90 04 05241 0
51. SUSSMAN, L.A. *The Elder Seneca*. 1978. ISBN 90 04 05759 5
57. BOER, W. DEN. *Private Morality in Greece and Rome*. Some Historical Aspects. 1979. ISBN 90 04 05976 8
61. *Hieronymus' Liber de optimo genere interpretandi (Epistula 57)*. Ein Kommentar von G.J.M. BARTELINK. 1980. ISBN 90 04 06085 5
63. HOHENDAHL-ZOETELIEF, I.M. *Manners in the Homeric Epic*. 1980. ISBN 90 04 06223 8
64. HARVEY, R.A. *A Commentary on Persius*. 1981. ISBN 90 04 06313 7

65. MAXWELL-STUART, P.G. *Studies in Greek Colour Terminology.* 1. γλαυκός. 1981. ISBN 90 04 06406 0
68. ACHARD, G. *Pratique rhétorique et idéologie politique dans les discours 'Optimates' de Cicéron.* 1981. ISBN 90 04 06374 9
69. MANNING, C.E. *On Seneca's 'Ad Marciam'.* 1981. ISBN 90 04 06430 3
70. BERTHIAUME, G. *Les rôles du Mágeiros.* Etude sur la boucherie, la cuisine et le sacrifice dans la Grèce ancienne. 1982. ISBN 90 04 06554 7
71. CAMPBELL, M. *A commentary on Quintus Smyrnaeus Posthomerica XII.* 1981. ISBN 90 04 06502 4
72. CAMPBELL, M. *Echoes and Imitations of Early Epic in Apollonius Rhodius.* 1981. ISBN 90 04 06503 2
73. MOSKALEW, W. *Formular Language and Poetic Design in the Aeneid.* 1982. ISBN 90 04 06580 6
74. RACE, W.H. *The Classical Priamel from Homer to Boethius.* 1982. ISBN 90 04 06515 6
75. MOORHOUSE, A.C. *The Syntax of Sophocles.* 1982. ISBN 90 04 06599 7
77. WITKE, C. *Horace's Roman Odes.* A Critical Examination. 1983. ISBN 90 04 07006 0
78. ORANJE, J. *Euripides' 'Bacchae'.* The Play and its Audience. 1984. ISBN 90 04 07011 7
79. STATIUS. *Thebaidos Libri XII.* Recensuit et cum apparatu critico et exegetico instruxit D.E. HILL. 1983. ISBN 90 04 06917 8
82. DAM, H.-J. VAN. *P. Papinius Statius, Silvae Book II.* A Commentary. 1984. ISBN 90 04 07110 5
84. OBER, J. *Fortress Attica. Defense of the Athenian Land Frontier, 404-322 B.C.* 1985. ISBN 90 04 07243 8
85. HUBBARD, T.K. *The Pindaric Mind.* A Study of Logical Structure in Early Greek Poetry. 1985. ISBN 90 04 07303 5
86. VERDENIUS, W.J. *A Commentary on Hesiod: Works and Days,* vv. 1-382. 1985. ISBN 90 04 07465 1
87. HARDER, A. *Euripides' 'Kresphontes' and 'Archelaos'.* Introduction, Text and Commentary. 1985. ISBN 90 04 07511 9
88. WILLIAMS, H.J. *The 'Eclogues' and 'Cynegetica' of Nemesianus.* Edited with an Introduction and Commentary. 1986. ISBN 90 04 07486 4
89. McGING, B.C. *The Foreign Policy of Mithridates VI Eupator, King of Pontus.* 1986. ISBN 90 04 07591 7
91. SIDEBOTHAM, S.E. *Roman Economic Policy in the Erythra Thalassa 30 B.C.-A.D. 217.* 1986. ISBN 90 04 07644 1
92. VOGEL, C.J. DE. *Rethinking Plato and Platonism.* 2nd impr. of the first (1986) ed. 1988. ISBN 90 04 08755 9
93. MILLER, A.M. *From Delos to Delphi.* A Literary Study of the Homeric Hymn to Apollo. 1986. ISBN 90 04 07674 3
94. BOYLE, A.J. *The Chaonian Dove.* Studies in the Eclogues, Georgics and Aeneid of Virgil. 1986. ISBN 90 04 07672 7
95. KYLE, D.G. *Athletics in Ancient Athens.* 2nd impr. of the first (1987) ed. 1993. ISBN 90 04 09759 7
97. VERDENIUS, W.J. *Commentaries on Pindar. Vol. I. Olympian Odes 3, 7, 12, 14.* 1987. ISBN 90 04 08126 7
98. PROIETTI, G. *Xenophon's Sparta.* An introduction. 1987. ISBN 90 04 08338 3
99. BREMER, J.M., A.M. VAN ERP TAALMAN KIP & S.R. SLINGS. *Some Recently Found Greek Poems.* Text and Commentary. 1987. ISBN 90 04 08319 7
100. OPHUIJSEN, J.M. VAN. *Hephaistion on Metre.* Translation and Commentary. 1987. ISBN 90 04 08452 5
101. VERDENIUS, W.J. *Commentaries on Pindar. Vol. II.* Olympian Odes 1, 10, 11, Nemean 11, Isthmian 2. 1988. ISBN 90 04 08535 1
102. LUSCHNIG, C.A.E. *Time holds the Mirror. A Study of Knowledge in Euripides'*

'Hippolytus'. 1988. ISBN 90 04 08601 3
103. MARCOVICH, M. *Alcestis Barcinonensis*. Text and Commentary. 1988. ISBN 90 04 08600 5
104. HOLT, F.L. *Alexander the Great and Bactria*. The Formation of a Greek Frontier in Central Asia. Repr. 1993. ISBN 90 04 08612 9
105. BILLERBECK, M. *Seneca's Tragödien; sprachliche und stilistische Untersuchungen*. Mit Anhängen zur Sprache des Hercules Oetaeus und der Octavia. 1988. ISBN 90 04 08631 5
106. ARENDS, J.F.M. *Die Einheit der Polis. Eine Studie über Platons Staat*. 1988. ISBN 90 04 08785 0
107. BOTER, G.J. *The Textual Tradition of Plato's Republic*. 1988. ISBN 90 04 08787 7
108. WHEELER, E.L. *Stratagem and the Vocabulary of Military Trickery*. 1988. ISBN 90 04 08831 8
109. BUCKLER, J. *Philip II and the Sacred War*. 1989. ISBN 90 04 09095 9
110. FULLERTON, M.D. *The Archaistic Style in Roman Statuary*. 1990. ISBN 90 04 09146 7
111. ROTHWELL, K.S. *Politics and Persuasion in Aristophanes' 'Ecclesiazusae'*. 1990. ISBN 90 04 09185 8
112. CALDER, W.M. & A. DEMANDT. *Eduard Meyer*. Leben und Leistung eines Universalhistorikers. 1990. ISBN 90 04 09131 9
113. CHAMBERS, M.H. *Georg Busolt. His Career in His Letters*. 1990. ISBN 90 04 09225 0
114. CASWELL, C.P. *A Study of 'Thumos' in Early Greek Epic*. 1990. ISBN 90 04 09260 9
115. EINGARTNER, J. *Isis und ihre Dienerinnen in der Kunst der Römischen Kaiserzeit*. 1991. ISBN 90 04 09312 5
116. JONG, I. DE. *Narrative in Drama*. The Art of the Euripidean Messenger-Speech. 1991. ISBN 90 04 09406 7
117. BOYCE, B.T. *The Language of the Freedmen in Petronius' Cena Trimalchionis*. 1991. ISBN 90 04 09431 8
118. RÜTTEN, Th. *Demokrit — lachender Philosoph und sanguinischer Melancholiker*. 1992. ISBN 90 04 09523 3
119. KARAVITES, P. (with the collaboration of Th. Wren). *Promise-Giving and Treaty-Making*. Homer and the Near East. 1992. ISBN 90 04 09567 5
120. SANTORO L'HOIR, F. *The Rhetoric of Gender Terms*. 'Man', 'Woman' and the portrayal of character in Latin prose. 1992. ISBN 90 04 09512 8
121. WALLINGA, H.T. *Ships and Sea-Power before the Great Persian War*. The Ancestry of the Ancient Trireme. 1993. ISBN 90 04 09650 7
122. FARRON, S. *Vergil's Æneid: A Poem of Grief and Love*. 1993. ISBN 90 04 09661 2
123. LÉTOUBLON, F. *Les lieux communs du roman*. Stéréotypes grecs d'aventure et d'amour. 1993. ISBN 90 04 09724 4
124. KUNTZ, M. *Narrative Setting and Dramatic Poetry*. 1993. ISBN 90 04 09784 8
125. THEOPHRASTUS. *Metaphysics*. With an introduction, Translation and Commentary by Marlein van Raalte. 1993. ISBN 90 04 09786 4
126. THIERMANN, P. *Die Orationes Homeri des Leonardo Bruni Aretino*. Kritische Edition der lateinischen und kastilianischen Übersetzung mit Prolegomena und Kommentar. 1993. ISBN 90 04 09719 8
127. LEVENE, D.S. *Religion in Livy*. 1993. ISBN 90 04 09617 5
128. PORTER, J.R. *Studies in Euripides' Orestes*. 1993. ISBN 90 04 09662 0
129. SICKING, C.M.J. & J.M. VAN OPHUIJSEN. *Two Studies in Attic Particle Usage*. Lysias and Plato. 1993. ISBN 90 04 09867 4
130. JONG, I.J.F. de, & J.P. SULLIVAN (eds.). *Modern Critical Theory and Classical Literature*. 1994. ISBN 90 04 09571 3
131. YAMAGATA, N. *Homeric Morality*. 1994. ISBN 90 04 09872 0
132. KOVACS, D. *Euripidea*. 1994. ISBN 90 04 09926 3